CHIRON IN LABRYS

An Introduction To
Esoteric Soul Healing

by
Kathy Jones

Published by
ARIADNE PUBLICATIONS
61 Tor View Avenue, Glastonbury, Somerset,
BA6 8AG, England

Cover Design : Alister Sieghart
The cover painting is an adaptation of Botticelli's painting of "Chiron and Pallas(Athena)", with the Goddess Pallas holding a Labrys.

Drawings by Jem Jarman and AnneMarie Hopper,
Typeset by Kathy Jones
Printed by Redwood Books, Wiltshire

ISBN 1 872983 18 9

To Bridie
She who is the Spirit of Healing

Acknowledgements

I would like to thank all the people who over the last twenty five years have given me the opportunity to develop my skills as a healer, as it is only through the practice of healing that we truly learn of its mysteries. I would also like to thank the students who have taught me to be clear about the principles and practice of healing. My gratitude goes to Cynthia and Mike for reading and correcting the proofs and to AnneMarie Hopper for illustrations. My thanks also cross 20 years to Jem Jarman who did the original illustrations for an early incarnation of this book, which just resurfaced.

Contents

INTRODUCTION

My healing experiences began over twenty five years ago during a time of inadvertent spiritual retreat in the mountains of south Wales. I found myself living alone on a hillside in a lovely old farmhouse which had a panoramic view of the Brecon Beacons. For five years I studied the esoteric teachings of the eastern and western spiritual traditions. I spent much of my time immersed in the beauty of nature, in gardening and chopping wood, in meditation and reading. I was in particular influenced by the writings of Alice A. Bailey and Jane Roberts. Since that time I have done many things. I am a writer, teacher, sacred dramatist, ceremonialist and priestess of Avalon. I am also an esoteric soul healer, tarot and psychic reader and for a time practised as a therapist using emotional regression.

At present I live and work upon the Isle of Avalon, the legendary Western Isle of the Dead, place of transformation, healing, death and rebirth. For twelve years I was involved in creating sacred drama for the deep healing of both individuals and communities. I am a co-founder of the Isle of Avalon Foundation, a registered educational charity, the Library of Avalon - a library of spiritual books, the Brigit Healing Centre and the Glastonbury Goddess Temple - a sacred space dedicated to the Lady of Avalon. I teach a year long intensive professional training in Esoteric Soul Healing for the Isle of Avalon Foundation, as well as a training to become a Priest/ess of Avalon.

In 1995 I suddenly found I was suffering from breast cancer and experienced the whole range of allopathic and complementary therapies including surgery, chemotherapy, and radiotherapy, as well as healing, massage, acupuncture, Chinese herbs, radionics, crystal healing, vitamin therapies, counselling and a few more. The whole experience brought home to me once again the realisation that disease and its healing are a spiritual as well as physical affair and that all healing is of the soul.

This book is based on my experiences both as a healer and as a patient. I began writing it about twenty years ago and it has been refined as my healing knowledge has grown. It is also in part a reworking of Alice Bailey's classic teachings on Esoteric Healing. At the time that she wrote her many esoteric volumes, *A Treatise on the Seven Rays (Lucis Trust)*, she felt it necessary to give information in a complex way that required students to search selectively through her writings to find the truths she wished to convey. She felt these truths could not be given out freely at that time as they might be misused. She wrote that a time would come when her teachings could be given in clearer forms to the world. That time is here now and I hope that this book is part of the unveiling of her mysteries making the practice of esoteric healing accessible to more people.

Introduction

My aim in this book is to bring some of her inspired work forwards out of the patriarchal, hierarchical context in which she wrote. I wish to incorporate some of her ideas on energy and healing within a balanced, egalitarian, non-hierarchical world view. My aim is to bring clarity and common sense to the subject of healing which can often appear vague and wishy washy or is put in such complicated language that few people can understand it and put it into practice. What I hope to show is that subtle invisible energies are not just amorphous and chaotic with no relevance to everyday life, but that they follow certain laws which can be discovered and used in healing disease.

Everywhere today we use the properties of non-material energies, such as electricity which give us light and heat, which we register with our physical senses, even though we still don't actually know what electricity is. In a similar way we can experience and use the non-physical energies of emotion, mind, consciousness and spirit to transform our lives, without necessarily knowing what those energies are. These subtle energies are not physically quantifiable, because they are not physical, but they have properties which we can register with the subtle faculties of the psyche which we all possess, although in some people they lie dormant. It is these subtle energies which we use in healing disease.

I hope to demonstrate that the illnesses which we contract are not just things that happen to us from the outside, although there are definitely external agents of disease, such as bacteria, viruses, poisons and carcinogens, which are being produced in ever increasing numbers by our industrialised societies. Disease has causes which are intimately connected to the reality of our nature as human energy beings. When we are whole and in harmony with ourselves, with our soul's energy, freely expressing what we sense, feel and think, then we are usually well and healthy. We don't *catch* the everyday germs that we breathe in with every breath. When we don't express ourselves, when we withhold our energy for whatever reason, we are likely to become ill - physically, emotionally, mentally, psychologically or spiritually. It is not usually a conscious choice to suppress our energy and disease is something that appears to happen to us from the outside.

Most of us have no conscious control over the expression of our energy. Some days we feel good, other days we feel bad. It often depends on how we feel when we wake up, on whether we have had good or bad dreams. We don't seem to have too much choice over how we feel. We often don't even recognise our own energy patterns. We don't know what it is to be conscious, we are just getting on with living. We are at the mercy of fate. As we begin to become conscious of our true Selves susceptibility to disease can lessen, though the possibility of unravelling deeper and deeper layers of personal karma also increases, again bringing with it a susceptibility to disease. Our bodies are also prone to the diseases of the world in which we live, to the karma of being a human being on planet earth in the twenty first century. We cannot hide from the fall out from Chernobyl if it falls on the place where we live or fail to breathe in the pollution in our cities and landscapes.

With this one great provision about the erratic and accidental effects of living in a polluted environment, the effects of our common human karma, the teachings of Alice Bailey state that disease comes whenever the energy of our Soul is inhibited in its expression. This inhibition can be minimal giving rise to the coughs and colds which we all suffer, or on a grander scale in the major diseases which maim, cripple and kill us.

Disease by its very nature changes the way in which we experience the world around us. A headache can completely remove the pleasures of a summer's day. A psychological depression can prevent us from getting out of bed in the morning, from relating to other human beings. A disease such as arthritis or cancer can immobilise us with pain, totally altering our everyday experience, confronting us with our human frailty and with death. The healing of such diseases requires radical transformations in our subtle bodies of emotion, mind and consciousness as well as our physical bodies.

In its positive aspect disease is associated with expanding consciousness. We are always changing, moving out from our spiritual centre towards greater personal fulfilment, reaching to the limits of our present physical and psychological forms. Whenever we near these limits or move faster than our personalities with their conditioned responses can cope, disease comes to accelerate the process and to help us break through into new awareness. Here disease and its healing help us see who we truly are as human energy beings and not just as physical creatures. In a sense disease itself is a healing experience.

A personal experience of healing is an initiation into new dimensions of reality for both the sufferer and the healer. It can bring with it the recognition that while we are mortal and human, we are also eternal, limitless Sparks of Life living in physical bodies. Healing brings the material and spiritual aspects of our humanity into sharp relief.

As healers our aim is to ease pain and suffering, to heal disease. In essence in esoteric soul healing our practice is to create an emanating energy field from within our own Soul, which allows the patient to come into contact with their own Soul's energy which flows through their non-material bodies into their physical form healing them of their disease. Our work as healers is to catalyse the process of soul contact for a sick person who may be too weak, distracted or withdrawn, to do it for themselves. Healing is a joint process in which both patient and healer are transformed by the experience. Essentially we all heal ourselves, but sometimes we need a little help from our friends.

The planetary body known as Chiron was first sighted in the heavens on November 1st 1977 moving in an orbit between Saturn and Uranus. Its recognition heralded an upsurge in interest in natural and complementary healing therapies. In mythology Chiron was a centaur, part human, part horse, part god. He was famed for his knowledge of earth magic and healing. The sons of gods and humans were sent to him for training in the heroic arts. One of these, Hercules, accidentally shot Chiron with an arrow tipped with the poisonous blood of the Hydra. This poison was normally fatal but because Chiron was an immortal (born of the gods), he could not die. The wound however would not heal and Chiron had to live with its pain for the rest of his life. He was eventually delivered from his agony by exchanging places with Prometheus who lay chained to a rock having his liver

Introduction

eaten out by a griffin vulture as a punishment for stealing fire from the gods. Through this exchange both Chiron and Prometheus were healed of their pain.

Chiron is known as the wounded healer - the person who through their own suffering knows the pain of others. S/he is one who can heal others and herself through generating and transmitting soul energy. Astrologically the position of Chiron in the natal horoscope indicates the placement of an individual's life wound, the karma that they are dealing with in this life. Transits of Chiron around the horoscope indicate opportunities to resolve the dilemmas this life wound creates.

The Labrys is the double-headed lunar axe which symbolises the phases of the moon - waxing, full, waning and dark, reflecting the cycles of the Goddess's nature. Goddess is the ruler of nature, the Matrix, the Mother from whom we all spring. She is the context in whom we live and move and have our being. Worshipped throughout the ancient world her epiphany in the great matriarchal civilisation of Krete was the labrys, used for decoration, large and small, in paintings and sculpture. The complementary image to this labrys was the symmetrical butterfly, symbol of the soul, transformation and rebirth.

CHIRON IN LABRYS is a book about transformation and the healing of disease in both the sick person and the wounded healer, within the context of the natural energies of our Mother the Earth and the laws, rhythms and cycles of Her Nature. This book is about healing in the sense of making whole, balancing all the energies of soul, consciousness, personality and form. Disease arises essentially out of the suppression of Soul energy which needs to be released, and sometimes our Souls too are in need of healing. As healers we use Soul energy to help catalyse the healing process in our patients. This knowledge is esoteric in the sense that it involves an understanding of non-material energies, which are by definition hidden from normal sight and this knowledge has not been readily accessible to the public until now. This book is an introduction to the subject which will allow you to begin to practice esoteric soul healing. Once you have some experience of this form of healing I suggest that you explore Alice Bailey's Esoteric Healing (Lucis Trust) for a deepening understanding of the subject.

In this book I shall attempt to give a description of who we are as energy beings, living out our lives in a material and spiritual universe whose underlying principle energy is Love. I shall give ways of getting in touch with and experiencing this Soul which we are and with the energy patterns and rhythms in which we all live and move and have our Being. We will look at the causes and nature of disease and describe two main methods of healing - Magnetic Healing using the energy of Prana flowing out through the hands and Radiatory Healing using the energy of the Soul flowing out through the aura. I shall also give information on specific forms of healing in the Emotional and Mental bodies, on Self Healing and on Death and Dying.

All the techniques given are stepping stones to the experiencing of certain energy states, which reveal the truth of the nature of our being and the worlds in which we really live. The methods themselves are not the Truth and should not be regarded as such. They are gateways through which we can contact the wisdom of our Souls and experience what is. It is here that we will learn Truth directly.

Once we know how to discriminate between different qualities of energy and recognise how they move and transform, the need to follow a particular method passes. We can heal in the flow of our intuition and inspiration which always comes.

Throughout the book there are exercises and meditations which are designed to transform the consciousness of the healer. The greater our personal Soul consciousness, the deeper our own inner explorations, the more we can assist other people on their journey of transformation. Our aim is ever to serve the healing spirit to whom in our hearts we are dedicated. That healing spirit has different names in different traditions. For some it is the Christ energy or the archangel Raphael or White Eagle. For me living here upon the Isle of Avalon, she is the Lady of Avalon, Goddess of Transformation. She is Bridie, Goddess of Healing. She is Ariadne, Arianrhod, Green Tara, Rhiannon, the Nine Morgens and Morgen la Fey.

CHAPTER ONE

The Basic Premises

We are all natural healers. When we are in good health healing energy naturally flows out through our bodies and auras, whether we are conscious of it or not. Whenever we touch another person with love, whenever we hug, caress or massage each other, when we stroke an animal, when we care for plants, when we create with our hands, when we smile, when we laugh, when we sing and dance, energy moves outwards from our centre.

The aim of this book is to encourage the conscious development of our natural healing abilities, by taking personal responsibility for the energies which are available to us as human energy beings. While we live in a physical universe which is bounded by time and space we are essentially energy beings - eternal, limitless and free. This energy is not something which is separate from us, a divinity which exists outside of us. It is an essence within which we recognise as our Source.

We begin with some basic premises about life and our place in the scheme of things. These premises are but one step beyond those currently accepted by science. Some of them you may find challenging to encompass with your logical mind but they are there to be tested by experience. They form a necessary basis for understanding the nature of energy and healing and will be amplified throughout the book

All is energy and energy is all there is

In purely physical terms we live and move and have our being in an eternal, infinite, interlocking system of energies and forces that compose our universe. Some of these energies appear to our five senses to be solid and have form, even though when we examine them closely they seem to disappear into nothing but space and energy.

We look at our hands. We see them with our eyes, we can touch them with our skin, we can smell them, we can taste the surface. If our ears were sensitive enough we could hear them living and breathing. When we look more closely we see the skin itself with its indentations, pigmentation, its transparency and underneath we can see the blood moving in our veins. Under a microscope we can see the cells which make up the tissues and the long chain molecules of which they are composed. Under the higher definition of the electron microscope, individual atoms become visible. When we examine these atoms more closely we find that matter itself seems to melt away and what we have left is energy. This energy acts at times as if it is pure energy without form and at other times as if it is composed of minute particles. This is true for any material form that we examine. Einstein formulated the relationship between energy and matter in the mathematical equation : $E = MC^2$, where E is energy, M is mass of an object, and C is the speed at which light travels. Einstein realised that energy and matter are interchangeable.

For all of us whether we are scientists, healers or ordinary(!) human beings, life is essentially an energy experience. None of us are focused in purely material reality. Although we must all eat food, drink water and breathe air to survive we actually spend most of our time in the non-physical worlds of feelings and thoughts, with occasional glimpses of a deeper world within and beyond. We are continually moved, swayed and transformed by energies which though physically immaterial, mould our actions and determine our behaviour and experience.

Energy, consciousness and form

For the healer the relationship between energy and matter is not just one of interchangeability. It is causal - energy always precedes a material form. To create a material form, energy which is organised in the form of Consciousness must be present. Consciousness or Being or Soul - *what IS*, is that coherent, integral, present, one and indivisible matrix of love energy shared by all forms in manifestation in our universe. Consciousness itself is organised into different forms, with different degrees of complexity. There are beings who ensoul planets, beings who manifest as plants, animals, as pebbles, and there are human beings.

The Soul is both individual and communal. We are each uniquely ourselves and we are all one and indivisible. The soul is the expression of divine life. It is governed by purpose and motivated by love.

All forms of consciousness appear to have a centre from which energy radiates, creating an energy field which surrounds them. This energy field is characterised by the quality of energy of the informing being and it is within this energy field that a physical form manifests itself and appears for us all to see.

As human beings we are Sparks of divine life expressing ourselves in a form of consciousness which is variously described in religious literature as the Soul, Psyche, Being, the High Priestess, the Christ within, the Goddess within, the Buddha within, etc., and in occult and psychological texts as the Self, the Deeper Self, the Higher Self, the Egoic Lotus, the Ego, the Charioteer, the Solar Angel and the Causal Body. In this book I shall use the terms Soul, Being and Consciousness interchangeably to describe our individual and collective what-is-ness.

The energy of the soul expresses itself in human form through the medium of mental and emotional energies, which condition seven (sometimes there are more or less depending on the system taught) major energy centres or chakras in the human etheric body. This etheric or light body is an interconnecting web of energy threads on which the atoms of physical matter find their place, allowing a physical form to appear.

Two streams of life and consciousness anchor into the body via a dual life thread, known as the sutratma. The life aspect of the sutratma anchors into the heart and the consciousness aspect anchors into the brain. A third stream, the earth thread, anchors into the base chakra, anchoring us in the physicality of Planet Earth.

Health, disease and healing

According to the teachings of Alice Bailey we are healthy when the energy of the soul is flowing freely through our minds and feelings, via the seven chakras out into the physical body. Disease comes when there is an excess, inhibition or blockage in the flow of soul energy through our mental and emotional bodies and into or out of the seven chakras, catalysed by both internal and external stimuli. Disease can be physical, emotional, psychological or spiritual depending on the location of the point of friction.

At all times it is our soul which determines our experience. The nature of the individual soul is to attract to itself the experiences it requires for the fulfilment of its purposes. These experiences can be positive or negative. We may be conscious of our soul purpose and identified with it or we may be completely unaware of it. It is the call of our soul to its expression, the personality, ever to expand to accommodate and express the soul's true nature, which at times creates points of friction and thus disease.

We begin to incarnate into physical life at the moment of conception, when two tiny human cells come together and unite to form one new whole person. Through life our physical bodies are constantly changing as we grow from helpless babyhood to adult independence, before we grow old and die. Emotionally and psychologically we also go through tremendous changes, growing through time into a fuller expression of our Self in the world through learning, remembering and experience. Potentially we have the opportunity to grow into greater personal fulfilment, happiness and joy through the expression of our unique and individual natures. Whenever soul expression is consistently impeded or distorted disease is likely to arise.

As esoteric soul healers our aim is to encourage soul expression in ourselves and other people. We work directly with consciousness and a person's energy field as well as the physical effects of the disease. We centre ourselves in our own being and consciously radiate soul energy. We create an energy field that allows the sick person to come into resonance with the energy of their soul which can heal them. Soul energy flows into their etheric body via the chakras , the sutratma and the earth thread clearing blockages, removing excess energy, stimulating the energy bodies and the immune system, allowing healing to take place.

When healing occurs a resolution of the energy imbalance takes place which can be felt by both the sick person and the healer within their own energy fields. This resolution may take place during the actual healing session or sometimes in the following days. When healing has not occurred there is usually no sense of resolution.

The Basic Premises

When we are unsuccessful in our efforts to heal we need to remember that although we can always improve our techniques, healing is truly in the domain of the patient's own soul. The cause of the disease may not yet have reached fruition. For the esoteric soul healer the secret of healing lies in an awareness of timing and the rhythms of being.

Experiencing energy

We experience physical energies through our five physical senses of touch, hearing, sight, taste and smell. Non-physical energies we register through subtle faculties connected to the chakras and the subtle energy bodies. We experience emotional and astral energies via our solar plexus chakra. We experience mental energies through the throat chakra and centres in the head. We also have faculties of clairvoyance and clairaudience through the centres in the head, which allow us to see and hear subtle energies. We can communicate with each other astrally via the emotional body, telepathically via our minds or causally, soul to soul. In most of us these subtle faculties are erratic, uncontrolled and indiscriminately used.

The key to understanding the nature of the soul and its emanated energy field lies in the development of the sixth sense - the intuition, the common sense which unifies all the others. The intuition is that state of awareness which is by definition, in tune with the laws of nature. It is the space where truth IS. Intuition is pure reason and is also known as buddhi. It is contacted via the antaskarana or rainbow bridge, which we build in mental and emotional matter, connecting our personality to the world of spirit via the soul.

This connection is developed whenever we create or act from our centre, our soul. Any creative activity into which we put our *heart and soul* calls forth intuition. It doesn't just have to be a *spiritual* activity like meditation, it can be cake-making, car maintenance, painting, writing, business, gardening, etc.., whatever we love to do. Through creative action we slowly build the rainbow bridge, even if we are unconscious of the way in which we use intuition in the process. We can also build the antaskarana consciously through meditation and the circulation of energy through the major energy centres in the head.

Primarily however we develop intuition by recognising its existence and its importance, by listening to it and acting upon the inner messages we receive about ourselves, other people, situations, ideas, etc.. The wonderful thing is that as soon as we act upon the information that intuition gives us, there is an automatic response from our environment which confirms its existence and truth. Our lives and the decisions we make about people and events begin to work for us. Life becomes easier.

Healing is an art and an esoteric science in which once we establish energy connections between ourselves and the patient, we work completely under the guidance of intuition. We don't try to think our way through the healing process, we don't wishfully hope for healing - although this may be difficult to exclude, we follow our intuition, our inner guide. This is our connection with the truth of being and when we follow it we act from that truth, allowing healing to take place.

Energy follows thought and feeling

Within the wider context of reality, we all help to create the world around us by our individual and collective thoughts, feelings and dreams. We are unique individual creative souls and we are part of the collective soul of the planet on which we live and move and have our being. The way in which we experience our world is constrained by the ideas that we have about the world. As we think and feel so the world is. On the personal level if we see the world as a hard place to live, that is usually how we experience it. If we can change our ideas, our feelings and thoughts about the world then our experience often changes too.

And it is by thought and feeling that we can change the world around us. Everything in existence begins as an idea in some being's consciousness. Fuelled by desire an idea gathers energy until it becomes concretised into form. Every thing that human beings create begins as an idea without form. Every building, every machine, every thing we wear, everything we design, everything we organise began as an idea. The United Nations Assembly began life as an idea in the consciousness of one or several human beings. It is an idea of unity in diversity between the peoples of the world, providing a forum for communication between people to bring peace to the world. It doesn't yet succeed in all its aims, but it exists and is alive and functioning. It began as an idea and evolved through feeling and thought, and it is materialising.

The power of creative imagination

Imagination is the creative faculty of mind and energy follows in its wake. It is the key to successful healing practice. Instead of dismissing imagination as a realm of fantasy as healers we recognise this faculty as a creative force in the healing process. The cancer patient who is able to visualise themselves as whole and well, who can see their cancer being destroyed by imaginary laser beams or sharks or pacmen, is much more likely to recover from their disease than the person who is conditioned by hopelessness and fear of the disease. So too the healer's active imagination helps create the correct conditions for the healing of the patient.

In the healing process we consciously use thought and feeling to visualise and to circulate energy. We use the power of creative imagination to generate a radiating energy field and to establish and maintain energy connections between ourselves and the patient. We visualise the release of blocked energy, the activities of devic and angelic forces and the healing energies doing their work.

In esoteric soul healing energy is envisioned as moving in triangles. As healers we generate energy by circulating energy through at least three points which we visualise with our imagination. These three points can be in the physical, etheric, astral , mental or soul vehicles, that is, in more than one dimension of reality. For example, one point may be in the healer's soul or consciousness, and the other two may be chakras in the etheric body, as shown overleaf. This particular triangle is used to generate the note sounded by our soul in the heart chakra.

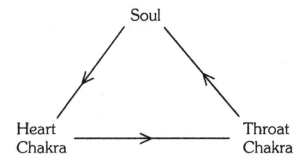

This requires facility in using the imagination to link through different energy dimensions, but after all this is what the imagination is for. This ability comes with practice.

Truth, beauty and goodness

There is a drive within all energy beings towards the experience and expression of three basic qualities of energy. These three qualities are *Truth, Beauty* and *Goodness*. How they are expressed and experienced depends on the degree of unfoldment in consciousness within any particular energy being.

Truth is what IS. It is that which accords with the laws of nature. In our human experience all truth lies in the moment and is relative. What is true for us today may not always be true tomorrow. It is true for humans, animals and plants that the sun *always* rises in the morning, shines through the day and sets in the evening. For the being who ensouls the galaxy of which we are a tiny part and who lives through aeons of time, our *always* does not last forever. Our sun is one of thousands that evolve from interstellar gases, shine for a span and then return to stardust. Our sun will not *always* shine.

In our everyday lives the drive to experience Truth shows itself in the ways in which we repeat psychological and physical patterns over and over again throughout our lives. These patterns are in our relationships, in our attitudes, in the way we see ourselves and our environment, becoming a framework of limitation. They spiral onwards until we recognise the Truth inherent within or denied by those patterns. We go on repeating ourselves until we experience and express what IS as far as our consciousness is able to take us. We know when something is true when the energy involved in resistance is released as all tension disappears and a piece of the jigsaw clicks into place.

We have all seen and felt the *Beauty* in a flower. We have all marvelled at the Beauty in a child's face and gasped at the beautiful sight of our the Earth viewed as one whole from space. There is Beauty which is skin deep and a quality of the matter which makes up the physical world and there is Beauty which comes from within and is a quality of the soul. This Beauty appears as we unfold into ourselves and begin to express our true nature in the outer world.

Again what we experience as Beauty is relative to our culture and perspective. Beauty is in the eye of the beholder. A large rounded woman is beautiful to an Arab man as she signals abundance and wealth, but she may be despised in western cultures as fat and out of control. A compost heap is beautiful to a gardener because she knows it contains nutrients essential for the next season's fertility, but that rotting heap is not necessarily beautiful to anyone else.

We all have within us the drive to express the Beauty of our soul and the degree to which we do so is the mark of our soul.

Goodness is a quality of essence, the divine Spark which we are. Deep within each of us, sometimes lying hidden, is the need to experience and express Goodness. This is not a moral value, although morality is one of the ways in which Goodness finds expression in the world. We all know a Good person when we meet one and they are not usually people who make judgments about other people's goodness or badness. Goodness is the jewel in the lotus of the soul. It is there in all of us waiting to be revealed.

In the etheric body Truth, Beauty and Goodness are expressed via the Throat, Heart and Crown chakras. Disease is often the result of our inability to recognise and/or express Truth, Beauty and Goodness within ourselves, in others and in the situations in which we find ourselves. As healers we attempt to assist our patients in finding what is Truth for them in their lives, to reveal the Beauty which lies within their own soul, and to express the Goodness which is their essence.

Harmlessness and non-interference

The principles of harmlessness and non-interference govern all our actions as healers. Our stance is to always act from a place of harmlessness where nothing that we do can harm another life form. This stance brings us face to face with our own limitations and pushes us onwards to become better human beings.

As healers we must always keep our will in check. The concentrated will of any individual or the directed will of a united group should never be used in healing. Will energy can greatly increase the patient's disease rather than healing it. It can stimulate the disease and disrupt instead of cooperating with nature's healing forces. Will is not used, only love.

In each of us there is a wisdom of being which guides our experiences for the fulfilment of its own purpose. This wisdom directs us towards those experiences which bring us ever into fuller expression of our soul's energy here on earth. As healers we assume that each person knows, somewhere within them, consciously or unconsciously, what is correct for them. We may not always be able to act upon that knowledge but when we do we know it is correct because it feels right.

Esoteric soul healing has powerful energetic effects within the human aura and should not to be used lightly as it can have definite, profound effects. If a person who is ill does not want to receive healing from us, then we do not attempt to interfere with their energy field for what may appear to us to be *for their*

13

good. We cannot, we do not see and know everything that is happening for anyone else, let alone ourselves. It is only the individual who can truly perceive and experience their own destiny and purpose. If someone does not want our healing assistance, we don't attempt to give it to them against their will. We respect the integrity of their choice. We are harmless and do not interfere.

EXERCISE:

The only way to learn about energy is to experience it. Non-physical energy cannot yet be measured by science, but nevertheless it is real and can be felt and experienced.

Feeling Energy - in the hands

Begin by holding both hands out in front of you, palms facing inwards towards each other, about one foot apart. Close your eyes and feel your hands from the inside out. Slowly bring both palms towards each other until there is only an inch or so separating them. As you move your hands inwards notice the sensations that you feel in your palms and in the fingers of both hands. Feel the texture of the air between your hands, feel its softness and its density. Sometimes it feels like you are squashing a ball of air. Hold your hands in that position for several moments and then move them slowly apart, again noticing all the sensations in your hands.

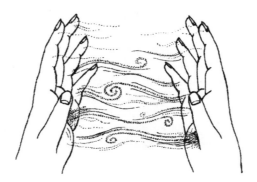

AMH

We all experience energy in different ways and particularly in our hands, which are one of the most physically sensitive parts of our bodies. There may be feelings of heat, pressure, pins and needles or a cooling in the palms and/or fingers. Energy is circulating through our physical and etheric bodies all the time and once we focus our attention on the energy flowing in our hands, we nearly all feel something. It is *not* a draught from a door or window, or the sudden heat of the sun. It is not *nothing*. Energy is moving through our hands. It is real. We all feel it and it can be used in healing.

Feeling Energy - between people
In Pairs

Sit opposite a partner, face to face and close enough for your hands to touch. Stretch out your arms and place your hands, one palm facing upwards and one palm facing downwards, below and above your partner's hands. Leave a gap of about a foot between the two pairs of hands. Close your eyes and feel the sensations in your hands.

Slowly bring your hands up and down towards your partner's hands until there is an inch gap between your palms. Don't actually touch hands. Hold them there for several moments and register the sensations you feel in your hands. Then, using your imagination, visualise a stream of energy in any form that you like - streams of white or coloured light, as threads or thoughts of energy flowing between the two pairs of hands. After a short time see if you can reverse the direction of flow. Feel the changes in sensation in your hands as you change direction.

AMH

When you are both ready slowly move your hands away from your partner's and register the limits of the sensation. How far apart can your hands be before the sensations disappear? Is the feeling there all the time waiting for your attention? Does it come and go? Experiment. What you feel is what is right for you. There is not just one way of experiencing energy. We are all different and experience things differently. Talk to each other about your experiences.

Three or more

Sit comfortably in a circle and hold your right hand out towards the person on your right, palm up or down. Hold your left hand out to the person on your left, up or down in the opposite direction. Repeat the process as given for pairs, registering all the sensations that you feel in your hands.

Using your creative imagination together direct energy around the circle of people, firstly in an anticlockwise direction and then later in a clockwise direction. Hold no fixed ideas about which direction is the *right* direction or which hand should direct or receive energy. Let yourself experience the energy flow before theories take over. After circulating the energy move the hands apart and discuss together what you have each experienced.

CHAPTER TWO

The Human Energy System

When healing ourselves and our patients we remember that we are in essence energy beings. Beneath and within the layers of the physical self we are energy expressing itself in different forms. The following is an energetic map of the human being based on the ideas of Alice A. Bailey modified by experiences in other traditions.

We are divine Sparks of Life expressing ourselves through a Spiritual Triad - a triangle of spiritual energies of Atma, Buddhi and Manas, which anchor into the Soul or Causal Body. The Soul is characterised by consciousness or Being, that energy which we share with every other being in the universe. The Soul in turn expresses itself through Personality, another triangle of energies - Mental, Emotional and Etheric energies, which condition the Chakras or Energy Centres in the Etheric Body, and then precipitate into an outer Physical form.

As human beings we live and move and have our being within the matrix of energies of the cosmic physical realm. See Appendix One for further information on the energy system of the universe, the seven rays and the cosmic physical realm of being, the energetic context in which we live as human beings..

Sparks

The Spark of Life is that divine essence of love, will and intelligence which we essentially are. It is an essence before consciousness of which we can know little. It cannot be experienced by us in physical incarnation, since experience implies a consciousness with which to experience it. It is an *Electric* energy with which we *Identify*.

Sparks also known as Monads, can be imaged as fiery sparks from an original divine fire or minute fragments of a divine mirror shattered at the moment of creation. They are differentiated according to the energy of the seven rays. There are 1st ray to 7th ray Sparks. Each ray represents a different kind of energy. At any particular point in time certain groups of Sparks are swept into incarnation following the rhythm of the Zodiacal ages through which our solar system travels. The majority of Sparks currently in manifestation are those of the 5th ray of pattern and 6th ray of devotion, predominant in the age of Pisces and those of the 2nd ray of love/wisdom and 7th ray of ritual which characterise the incoming Aquarian age. There are also smaller groupings on other rays.

The Human Energy System

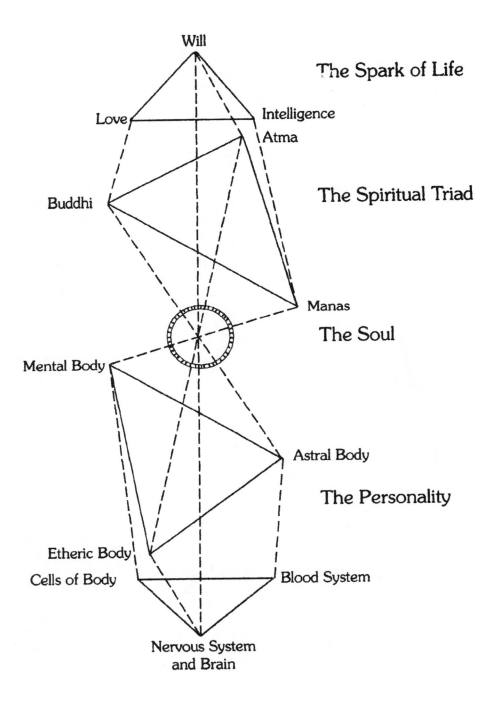

Will

The Spark of Life

Love   Intelligence

Atma

The Spiritual Triad

Buddhi

Manas

The Soul

Mental Body

Astral Body

The Personality

Etheric Body

Cells of Body   Blood System

Nervous System
and Brain

The Spiritual Triad

The Spiritual Triad is a triangle of the three energies of *Atma, Buddhi* and *Manas*. *Atma* is Spiritual Will, *Buddhi* is Wisdom and *Manas* is Mind. These three are the first expressions of the essential energy of the Spark of life. We come into resonance with these energies in meditation and thereby are able to experience them. We contact them through the agency of the Soul and through building the Antahkarana or Rainbow Bridge which connects the Spiritual Triad to the Personality.

Soul

Soul, Being, Consciousness, Isness is an energy state which we all share. It *is* everywhere in all beings. It is the basis of the truism that we are all One. Within the individual this consciousness is known as the Soul, Self, Being, Goddess or God Within, Deeper or Higher Self, Causal Body, Egoic Lotus and the Solar Angel. We are all one - we all have the same consciousness, yet we are individual and unique.

The Soul or Causal Body is itself a subtle vehicle for the energies of the Spiritual Triad, allowing them to be expressed in the worlds of form. Technically the soul is composed of matter of the abstract levels of the mental sphere and carries the seeds of karma which ripen through our lives..

Symbolically the soul is imaged as a Lotus Blossom with twelve petals which hide a central jewel - the *Jewel or Spark in the Lotus*. During incarnation the petals of this lotus unfold through time and experience revealing the *Colours* and *Qualities* of each of the twelve petals until the jewel, which is our essence, is revealed. These colours can be seen within a person's aura and as the lotus opens the Light emanating from the jewel becomes visible and the aura becomes correspondingly luminous. This colour and light give us an idea of a person's current pattern of unfoldment. At any one time certain petals are highlighted and others are dormant depending on the rhythm and pattern of the unfoldment of the Soul and its Purpose in this life.

Personality

Personality is composed of our *Mental, Astral/Emotional* and *Etheric/ Physical Bodies*. It is in one sense a reflection of the energies of the Spiritual Triad in the denser energies of physical incarnation. We express the invisible energies of our soul through the medium of our personalities.

We come into incarnation with some aspects of personality, our character, already formed - some children are naturally happy and easy going, some have a lot of energy, some are slower and others find life immediately difficult. This character is created from a combination of our physical genetic make-up received from our parents and our individual psychic karmic inheritance. Character is represented in our astrological birthchart, the pattern of the heavens at the moment of birth, which in the hands of a skilful astrologer can tell us much about who we are, our motivations and behavioural tendencies.. Some parts of the personality grow and flourish during incarnation others are diminished by adverse experiences. We do not always live out our lives to their full potential. In describing the processes of character development we must necessarily make generalisations which do not apply to all individuals but give us a sense of the patterns of growth in the personality.

As we grow through childhood and adolescence the three aspects of our personality, of the mind, emotion and physical form develop and strengthen at differing rates. For example we grow physically extremely quickly before and after birth for our first year or so, and also again during adolescence. We grow at a more moderate rate in between. Later in life we stop growing altogether and our physical bodies decline. So too we develop mentally and emotionally at differing rates, depending on our genetic make up, on what's happening to us in our environment and on input from our souls. Usually by the age of twenty one the three aspects of mind, emotion and body are becoming integrated and begin to form a functioning whole. From this time onwards personality strengthens and becomes dominant in our lives.

Through life experience the personality consolidates, integrating memories, sometimes becoming fixed, loosening, expanding and changing with endless variation, but on the whole personality is quite a stable function. We remain recognisably ourselves with our likes and dislikes and characteristic quirks. What we like about ourselves we hold to be truly us. What we disapprove of becomes relegated to unconsciousness and becomes part of our Shadow.

Every so often in life in its own purposeful rhythm the soul calls to the personality for greater Self expression. We experience this calling in many different ways, but it triggers a crisis, a loss of self confidence and a struggle for identity. When we are young we may not yet have had a sense of self to identify with. When we have a sense of self we can lose it, feeling lost, alone and out of control. Such feelings are signs that a meeting or confrontation is taking place between the energies of the personality and those of the soul as the vehicle for the energies of the spiritual triad. This meeting is occasionally conscious, but more often it is unconscious and therefore uncomfortable and disturbing for the person experiencing it. It is often accompanied by dis-ease.

Such a confrontation is described in the spiritual text of the Baghavad Gita between Arjuna the personality and Krishna the soul, who meet on the burning ground of the Kurukshestra, which symbolises the Astral or Emotional Body. This confrontation is experienced as an internal emotional battle in which we don't know which part of us will win, the destructive or the creative, the *bad* or the *good*. In Western esoteric terms this confrontation takes place between the Dweller on the Threshold - the Personality in its Shadow form and the Solar or Guardian Angel or Soul. Such crisis points often take place at the time of strong astrological transits, such as that around the age of twenty eight at the time of the astrological Saturn return, when Saturn the limiter and teacher, returns to its original place in the individual's natal horoscope, vibrating the karmic birth seeds.

Initiation

Each time a face to face meeting between soul and personality comes to a crisis point and opposing energies are hopefully integrated with each other, there is an expansion in consciousness within our everyday lives, known as an *Initiation*. At each initiation the petals of the Heart Chakra unfold to a greater degree allowing more soul energy to be expressed in the material world. To initiate something is to begin a process of change and there are many minor and major initiations in our lives here on earth. With each initiation we pass through we are more able to express the energy of the soul and of life itself through the vehicle of our personalities.

In her work Alice A. Bailey described a series of initiations which aspiring disciples should aim for in a linear progression. By climbing this spiritual ladder disciples eventually rise to the top of a tree of perfection to become enlightened. I have not included descriptions of these initiations here since most human beings are currently approaching the initiation in which we begin consciously to recognise and express soul energy. Trying to work out where you or anyone else is on the spiritual ladder seems to lead mainly to competitiveness amongst aspiring personalities rather than enhancing the pool of spiritual knowledge. You can read about the major initiations in Alice's books.

My personal feeling is that the spiritual ladder of achievement is not an accurate presentation of spiritual development but part of the patriarchal/ hierarchical worldview within which Alice wrote. I favour a more Jungian approach to the subject in which there is a field of spiritual potential out of which different and equal challenges arise at different times throughout one's life, which need to be met and integrated. What we are attempting to deal with at any time is what we should be facing. There are many earthplane initiations which all add to the expansion of our consciousness, and which can help us to become better human beings.

The Mental Body

The Mental Body is the particular set of mental energies through which our soul expresses itself as a personality. It is not a body in the sense of having a fixed shape and size, but is a range of mental energies available to us through our degree of soul unfoldment, karma, genetic make up and interaction with the energetic environment in which we live. These mental energies normally include the dense, liquid, gaseous and 1st etheric levels of the mental sphere and in awakened individuals can include the full range of energies including soul energies (see Appendix One). The mental body anchors into the physical/etheric body principally via the throat chakra and the centres in the head. Our mental bodies give us the capacity to be conscious, to think, to be intelligent, to use language and symbols to communicate verbally and telepathically with each other and with other intelligences in our universe. Imagination is the creative faculty of the mental body.

The mental body is given character from the moment of conception through learning, acquiring knowledge and by interaction with the environment. Through time some of these mental energies become fixed forming the foundations of our personality, while others remain fluid and continue to change. As we get older repeated patterns of thinking act like grooves on a record - put the needle on the record and the same tune plays over and over again. This can be very useful in some situations where we need to respond automatically, say when driving a car. but it can also mean that we stop thinking creatively. These limitations in mental activity create blockages and conflict, which finding no resolution in the mental body are reflected into the astral and physical bodies and are experienced as emotional and physical, as well as mental difficulties. Certain chronic diseases, such as arthritis, rheumatism and joint diseases are the effects created by the rigid grooves in our mental attitudes and habits.

Conflict within the mental body can be resolved with esoteric soul healing, using psychic reading which speaks directly to the mind and its strictures. The many psychotherapeutic techniques, including transactional analysis and neurolinguistic programming are also useful. Transpersonal psychological approaches use the creative imagination and recognition of the soul and its transpersonal energies to loosen the limitations in the mind. All of these latter techniques are enhanced by consciously working with healing energy as part of the process.

Astral or Emotional Body

The Astral or Emotional Body is the Soul's expression within the Astral Sphere of energy. Again the astral body has no defined shape although it is sometimes imaged in the form of a large bodily sphere surrounding and including the whole of the physical body. The emotional body anchors into the physical/ etheric body primarily via the sacral, solar plexus and heart chakras. It is conditioned by our genetic and karmic inheritance, both individual and collective, and through our emotional experiences from the moment of conception. It is a very fluid body constantly interacting with the outer world, with other people's emotional bodies, as well as the world of the collective unconscious. It can include all the emotional states which characterise our lives as human beings from joy to fear, from rage to grief, bliss to sorrow.

From the moment we are conceived we are responding to emotional energies and developing our astral bodies. As we develop and grow within our mother's physical body we also grow within her emotional body. At this stage of development there is no emotional separation between mother and child. We take in our mother's emotions and reactions automatically and make them our own. This process is unconscious and part of the way that familial patterns continue through the generations. It happens to us all.

The process of birth itself is especially important in laying down the psychic seeds of our future emotional development. The activity and feelings experienced by the baby at the time of birth cliché the emotional, mental and physical patterns which will later be amplified and repeated throughout our lives. They are an expression of the seeds of karma which we carry from life to life within the causal body. Just as an astrological birthchart gives us an external picture of our future character by pinpointing the moment of birth in relation to the coincidental movement of the heavens, so the way we are born gives us an internal cellular level picture of our karmic inheritance. This picture remains unconscious until we begin to explore our own past and make it conscious.

We can return to this birth experience in order to release ourselves from our chosen emotional patterning. We can find out who we really are beneath our automatic reactions and conditioning. There are several methods of emotional regression which help us to remember our birth experience. These include hypnotic regression and rebirthing, a breathing technique described by Leonard Orr and others. These methods allow us to remember and re-experience the delight and/or the trauma of our birth into this world. We can become conscious of the ways in which we have set up our emotional habits and choose consciously whether we wish to continue to repeat the same old patterns or whether we can do something different. See Chapter Seven on *Emotional Healing through Regression*. Sometimes we have flashbacks of birth trauma in dreams and waking visions, when we are caught up in present day dramas. Their purpose is to bring to consciousness the source of our anguish and so help to release us from the wounds of our karma.

When conflict arises in the emotional body which is unexpressed or unresolved it seeks expression in other ways, reflecting onwards into the etheric/physical body and appearing as disease. The severity of the disease depends on the degree of conflict. Diseases resulting from emotional suppression are numerous and include heart disease related to fear and lack of generosity; cancers, digestive disorders and ulcers related to stress and anxiety; and sexual diseases caused by the inadequate or inappropriate expression of sexual energy. The majority of diseases suffered by human beings at the present time are caused by the suppression or distortion of soul energy as it flows into and through the emotional body. This is in conjunction with the increase in environmental toxins caused by the loss of our conscious spiritual, emotional and physical connections to Gaia, our Mother Earth and her Nature.

Thoughtforms

Thoughtforms are agglomerations of emotional and mental energy given life through desire and need and fuelled by the energy of the individual and collective unconscious of all human beings. During our lives on earth our emotional and mental bodies are conditioned by huge collective thoughtforms which surround the planet. These thoughtforms are constantly influencing our individual thoughts and feelings without us noticing them. For example, our planet is conditioned by a thoughtform which says that inevitably every year several million people will starve to death, and every year they do, despite the fact that first world countries destroy huge quantities of excess food. This thoughtform conditions the ways in which we use our energy to solve the problem. Advertising too takes advantage of our susceptibility to thoughtforms.

Thoughtforms die from lack of energy or because the energy which fuelled them has been redirected to a stronger thoughtform. Werner Erhard who created EST, the Erhard Seminar Training Programme which was very popular in the 1980's, set up the Hunger Project to specifically counteract this starvation thoughtform. Werner together with millions of other people throughout the world, consciously began creating a thoughtform which says there is enough food on the planet for everyone and no-one needs to starve to death. Over twenty years through education and communication, through the desire energy of millions of people, this new thoughtform will take over and the old will die away and people will no longer starve because of lack of food.

Another thoughtform which currently conditions humanity is that of environmental catastrophe through pollution, holes in the ozone layer, greenhouse gases, etc.. This thoughtform which originates as information and a desire to do something to change the habits which are destroying the environment, is fuelled by the fear that it generates. This thoughtform has become increasingly powerful at the turn of the twenty first century and has the potential to produce both positive and negative effects

The Etheric Body

The human Etheric Body has been described as a *network of fire*, a *shining web* animated by light, a *shimmering veil,* a *Golden Bowl*, and a *Chalice*. The etheric body is the energetic mould for the Physical Body, an archetype of energy on which the dense physical atoms place themselves creating the physical form which we can see with our eyes. The etheric body is a web or network of fine interlacing energy channels, called nadis or meridians, made from etheric matter and built into a specific form. Etheric energy flows along the meridians and out of the body creating the health aura, which can been seen physically using Kirlian photography. The aura follows the contours of the physical body and its colours can be seen clairvoyantly. The extent of the aura depends on the healthy outward flow of energy.

The etheric body is a reflection in etheric matter of the energy of the soul which flows in via the mental and astral bodies. *Life* energy flows into the etheric body via the *Sutratma*, the dual thread of *Life* and *Consciousness* which enters the body through the Crown Chakra on top of the head. The life thread anchors into the heart while the consciousness thread anchors into the brain. The etheric body is given life by the energy that enters via the sutratma. It is also energised by the energy which enters the body through the *Earth* thread via the Base Chakra.

Prana is the energy which connects all living beings on the planet. Every time we breathe in air we also take *Planetary Prana* into our etheric bodies, as we absorb oxygen into our lungs. So too do the animals, birds, fishes, insects, trees and plants, as well as the oceans, rivers, land, earth and rocks. When the sun shines we absorb *Solar Prana* as it radiates directly from the sun into our etheric body - one of the reasons why sunshine makes us feel good. Prana enters the etheric body via a triangle of minor chakras or energy centres at the spleen, the centre at the diaphragm and one between the shoulder blades. This prana is also known as *Active Radiatory Heat*. It is assimilated in the spleen, coloured by our individual Qualities and transmitted outwards again through the etheric body to be seen as the health aura. *This Active Radiatory Heat is the energy we use when healing with the hands.*

During incarnation the etheric web or veil forms a barrier between our astral and physical bodies, which prevents us from clearly recollecting our dreams, which occur in the Astral Sphere. It also protects us from influxes of astral energies which can harm the physical body and causes the momentary unconsciousness of death. Through meditation and using the active imagination we can slowly expand our consciousness to the point where the limits of the dividing web are transcended and subtle energies can be included harmlessly in our everyday awareness. We can see through the veil that separates the visible and invisible worlds. Then there is continuity of consciousness, we can remember our dreams clearly, we can travel in the formless worlds and we have the opportunity to die consciously.

Excessive use of alcohol, narcotic and psychedelic drugs; physical accidents traumatic experiences; certain supposedly therapeutic practices such as electroconvulsive therapy (ECT) for depressed patients; or the premature awakening of the Kundalini energy latent in the Base Chakra can all lead to the destruction of the protective etheric web. Holes or tears appear in the web allowing astral energies to enter the physical body. The patient hears voices, has hallucinations, feels depressed and overwhelmed by outside forces, thinks s/he is truly Mary or Morgana, Jesus or King Arthur.

Left to its own devices without further damage the etheric web can over a long period of time heal itself, but this can take at least seven years after the damage was first inflicted. Also once the web is damaged other forces are likely to enter and cause more damage. Seven years is also the time taken for the physical body to replace all its cells. With healing and the help of devic forces this process can be considerably speeded.

When the will-to-live disappears and a person is ready to die, the radiant fire of the etheric body is withdrawn from the body through one of the exits in the web, which are situated at the crown, the heart and the solar plexus. The Sutratma is broken, the pranic life is abstracted bodily out of the physical body, the framework of etheric matter breaks down and the dense physical body quickly falls apart.

The Chakras

Throughout the etheric body there are energy vortices known as *Chakras or Energy Centres*, where different types of energy enter the etheric body and are given physical expression. In the system I am describing there are seven major chakras and twenty one minor chakras. The seven major chakras are the Base, Sacral, Solar Plexus, Heart, Throat, Ajna and Crown. In other systems different numbers of chakras are given, e.g. Tibetan Buddhists work with five main chakras, combining the functions of the Base and Sacral Centres and the Ajna and Crown chakras. These centres also exist in the astral and mental bodies and are centres of translation of one form of energy to another.

Positions of the Seven Major Chakras

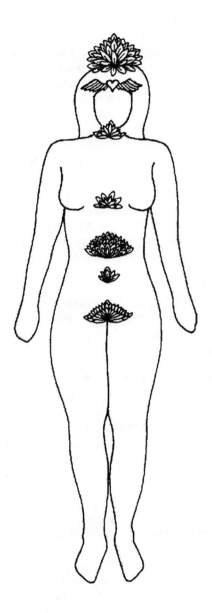

AMH

Each of the seven major chakras is directly related to one of the main endocrine glands in the physical body and via those glands to the physical organs and tissues in the surrounding areas of the body. The chakras control via the nadis or meridians, the energy channels also used in acupuncture, and via the nervous, endocrine and blood systems. As healers we work with the chakras in the etheric body. We deal with causes in the energy bodies and not merely symptoms, with areas in the etheric body as well as physical organs, with energies and their distributing points.

Each of the major chakras carries a different quality of energy into physical expression. For example, the Solar Plexus carries primarily emotional energy, the Throat Chakra carries mental energy, etc. For most human beings at any one time consciousness is polarised or focused either in the mental body or in the astral body. Only rarely are we polarised purely physically or in our souls. This polarisation is determined by the will of our being for its own purposes and is reflected in the condition of the chakras in the etheric body.

For example, when we are polarised in our emotional bodies we experience life through our emotions, reacting along the astral threads of feeling which connect us to other people. Our minds have little control over our reactions. When we are focused in our mental bodies we experience life through the mind and the throat chakra, often blocking feelings and intellectualising our experiences, explaining away emotions which we don't wish to feel. We may be mentally or astrally polarised, focused mainly in one or two chakras for a whole lifetime or for a few days or months at a time. The duration is determined by our soul's purpose and the unfolding of the experiences which such a focus brings to us.

Each chakra carries a predominant quality of energy and therefore appears to have a different colour. Quality and colour are interchangeable in the psychic world. A word needs to be said here about colour and the meanings given to it.

We all see colours differently, whether we are looking at them physically or psychically. One person may look at a red and call it orange, while someone else sees it as brown and another who is colour blind sees green. People who work with colour dyes are able to discriminate between a much wider range of colours than you and I by naming them. Psychically too we tend to see colours differently depending on our point of perception and experience. Some people only dream in black and white, while others dream in a more vivid than life, technicolour.

Certain standard colours are given by healers and occultists for particular qualities of energy. For example, yellow is often said to be a colour of the mind, green is healing, while orange is a colour of devotion worn by sanyasins devoted to a guru. Energy however is qualified by the matter through which it is passing. It is not simply that one colour means only one thing, the same colour can mean different things depending on whether it is in say the etheric or mental sphere, whether it's vibration is dense or atomic.

We shall use standard colours to represent qualities of energy, to show how we work with colour in healing, but they are not necessarily *true*. You may find that you also perceive these colours within your own and other's energy fields and in the world, but you may well find that you perceive a completely different set of colours that are yours. Your vision may be different to mine or anyone elses and *its important to follow your own vision*.

The Human Energy System

The only real way to learn about the chakras and the energy they carry is to feel them within your own body and to experience their energy. This can be done by locating each chakra at a specific point in the physical/etheric body and using your imagination to feel the energy in the chakra beating like a pulse at about the rate of our heart beat - bip....bip.... bip....bip....bip....bip ....bip....bip. For example, locate the solar plexus at the navel and feel its beat. For more details see exercises in the following chapter.

The energy of the chakras can be visualised in different ways. They can be imaged as small separate points of coloured light, as larger spheres of colour which grow in size overlapping and blending with each other, or as particular coloured shapes. Traditionally in eastern teachings chakras are depicted as lotus blossoms. When the lotus is in bud the energy in the chakra is dormant and unexpressed. When the lotus is in full bloom soul energy is flowing freely into expression. For example, when the heart lotus is in bloom the soul's energy flows directly out through our love nature. It is felt by other people as warmth, compassion, love and empathy. Choose whichever symbol for the chakras is meaningful to you.

The chakras are connecting points between one dimension of reality and another. They are psychic spaces where energy flows from one vehicle or body into another and where energy in one form expresses itself in another. For example, at the solar plexus emotional energies are translated into physical energies and are expressed through the digestive system. When we are anxious - an emotion, we feel a tightening in our stomach muscles - a physical expression. If the emotion becomes stronger the feeling of *butterflies in the tummy* soon becomes a harder *knot*. Emotional reactions such as fear and panic, can cause strong physical reactions stimulating a survival response where the physical body is prepared to flee or fight. When such emotions are present most of the time and when we try to control or suppress them, physical diseases, such as ulcers and cancers, result as a way of bringing such imbalances to consciousness for healing.

The chakras are connected to each other via three main energy channels which run through the etheric body. There is a central channel called the *Sushumna,* which passes directly from the Base Chakra through the Sexual Centre, Solar Plexus, Heart Chakra, Throat Chakra, Ajna Centre up to the Crown Chakra. Around the sushumna there are two side channels, the *Ida* and *Pingala*, which run on either side of the central channel and encircle the sushumna at the each chakra.

In most human beings energy is flowing mainly in the ida and pingala, which as they fill constricts the flow of energy in the central channel where they encircle it at each chakra. Filled with energy the ida and pingala form knots at each of the chakras which hamper the free flow of energy in the chakras and through the body causing disease. One of the purposes of meditation and chi and prana exercises is to redirect the flow of energy from the ida and pingala into the central sushumna, which helps release these knots enhancing the flow of energy in the chakras and bringing good health.

30

The Sushumna, Ida and Pingala
connecting the Chakras

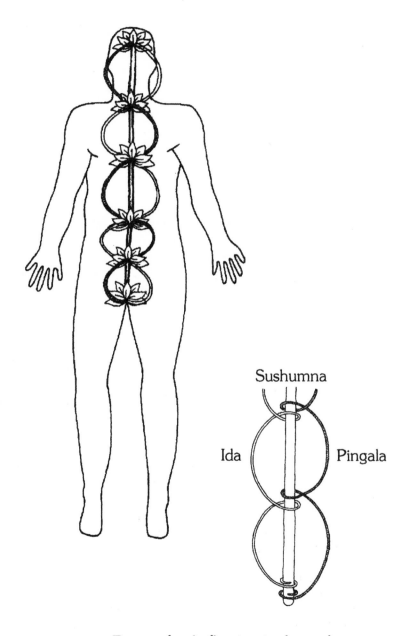

Sushumna

Ida

Pingala

AMH

Energy freely flowing in the sushumna

The Physical Body

We each have a physical body and there is a vast amount of information available on the body through the researches of medicine and science, although little is known about the connection between physical and non-physical energies. The physical body is the material vehicle for the expression of the energies of the Soul. It is the Temple which houses the divine Spark of Life. It needs our care and attention. It needs good unpolluted food, clean air to breathe, clear water to drink, exercise and sunshine to remain healthy. A detailed knowledge of anatomy and physiology of the human body is very useful to the healer who works consciously with energy, although our emphasis here is on the energy bodies and their development, interaction and transformation.

Essentially we work with our patient's energy field and aura, as well as bringing immediate relief to discomfort or pain by putting our hands directly on the physical body. This brings the comfort of physical touch as the energy moves through to heal the disease.

Human Unfoldment and Development

During our lives on earth our soul energy unfolds through several different rhythms of growth and development, all of which are in progress at the same time. Each is determined according to our soul's purpose and all are inter-related. Encompassing the whole process is the specific *Life Purpose* for which we have incarnated - why we are here alive on the earth now - the *Cause* for us. This process of unfoldment is imaged in the unfolding of the twelve petals of the Egoic Lotus, of the Soul to reveal the Jewel in its centre which is the Spark of Life.

In order to fulfil our Life Purpose we follow particular patterns and rhythms of development which are our own and unique, but which are also connected to those of other people, such as family groups, soul groups, those on similar Rays, those incarnating in the same culture, in the same astrological generations, etc.. These inner patterns of development are mirrored externally in planetary transits of our natal horoscopes throughout our lives, for example, in the 28 year cycle of Saturn which affects us every seven years when it squares, opposes and conjuncts our natal Saturn. The 52 year Chiron cycle brings us the healing experiences we need while generationally the longer cycles of the outer planets, of Uranus, Neptune and Pluto reflect deep changes in the individual and collective human psyche.

Anything which is said about patterns of human unfoldment is necessarily a generalisation and cannot be applied to individuals in a fixed manner. However used with discrimination they give a framework for exploring our own development and that of our patients.

From nine months *before conception* the Spark of life which we are, begins its journey into physical expression building for itself the solar, mental and astral bodies which will be modified by life in the physical sphere. During this time we are attracted to parents whose energy is such that they will provide for us the best conditions through which we can begin life, grow and fulfil our life purpose. We choose our parents for the way they are. This choice is made purely in terms of energy, karma and a synchronous vibration. During this time our future parents begin to dream about us and prepare for conception.

At *conception* the incarnating soul takes its first step into physical manifestation. This process once begun is usually completed through the creative impulse of the spark of life and the vitalising energy of matter itself. In the womb the soul begins to build its new physical body, modified by the genetic make up of the physical cells contributed by both parents and conditioned by the mother's mental, emotional and etheric energy bodies and her experiences during pregnancy.

At *birth* the baby emerges physically independent though not self sufficient, with a blueprint for emotional experience already imprinted in the emotional body and with a fledgling mental body which has an innate capacity to learn from experience.

From birth it takes most of us approximately twenty eight years for our consciousness to fully incarnate into life in the physical sphere. During the first seven years we are anchoring into physical expression. We are getting used to having physical bodies and developing our emotional and mental bodies, laying the foundations of our character. By the time we reach *puberty* around fourteen years we have anchored into emotional expression, the patterns are on the whole set for our future relationships. This is not to say that they cannot change but the repeating cycles of relating have begun. Many of us get stuck at some point in our emotional development and do not fully anchor until we are much older, say thirty five or forty two, if at all.

It normally takes twenty one years to fully develop the capacities of the mental body though again this can take a shorter or much longer time and we go on learning the whole of our lives. We may be mentally agile as children or our mental capacities may expand as we get older and learn to have more confidence in ourselves. By the time we are twenty eight our personality has become integrated and whole and we have begun to recover knowledge from the past held within our soul, the residues of experience from previous incarnations. We become aware of our soul energy and can bring it consciously into expression.

Around twenty eight we experience what is known astrologically as the Saturn return, which is often characterised by a crisis within a person's emotional, mental and/or physical life. It is at this time that the personality and the soul confront each other on the Burning Ground of the Kurukshestra often with a lot of emotional and mental turmoil. Once this crisis is resolved one way or another we usually feel happier about who we are and what we are doing in life. We have begun to understand our limitations and appreciate our qualities as human beings. We can move more actively into creation now and in the future rather than being governed by past experience. We become more ourselves and less dominated by family and cultural conditioning. The ages twenty eight to thirty five are a time of consolidation of character with a move outwards into expression. We can now be truly creative in the world although some of us never reach this point and spend our whole lives dealing with the problems of incarnating fully.

The *midlife crisis* comes between thirty five and forty two and is paralleled by a set of major planetary transits of Neptune, Uranus and Pluto which all human beings experience. Now there is a definite call from the soul to fulfil its purpose in incarnating, which can result in complete changes of direction in life, major ill health and/or premature death. Life begins at forty as they say, and forty two to forty nine is a time of activity and often powerful self expression.

Around fifty to fifty two years the *Chiron return* brings us face to face with our life wound, the karmic knot we have come into life to resolve. This is also the time of menopause in both women and men with its loss of direction and certainty, its direct access to the numinous inner worlds, and an acceptance of the processes of aging and the inevitability of death. The double Saturn return at fifty six years of age heralds the beginning of the crone cycle in women and the sage cycle in men.

At each of these challenge points we are more likely to face illness and disease as we struggle to integrate conflicting forces. As healers we need to be aware of our own patterns of unfoldment as well as those of our patients. Disease is the result of the actions of forces working from the longer term perspective of our whole lives, as well as with the short term and present conditions.

EXERCISE:
Sensing the non-physical energies of the body using the Hands

As well as being powerful transmitters of energy our hands are also sensitive energy receivers and can be used to feel the extent and presence of non-physical subtle energies in the human body. Following from this they can be used to diagnose disease and disturbances in a person's energy field. This exercise is good for beginners and can be practiced on a friend who is happy to let you sense into their energy bodies and who will give you reflection on what you see and sense with your hands.

In this exercise use your hands as if they are mirrors in which you can feel/see radiations coming from a person's body and can register them. Ask the person to stand in the middle of a space in which you can move all around them. Begin by sensing the health aura, the natural radiance of the etheric body.

Sensing the Aura

1. Stand behind the person with your hands on a level with their heart at the back. Hold the hands with the palms towards the person and notice the sensations that you feel with your hands. Become accustomed to the energy field in the space around the patient's heart. Close your eyes if it helps you to concentrate more easily on the sensations in your hands. You may notice feelings of heat and cold, tingling, pins and needles, prickling, energy streaming, impressions of colours,

AMH

shapes, feelings and other images. These sensations may be strong or more usually subtle. Note all sensations no matter how small.

2. Move your hands towards the patient's body and see how near you can get to the surface of their clothing before there is a definite sensation of pressure in the hands. This may be an inch away from the body or five inches or it may gradually fade out at a few feet.

3. Slowly move the hands up through the space around the chest, shoulders and neck. Again register all sensations and sensings that you feel with your hands. The aura and consequently the hands may dip inwards towards the neck showing perhaps how the patient separates their head from their body; or the aura may bulge outwards over the shoulders showing the weight they carry. Note all impressions however fleeting. Often the more fleeting the impression the more information it carries. Intuition moves at great speed and the slower brain mechanism often does not register the passage of Mercury's swift feet or we dismiss it with our minds as unreal.

4. Move the hands up over the head and notice the sensations that you feel around the head. Bring the hands up over the top of the patient's head and then down the front of the body noticing any perceptions felt with the hands. Move the hands over the the throat area and down over the heart and breasts, over the abdomen and pelvis and down the legs to the feet. Then come back up the sides and backs of the legs and up the back of the body to the level of the heart, sensing the condition of the whole aura.

5., Use your intuition to help you interpret the sensations felt in your hands. Trust that what comes immediately to you is correct. Don't think about interpreting the information, listen for the interpretation. Be prepared to make some mistakes. Tell the person what you have felt with your hands and what you sense that might mean for them. Listen to the feedback from them. Dare to be right, and wrong.

In some patients the aura will feel distorted in certain places. It may bulge or it may feel constricted. You may sense bright colour in some areas and dark spots in others or lack of colour altogether. It is a good idea to draw and paint the colours, shapes and images in the aura using the act of drawing as a means of expressing the intuition, not your skill in drawing. More ideas come to mind as the right brain expresses itself through the hands.

Sensing with the hands can be carried out rapidly in a matter of minutes to gain an impression of the overall state of the aura and the energies which the person is expressing or repressing. It is used as a means of fine-tuning the mind to respond to the flashes of the intuition. All impressions no matter how fleeting and ludicrous they may appear, should be noticed.

When used more carefully, sensing with the hands helps us become more attuned to the self, centred in our being and therefore in touch with intuition. Intuition is the key to the accurate diagnosis of the causes of a disease and from there its healing. In a healing session we use this method of sensing with the hands as a means of diagnosis of disease and its invisible causes.

Repeat the process to feel the radiance of the emotional body and of the mental body. First hold in your mind the idea that you are trying to feel the radiance of the emotional body and use the hands to find its shape and colour, and repeat to find the mental body. Write down or draw what you see/feel. Talk to the person about your perceptions and listen to their feedback.

CHAPTER THREE

The Chakras

In the system I am describing here there are seven major Chakras or Energy Centres and twenty one minor Chakras in the human etheric body. Each major chakra in the etheric body carries a different quality of energy into physical expression and has a different colour. I have given a set of basic colours for the chakras imaged as radiant spheres of energy. Each chakra is at a different stage of unfoldment at any one time and this can be registered as intensity of colour, as heat, light and as a visual impression. With practice we learn to see, feel and sense these energies within our own chakras and within those in other people's bodies.

I have also given the traditional colours and numbers of petals from the Tibetan system for each of the chakras imaged as a lotus. These are the healing colours with which the individual chakras can be balanced and healed. You will note that sometimes the colours given for the chakra spheres and the lotuses are different. For example, to invigorate a muddied Base Chakra, which is imaged as a dull red-brown sphere, we would visualise green healing lotus energy pouring into the chakra to clear out the muddiness. The lotus colours are also used in personal meditation for self healing.

Normally energy flows into the chakras in the etheric body from the mental and emotional bodies, from other chakras, via the life, consciousness and earth threads and via the sushumna, ida and pingala, the central channels in the etheric body. Energy moves out of the chakras into the dense physical body. Restrictions in the energy flow through the chakras can occur in three places - as energy is flowing into the chakra, within the chakra itself due to lack of unfoldment and personal development, and as energy flows out into the dense physical body. In the first case the chakra will be poorly energised and will appear psychically as being small in size, and be expressed as weakness in the physical body. When the chakra itself is not awakened it will also appear small, pale and dull, expressed as a weakness in personality and character. When there is constriction as energy is flowing out of the chakra, the chakra becomes over-energised and appears excessively bright or muddied and enlarged. These are unstable conditions which can all create disease and need healing.

The following are descriptions of the seven major chakras in the etheric body, with their energetic functions, their related endocrine glands and organs in the physical body and some of the common diseases associated with them which we can suffer as human beings.

CENTRE	CHAKRA	GLAND
CROWN	SAHASRÂRA	PINEAL ~ BRAIN
AJNA	AJNA	PITUITARY ~ EYES, EARS, NOSE.
THROAT	VISHUDDHA	THYROID ~ BREATHING & VOCAL SYSTEM
HEART	ANÂHATA	THYMUS ~ HEART, VAGUS NERVE
SOLAR PLEXUS	MANIPÛRA	PANCREAS ~ LIVER, STOMACH, GALL BLADDER
SACRAL CENTRE	SVADHISHTHÂNA	GONADS ~ REPRODUCTIVE SYSTEM.
BASE or SPINE	MULÂDHÂRA	ADRENAL ~ SPINAL COLUMN

The Base Chakra

The Base Chakra is known as the Root, Secret, Base of the Spine and Muladhara Chakra. It is located in the area of the perineum which lies between the vaginal opening and the anal sphincter in women and the scrotum and anus in men. It can also be felt at the bottom of the coccyx or tail bone. The Base Chakra can be visualised as a slow burning piece of coal which when awakened begins to glow red hot, burning with fire. This fire is energy, the Kundalini or Fire of Matter which lies dormant in the base chakra. As a lotus the base chakra has 32 petals and its healing colour is bright green.

The Base Chakra carries the energies of the earth which enter the body directly through the earth thread and up through the feet and legs. Through it we feel our connection to the earth beneath our feet and to the world around us. It is the energy which allows us to feel Present, Here and Now. It carries a quality of energy which is described as the Will-to-be-our-Self. When the energy in the Base Chakra is dormant and unexpressed, we feel ungrounded, often fearful and jealous, disconnected from the world in which we live, as if we don't really belong here on Earth, as if we come from somewhere else. We live in a world of plans and ideas which rarely come to fruition and have difficulty living in physical reality. We don't know where we are going in life and what we should be doing. We feel lost in an alien land.

The energy in the Base Chakra allows us to express our Self within the physical world. It is the energy which can manifest our dreams and ideals and bring them into physical reality. Without it we can dream of utopia, but we cannot make it happen. With it we can bring spirit into matter. Viewing our energy system vertically it is the deepest major chakra within the etheric body, the deepest reaching of the energies of the heavens into the earth of our bodies. In order to fully incarnate our energy must reach down to this deepest place of being. Many people live their lives as if they are half way out of their bodies, living in the space above their heads. Energy flows in the upper chakras, but is greatly constricted in the lower ones. Many patriarchal spiritual systems place great emphasis on the activation of the centres above the diaphragm with the suppression of those below. This leads to imbalance, a lack of wholeness and an inability to live in the world as it is. The Sacral Centre below the diaphragm is one of women's power centres which has been largely rejected by male teachers who are themselves more comfortable being out of their bodies. This has led to a denial of women's spiritual experiences which are often in the body.

The activities of the Root Chakra give us two of the most complete and whole experiences - spiritual, emotional and physical, perhaps not mental, of life in the physical sphere that it is possible to have. These are being born and giving birth. At the time of our own birth the life energies reach down to our Root Chakra, we push with our legs and abdomen, and we enter physical existence through the gateway of our mother's Root Chakra, whose petals unfold and expand allowing the vagina to open fully. For us to be born naturally our mother's perineum has to stretch fully to allow the baby's body to negotiate the vaginal canal. This is the physical manifestation of the flowering Base Chakra. This expansion of the perineum can be aided using massage and oils to prevent unnecessary cutting and tearing.

For both mother and child birth can be a truly ecstatic experience in which we can feel and know the complete range of energies which are available to us as human beings in the physical sphere. Being born and giving birth are processes of initiation into the mysteries of life and death. It is a time when both mother and child face life and death head on, because we can both die and be born with new life. In our culture birth is not recognised as an initiatory rite of passage, but is treated as a mechanical process, thereby losing a great opportunity for spiritual development. Fortunately things are beginning to change slowly as women reclaim our rights to our own bodies and the ways in which we wish our children to be born.

The Base Chakra is the home of the Serpent Fire of Kundalini - the latent fire of matter. When aroused this fire travels from the Base Chakra up through the central etheric channel of the sushumna which connects all the major chakras, to the Ajna Centre. This process is symbolised in the Caduceus of Mercury with the heart and wings symbolically representing the Ajna centre. The energy raised is then blended with spiritual energy in the Crown Chakra.

As the Kundalini fire rises through the central channel there is an energy transformation within the matter of the etheric, astral and mental bodies, since Kundalini is one of the Fires of Matter. When the Serpent Fire rises through the chakras to the Crown consciousness expands beyond its current limits and this expansion is permanent. When it happens we know it has happened. It is a strong electric experience of pure fire.

The Kundalini rises slowly and safely through everyday experience and through our interaction with the physical and non-physical worlds. The matter of our vehicles is daily transformed through living, the passage of kundalini keeping pace with our slowly expanding consciousness. The awakening of Kundalini can be accelerated through certain forms of yoga, pranayama (controlled breathing) and energy visualisations and meditations. (Some are contained in this volume) The purpose is the rapid transformation of both consciousness and material forms.

Caduceus of Mercury

One of the aims of Tantric or sexual yoga is the mutual raising of the Kundalini energies and an expansion of consciousness for both partners. Traditionally the man's physical orgasm is withheld by putting physical pressure on the Base Chakra. The woman's multi-orgasmic energy is absorbed by the man and his own orgasmic energy is redirected so that it travels back up through the his sushumna rather than being given out physically to the woman partner. Union or yoga takes place within the man. The woman serves the spiritual man.

In the Tantric forms of this age the two partners seek to embody and become as Goddess and God. The orgasmic energies are released by both partners to each other, as a bodhisattvic act of grace for the raising of Kundalini in the other, woman or man. The aim of the practice is to generate at-one-ment between the energies of the Physical and Spiritual Spheres with another human being, extending the duration of that moment of union when we know we are One. Understanding of the spiritual and transformative nature of sexual energy has been much debased in our society and its power denied by patriarchal religions and practices. In essence sex connects us directly to the creative, generative pleasure-giving power of the universe, which is the basic reason for its primary place in our lives.

The fires of matter are destructive to physical forms which do not resonate at the same frequency. Normally Kundalini awakens slowly with the gradual expansion of our consciousness through living - our consciousness determines the quality of matter within our vehicles. As we grow to maturity, anchoring into the Base Chakra, Kundalini fire begins to glow and rise up the spine. Many traditions give dire warnings about the premature raising of the Kundalini fire, but how do you determine what is premature? If you should decide to attempt to raise Kundalini consciously always listen to the voice of your intuition and follow what it tells you to do. Stop when it says stop and continue when it says continue. Intuition is your channel of communication to your own soul and its purpose for you. If you do not follow your intuition the fires of matter can cause severe physical damage to the body. Certain types of continuous back pain are the result of the Kundalini fire burning through at the level of the spine to which it has been raised. This should not normally happen and healing is needed with energy adjustments within the non-physical bodies to ease the burning sensation.

The energy of the Base Chakra manifests itself through the Adrenal Glands which are situated on top of the kidneys. The major secretion of the adrenal glands is adrenalin, which prepares the body for *fight or flight* in response to attack or shock. Adrenalin increases the heart rate and the rate of breathing, bringing more oxygen to the muscles so they are prepared for movement. Blood vessels to the muscles dilate so oxygenated blood can flow rapidly to where it is needed and blood vessels in the skin constrict - the person goes white with shock.

When there is excess energy in the Base Chakra, when the energy does not flow out into activity but is blocked in the chakra, this is reflected in the adrenal glands which are in a permanent state of arousal. The level of adrenalin flowing in the body is increased and we are in a constant state of fear, anxiety and anticipation, ever ready to fight or flee whatever situation we are in. When the energy in the Base Chakra is reduced or constricted, this is reflected in a reduction in the amount of adrenalin flowing in the body. The heart rate slows, the breathing rate slows, both of which can be a good thing in themselves reducing anxiety and stress, but if the chakra becomes too constricted, the body becomes sluggish and unprepared for the experiences that come to it. We have a feeling of distance from our experiences, we are not present, we are somewhere else.

The Base Chakra also governs the lower part of the body, including the organs of elimination - the kidneys and the bowel, the bottom of the spine, the legs and the feet. All diseases found in these areas are healed through working with the energy in the Base Chakra, as well as those of the minor chakras at the kidneys and in the legs and feet as necessary.

The energy in each of the major chakras is particularly related to the energies in one or two of the other major chakras. The energy in the Base Chakra is related to that in the Crown Chakra. As the Base Chakra carries the physical Earth energy so the Crown Chakra carries the energy of Atma or Spiritual will. When working with a particular chakra we usually also balance its related chakra.

The Sacral Centre

The Sacral Centre is also known as the Sexual Centre or the Svadishthâna Chakra. In some traditions it is regarded as a minor chakra but we will consider it as a major chakra. The chakra is located centrally in the body above the perineum in the womb space in women and that same space in men. It can be felt in several places - in the womb space in women; on the sacrum - the flat bony part of the spine between the hip joints which can be felt at the back of the body; or it can be felt through its sexual expression in the clitoris in women or the penis in men. The energy in the chakra can be felt as a pulsation that moves at the rate of the heart beat. The Sacral Centre is visualised as being violet in colour with a tinge of bright green energy.

The Sacral Centre carries sexual energy, the energy of sexual attraction, physical creation and of gender identity. It is this energy which amongst other things ensures the continuation of the human species. This energy moves into expression at puberty reaching a peak of physical focus in adolescence and the twenties, before becoming more fully integrated into the personality in the thirties and forties. Its most complete expression often comes in midlife as we experience and learn of the mystery of its ways.

Our sense of who we are as women and as men is vital for personality and soul development. This important sense of gender identity governs many aspects of our psychological and spiritual development even if we view the soul as being genderless. In incarnation we are all born with physical bodies of one sexual form or the other and express our inner nature through these forms. The energy of the Sacral Centre plays a role in how we see ourselves and in who we are.

During sexual arousal and orgasm the petals of the Sacral Lotus temporarily unfold and open allowing the energy of the Soul to flow directly into the physical body. We feel completely relaxed and have a great sense of well-Being. This is the power and the lure of sex for us all. It gives us an experience of our Soul which many of us have no other way of having, and it is a shared human experience.

We surrender the barriers which usually separate us from each other. We no longer feel isolated and alone. We share our Soul essence as well as our physical bodies with another and experience our Oneness as human beings. Sex without such surrender is Soul-less and mechanical.

The Sacral Centre expresses itself physically through the sexual glands, which control both the experience of sex and the reproductive cycles in men and women. In men these glands are responsible for creating erections, orgasms and mobile, fertile sperm and in women for the engorgement of the vagina, orgasms, the production of eggs, the menstrual cycle, pregnancy, the development of the foetus and the birth of a healthy baby. During a women's reproductive life between the onset of menses and the menopause, our attention is returned in a monthly rhythm to the Sacral Centre and its creative energy. This rhythm is reflected in the menstrual cycle.

Ovulation is the time when the creative energy of being flows into and out of the Sacral Centre. We become more attractive, both energetically and physically, we wear fewer clothes, we show more flesh. If this focusing of attention does not result in conception then this creative energy is available to be used for other purposes. During menstruation our focus of attention turns inwards to the creative realms of the inner worlds. We commune with our Souls and with our Divine Feminine Nature, with the Goddess. When this time of communion is unrecognised and suppressed, the energy of Being cannot flow freely into the Emotional Body and so we feel irritable and *emotional* and sometimes physically unwell.

The menstrual cycle is the physical expression of a natural movement within the psyche from an inner communion to an outer expression. The cycle parallels that of the moon as it moves through its phases, waxing from new moon to full, then waning until the moon disappears into darkness before the new moon appears once again. Ovulation often occurs at the time of the full or new moon with menstruation at the opposite pole of the new or full moon. Women who live in community, such as nuns, and those who work together in the same place, often ovulate and menstruate at the same times, indicating that they have synchronised their internal psychic as well as physical rhythms. As consciousness develops we become more attuned to natural rhythms - the rhythms of nature, and our menstrual rhythm synchronises with the lunar cycle.

When conception occurs the creative energy released with ovulation moves directly into physical expression, preparing the mother's body to provide a nurturing environment for the growing embryo and providing the materials from which the incarnating soul builds its vehicles of manifestation, again all under the domain of the Sacral Centre. During pregnancy the mother's attention shifts from wherever it was previously located into her emotional and physical bodies. This is expressed as a focusing of energy in the Solar Plexus and Sacral Centres. This shift ensures the well-Being of the mother and the child. As mothers we experience this change in focus as *feeling emotional*, as a increasing lack of interest in outside events, lowering of mental creativity, increased emotional and intuitional sensitivity and being unable to sustain much interest in anything other than babies.

When the mother is about to give birth her soul energy moves directly into the three chakras governing the lower part of the body - the Solar Plexus, Sacral Centre and Base Chakra. If the mother is completely relaxed and flowing with her own energy, the process of birth is a natural unfoldment of the petals in these three lotuses. It is a spiritual, emotional and physical experience of great power as the energies of Life flow out into physical expression with the birth of a new Life. Where there is resistance to the Soul's energy for any reason either internally in the mother's own thoughts, feelings and physicality, which may be conscious or unconscious, or externally through the insensitive, mechanical handling of the process of birth by doctors and midwives, then the waves of energy will be experienced as painful resistance.

Birth is one of the most spiritual experiences that it is possible to have in a physical body on the earth, shared by two people - mother and child, as well as those who attend them. Its importance is unrecognised and undervalued in our patriarchal society because it is a woman's mystery and because it is so commonplace.

In men sacral energy is expressed through a strong sexual focus expressed as sexual desire and attraction. Whereas this energy in women is partially refocused in the menstrual cycle and motherhood, in men it remains mainly directed towards sexual activity or sublimated into physical prowess, sport and adventure. Through dangerous sports and explorations of the earth and of space men are brought face to face with a similar death and life initiation to that experienced by women in giving birth. It is the unconscious striving for such initiatory experiences that leads to the excesses of violent behaviour and war.

When there is excess energy in the Sacral Centre its appears as a vivid purple. When the energy is restricted the colours darken, become muddied and pale. Disturbances in the Sacral Centre are quite common in our culture and at some time or another we all experience confusion in our sexual lives. Sexual energy is one of the prime moving forces for human beings since it is so intimately linked with our survival as a species and our identity as individuals. As we unfold we face various crises of identity and these are often reflected in disturbances in our sexuality as a creative expression of the Self.

Suppression or excess of energy in the Sacral Centre expresses itself physically as disease associated with the ovaries, womb and vaginal tract, with the prostate gland, testes and penis, including dysfunction of the sexual organs, infertility and venereal diseases. The Sacral Centre also governs the sacrum and the hips. One of the common effects of suppressed sexual energy is lower back pain and displacement of the hips. These can often be healed by releasing the suppressed energy and allowing it to flow freely and by recommending to patients that they increase their level of sexual activity.

The energy of the Sacral Centre is related to the energy in the Throat Chakra. Both express creative energy in different forms. The Sacral Centre governs physical reproduction while the Throat Chakra governs mental creativity and all activity involving the arms and hands and/or the voice. When there is an excess or inhibition of Soul energy in either chakra it will be reflected in the other. For example, when there is congestion in the Sexual Centre we often suffer corresponding diseases connected with the Throat Chakra - sore throats, laryngitis, toothache, etc. When we suppress the Truth which the Throat Chakra expresses, there is often a corresponding depression in our sexual lives with loss of periods, impotence and infertility.

The Sacral Centre is also related to the Ajna Chakra, the Centre between the Eyebrows. (See later). The Ajna Chakra is the synthesising centre for the whole Personality, bringing together and integrating all of our many aspects. The Ajna Chakra expresses itself through the Pituitary Gland, which is the gland in the brain which controls all the other endocrine glands and which regulates levels of sex hormones in the blood. The relationship between the Sacral Centre and the Ajna Chakra is expressed in the relationship between the sexual hormones which are secreted by the pituitary gland and those secreted by the ovaries and testes. The hormones from both glands complete the reproductive cycle. Dysfunction in the Sacral Centre will be reflected in the Ajna Chakra and vice versa; i.e. sexual problems will reflect in difficulties in personality integration and vice versa. Since many of us are focused on personality integration we can expect to experience sexual difficulties at one time or another.

The Solar Plexus

The Solar Plexus is also known as the Manipura Chakra. It is the golden yellow plexus of the sun, which glows with the warmth and light. When its energy is flowing unimpeded we feel warm, affectionate, generous and open to life. When restricted we can feel miserly, cold and full of pride. In excess its colour is inflamed with orange and red. The Solar Plexus can be felt as a pulse at the navel. Its sphere of influence extends to the Sacrum below including the Hara or One Point on which many physico-spiritual exercise systems centre their energy, and to the diaphragm above at the bottom of the ribs. As a lotus the Solar Plexus is imaged as having 64 golden petals.

The Solar Plexus carries emotional or astral energy. This is where we feel laughter, happiness, sadness, pain, anxiety and tension, where our needs show themselves. An emotional reaction to a situation is felt in the Solar Plexus. It is experienced in the physical body as a tightening, tension or release in our stomach muscles, which spreads to other parts of the body. Our emotions are conditioned, i.e. set in patterns, during the time we spend in our mother's womb and then fixed at birth by the way in which we are born. They are amplified and repeated throughout childhood and adolescence. This conditioning can be experienced and released through specific healing in the emotional body. (See chapter on Emotional healing)

During our time in our mother's womb we receive food and oxygen necessary to establish our physical life via the umbilical cord that enters the body at the navel. There is also an emotional cord built in astral matter from our mother's emotional body, connecting and nourishing us emotionally, which enters our emotional body via the Solar Plexus. Within a few minutes of birth the physical umbilical cord stops beating. Once the cord is cut physically it begins to shrivel and within a few days dies away. The astral cord connecting us to our mother nourishes us emotionally for many years and is very important for our emotional development and well being into adult life. This astral cord is usually reduced in adolescence as we assume an independent physical and emotional life. If as babies we lose or have an unsupportive mother and there is no nourishing astral cord, we become emotionally damaged and find it difficult to form successful personal relationships as adults. The astral cord to the father grows through emotional interaction between the child and its father.

The needs which we establish at birth are expressed and fulfilled through our relationships with our parents, siblings and families, and in the intimate love relationships we have later in life. We send out emotional threads from the Solar Plexus to the people we desire to be close to, often in the hope that they will fulfil our needs. It is these astral threads which often have hooks attached to them, which tie and bind us together in pleasant and unpleasant ways. We become emotionally codependent upon one another, each expecting the other to solve our emotional problems. However our needs are our own and we are the only people who can truly satisfy them.

Many human beings in first world cultures have been emotionally scarred by the trauma of the technological processes of birth and through their childhood experiences. The result of this scarring is that we hold negative emotional attachments to our parents over many years in an attempt to heal those scars. Emotionally many of us remain as children long after we should have grown up. The majority of people in incarnation are emotionally focused and exploring consciously or unconsciously the mysteries of emotional energy.

During sleep consciousness leaves the body usually via the Solar Plexus, although it can also be through the Heart or Head Chakras. We remain attached to our physical body via a thread of etheric energy which ensures that our physical and etheric bodies continue to function while we are asleep. In our dreams we travel in the Astral Sphere experiencing the hidden expanses of our own emotional body with all its complexities, as well as those of the collective unconscious. In our dreams we can resolve emotional difficulties, receive symbolic insights and have contact with astral entities and energies. Astral pathworking is a method of using particular symbols from the collective unconscious to negotiate one's way through the astral worlds and to travel safely into a space of learning, precognition and contact with our resonant being. We can wake in the morning feeling wonderful or sad, depending on our dream journeys. Keeping a dream diary is a good way to explore the Astral Sphere.

The outer physical expression of the Solar Plexus is the pancreas which amongst other activities secretes insulin. Insulin reduces the level of sugar in the blood. Many of the foods we eat are broken down into sugars through the digestive process. These sugars are transported around the body in the blood stream and used to give us energy. If we produce too much insulin, sugar is broken down and excreted and the level of sugar in the blood falls. With a low blood sugar level we feel dull and lifeless and have little energy. When the Solar Plexus is overactive, we feel emotional, needy, vulnerable, angry or sad. There is an increase in the production of insulin in the pancreas and a lowering of blood sugar levels. As a result we go on sugar binges - eating chocolates, sweets, cakes, etc., smoking cigarettes in order to raise our blood sugar levels back to normal. This works in the short term but not if the Solar Plexus is consistently over stimulated. The excess sugars in the cakes and sweets are converted into fats and we become overweight making us feel worse and reinforcing the cycle. In Britain and North America we live in societies where emotions are not honoured or allowed appropriate expression in our lives. Sugar is added to most foods because the manufacturers know we have a *sweet tooth*. This is actually a cultural adjustment to our constricted emotional bodies.

In diabetes the pancreas produces lower amounts of insulin than normal, i.e. energy flowing from the Solar Plexus into the pancreas or from the emotional body into the Solar Plexus is inhibited or repressed. When the level of insulin is low in the body there is a rise in blood sugar levels and the danger of hypoglycemia, which can result in the patient going into a coma. Diabetics therefore have to control their intake of sugar so it parallels their lower levels of insulin. They may also have to inject insulin into the blood stream in order to supplement their own small supply. As healers we work with diabetic patients in adjusting the energy flow from the emotional body into the Solar Plexus and from the Solar Plexus into the pancreas. We also make them aware of the underlying need for emotional expression, for love, comfort, affection and generosity of spirit, which is being repressed. This may call for specific healing in the emotional body.

The Solar Plexus also governs the stomach, liver, gall bladder and the organs of digestion. The condition of these organs are directly affected by our emotional state. Sometimes there are things that we just can't stomach.

The Solar Plexus is related to the Heart Chakra. Where the Solar Plexus carries emotional energies, the Heart carries the energy of love and of the soul. The point of transformation for these two energies takes place at the minor chakra at the diaphragm. This is where we hold our breath when we don't want to feel pain, when we don't want to feel what is happening to us. It is here too that pain can be released into bliss and where astral and soul energies can meet and blend.

The Solar Plexus is also related to the Throat Chakra. Where the Solar Plexus carries the energies of the emotional body the Throat carries the energy of the mental body. When we are emotionally disturbed, our minds are usually thrown into a whirl as well. When we *fall* in love, when we are emotionally attracted to someone, we suddenly stop being able to think clearly about anything else. Similarly so when we experience other strong emotions, such as anger or fear. The two energies are balanced around the Heart, which is the space of love which allows the resolution of such disturbances.

The Solar Plexus and the Throat Chakra have a reciprocal relationship. When one is overstimulated the other is often inhibited or repressed. In western patriarchal culture women are often thought of as *emotional* while men are considered *intellectual* with more social value being given to being *intellectual* and male, rather than *emotional* and female. The women's movement and the alternative culture have brought considerable changes in emphasis for both genders. As a generalisation women have become more mentally aware as men have become aware that they too have emotions which need positive expression. There are transitional swings to the opposite polarities in both women and men before a balancing takes place between emotional and mental energies.

One of the ways in which we repress our emotions is by staying in our heads rather than feeling through our bodies. We attempt to think our way through our emotional problems rather than feeling them. This doesn't work. The difficulties remain latent in our consciousness and active though repressed, resulting in diseases of the digestive system, e.g. liver disorders, gall stones, etc.. Many of us are emotionally focused, having an overactive or constricted Solar Plexus, creating ulcers and cancers, while the mind itself is under-used and the energy of the Throat Chakra is unexpressed.

The Heart Chakra

The Heart Chakra is also known as the Anahâta Chakra. It is electric blue in colour with a light filled centre. It can be imagined in the centre of the body on a level with the physical heart, beneath the breast bone at the front of the body and between the shoulder blades at the back. Its sphere of influence extends to the diaphragm below and to the top of the ribcage. As a lotus it has eight or twelve electric blue petals depending on the system described, enclosing a light-filled jewel in the centre, the Jewel in the Lotus.

The Heart Chakra is the Seat of Life in the etheric body. It is the place where the Life aspect of the sutratma, which holds us in life and in form, anchors into the etheric/physical body, The Heart Chakra carries the energy of Love which powers the universe and which makes us vulnerable, loving, compassionate and uniquely human beings. When the energy in the heart is flowing unimpeded we lose our feeling of separateness and merge into the realisation of our unity with the divinity within us, with each other and with all beings in all forms in nature. This love energy springs from the Spark of Life which we are and flows via the Soul into the Heart Chakra. When the Heart is open we have a sense of our Self and the Life within us. Anger and hatred disappear and we feel compassionate, open and alive. When our hearts are closed we feel unloving, unloved, mean, angry, depressed, confused, unclear and we easily become ill.

When we are born the openness of our Hearts as with all the chakras, depends on our karmic inheritance and the degree of unfoldment in our Souls. Many babies are born with open love-filled Hearts, which then close down due to adverse circumstances in childhood. The love lotus can then take a long time to expand to its birth place. The Heart Chakra unfolds its petals slowly through time and through particular heart-rending and heart-warming experiences. The Heart is the central chakra in the body and its expansions and contractions reflect change and transformation within the Soul itself.

In esoteric language the first opening of the inner ring of three petals out of the twelve, to reveal the central Jewel in the Lotus of the Heart Chakra, is known as *the birth of the child in the cave of the heart.* This is termed the first initiation and was expressed mythically in the birth of Jesus Christ in the stable or cave in Bethlehem. An initiation is a lasting expansion of consciousness, catalysed by life experiences, which mark the beginning of a new way of being in the world. We move from being concerned about ourselves and focused purely in our personality vehicles to being able at times to focus in our souls, to being of service to others and to transmit the energies of the spiritual triad. We begin to experience an inclusive love for all beings in nature, human and otherwise. In successive initiations personality and soul become increasingly integrated with each other and consciousness continues to expand.

The energy of the Heart Chakra precipitates into the physical body through the thymus gland, the physical heart and the lungs. The thymus gland controls the defence systems of the body, regulates muscle tone and the general well-being of the physical body. It ensures immunity against certain diseases in childhood and regulates the auto-immune system in adults. When the flow of heart energy is impaired there is an immediate susceptibility to diseases of all kinds. This is the reason why when we are going through major life crises involving changes which are central to our being, and therefore affected by the flow of energy through the Heart Chakra, we often become ill with common diseases such as colds, coughs, flu, stomach upsets, etc.. Major Heart Chakra diseases, such as angina, heart problems, lung disorders, etc., bring us face to face with who we are and our purpose in being alive on the planet at this time.

The Heart Chakra governs the physical heart and the blood system which is responsible for carrying food and oxygen - physical energy, as well as prana - etheric energy, to all parts of the body. It is the Life support system. It also carries waste products and toxins to the organs of excretion and elimination, primarily the liver, kidneys and large intestines. Together with the lungs which absorb planetary prana with every breath, the heart ensures the vitalisation of the whole body both physically and etherically.

Diseases of the heart are caused by an excess or inhibition of Life energy as it flows through the Heart Chakra into the physical body. A heart attack is due to a sudden upsurge or diminution in the flow of energy into the Heart Chakra and thence into the physical heart. The muscles of the heart are over- or understimulated and go into spasm, so that they fail to beat with their natural rhythm. This sudden spasm produces the pain of a heart attack. As the heart fails to beat rhythmically, so blood, oxygen and prana fail to circulate in the body and death can result.

Hardening of the arteries is the physical expression of a persistent constriction of the flow of love energy through the Heart Chakra. High and low blood pressure are expressions of resistance to the flow of heart energy from the soul into the Heart Chakra or from the chakra into the physical heart. These conditions respond to healing energies, but care must be taken not to over-stimulate the heart as this can precipitate physical death. Healing is given by the balancing out of heart energies between healer and patient.

The Heart Chakra governs the lungs under the direction of two minor chakras, one in each lung. When we resist our life energy we catch colds, coughs, flu, bronchitis, asthma and lung cancer. Each disease is created by a slightly different set of conditions in the patient and their environment but the essential constriction on the Life energy is the same. The disease can be karmic as well as being environmentally determined.

Cigarette smoking is one way in which human beings deal with stress. Stress is too much excitement, too much aliveness or too much fear of life. We learn to suppress our life energy by reducing the amount of prana we take into our lungs by smoking while breathing. We have developed a way of preventing ourselves from feeling too excited, disturbed and emotional about our lives. In essence we are stopping ourselves from feeling our own heart energy, our own life force. We are afraid to live. In many cases smoking leads to lung cancer and finally death - the ultimate solution to a fear of living.

Asthma is an allergic reaction in the lungs and respiratory tract to certain antigens in the air we breathe. This reaction often originates in stressful circumstances in childhood and an asthmatic attack is exacerbated by stress as well as by antigens in the air. It is compounded by the fear of being unable to breathe and therefore live through an attack. This fear of being unable to breathe may have been conditioned at the time of birth if the umbilical cord was cut too soon before the baby was ready to breathe independently and while the air passages and lungs were still filled with mucus. For a few moments we live in terror of dying from lack of oxygen before we have been born into life. This terror returns in stressful situations as an asthmatic attack.

The Heart Chakra occupies the central position of the seven major chakras. All expressions of being revolve around the Heart. Viewing ourselves vertically the Heart Chakra is a gateway between the energies of the Base, Sacral and Solar Plexus Chakras and those in the upper part of the body - the Throat, Ajna and Crown Chakras. Viewing ourselves horizontally the Heart is the space where we expand outwards from our Selves into the world around us. This pattern of energies is imaged in the Rosicrucian equal armed Cross which has a rose at its centre. Rose has long been recognised as the perfume of the heart.

The Heart Chakra is directly related to the Pituitary Gland, one of the physical centres in the brain. The Pituitary Gland is the main endocrine gland in the body which regulates the secretions of all other glands and directly links the chemical endocrine system and the electrical nervous system. The Pituitary Gland represents the energy of the Heart or buddhi within the head. Together with the Pineal Gland which carries atmic or spiritual energy and the Carotid Gland, which carries manasic energy, these three glands in the head are physical expressions of the Spiritual Triad. When this triangle of energies is awakened and vivified it results in the opening of the Third Eye, which allows us to see clearly in non-physical spheres.

The Throat Chakra

The Throat Chakra has two aspects. One is the Throat Centre or Vishûddha Chakra found at the throat and the other is the Alta Major Centre situated at the back of the head where the spinal cord enters the brain. If we imagine the chakra as a lotus, then the unawakened Throat Chakra appears as a red lotus bud hanging downwards at the throat into the body. As the energy in the Throat Chakra comes into expression the sixteen petalled red lotus slowly blossoms turning its head up to receive the energies coming in from above, bringing into play the energies of the Alta Major centre.

The two aspects of the Throat Chakra mirror the two aspects of the Mind which are connected through building the Antahkarana or Rainbow Bridge in mental matter. The Antahkarana connects everyday thought to subtle mental capacities. Imagination is transformed into mental discrimination and thereby becomes receptive to intuition and buddhic energies. Energy flowing into the Alta Major moves through the Throat Chakra and from there directly into activity. We become inspired in our words, painting, music, cooking, building, dressmaking, performing - anything that we do. The energies of the Spiritual Triad can come into expression.

The Throat Chakra governs the expression of Truth in our lives. As we all know, truth is relative and changes with our perspective. The Truth we are talking about here is the Truth of our own Souls, whose expression allows us to *walk our talk* and live our Truth.

The Vishûddha or Throat Centre

The Throat Centre is green in colour with a violet streak spiralling through it. Psychically green is a colour of activity, mentality and truth. When disturbed the violet deepens to purple and black and the green muddies to brown. The centre can be felt as a pulsation in the throat on a level with the larynx. Its area of influence extends to the collarbone below, including the shoulders, arms and hands, and to the base of the skull above including the mouth and jaw. Imaged as a lotus it has sixteen red petals.

The Throat Centre carries mental energies into physical expression. These

The Chakras

mental energies are expressed as a desire for facts and information beneath which lies the quest for Truth. The Throat Chakra governs all activities carried out with the arms and hands, which in humanity have developed a unique sensitivity. We use our arms and hands to feel, touch, love, create, build, nurture, destroy and kill. The way in which we carry out any of these activities is determined by the degree of unfoldment within the Throat Centre and the extent to which we have begun to build the Rainbow Bridge.

The Throat Centre externalises through the Thyroid Gland which governs the growth and development of the human body and its metabolic rate, i.e. the rate at which we use physical energy, through the production of thyroxine. When there is excess energy in the Throat Centre, the Thyroid Gland secretes larger amounts of thyroxine, the hormone which maintains our normal metabolic rate and our consumption of oxygen. As a result we become hyperactive and speedy and we lose weight. When the energy in the Throat Centre is reduced the production of thyroxine slows, metabolic rate decreases. We feel sluggish and slow, our bodies thicken and we put on weight. In extreme these are the symptoms of hypo- and hyperthyroidism. A deficiency in thyroxine in the young stunts growth creating dwarfism and slowing mental development.

In healing we often find that this centre is congested in one way or another. The mental faculty is developing throughout the human race and as our mentality struggles to express itself consciously and unconsciously, we experience difficulties which reflect themselves as physical diseases. We commonly catch viruses which result in sore throats, colds, laryngitis, tonsillitis, etc.. There is a reaction in the Throat Chakra whenever we constrict its energy flow. We can feel this tension physically, initially as a tickle in the throat, as sudden excess fluid in the mouth - we swallow, gulp and cough. If this tension continues a minor illness comes to express and resolve the tension by changing our state of mind.

The Throat Centre is related to the Solar Plexus, the seat of the emotions. The relationship centres around the Heart Chakra or the centre of being, which allows the resolution of most emotional and mental conflicts. When there is congestion in one of these centres it will usually be reflected in the other. As we all know, our minds and emotions are mixed up with each other.

At times many of us feel ourselves to be separate from our bodies and removed from our feelings. We live in our heads and cut ourselves off from the energy flow at the Throat Centre. As a result the energy of the chakras in the lower part of the body, in particular the Solar Plexus becomes depressed and the energy flowing through the head chakras has no means of expression in the body. This constriction in the Throat needs to be released, usually with a corresponding release of emotion and feeling, before we are able to be fully alive on the earth. This point of constriction is located physically in the body on the chest where the collar bone meets the breast bone. It is here that energy needs to be released by circulation of energy through the Heart, Solar Plexus and Throat Chakras.

The Throat Centre is related to the Sacral Centre. Both are associated with creative energy - one with the creation of physical children and the other with the creation of the children of the mind - ideas and thoughtforms, some of which are strong and precise enough to continue onwards into physical expression.

54

Mental creativity and sexual activity are directly linked. Where there is an erratic creative life, there is often an erratic sexual life - *the artist in the garret* character. There is also a reciprocal relationship between the two centres. When one is active the other may be sublimated to generate more energy for the other. This works both ways. Many religious teachings recommend celibacy so that the unexpressed sexual energy may be *raised* and transmuted into creative mental and spiritual energy and put into good works. The ascetic attempts to sublimate their sexual desire through mental discipline, prayer or plain lack of attention, Instead they focus their attention on the chakras above the diaphragm which patriarchal religions have long regarded as being of superior merit.

Concentration on any one chakra, which may mean withdrawing our attention from other chakras, allows for its specific development. This may be a period of weeks, years or a whole lifetime and is a part of our life's purpose. However all chakras carry the energy of being in their own unique way which needs direct expression. We are here on earth to live in all our ways of being, not just those which are valued by the current ruling religious culture.

The Alta Major Centre

The Alta Major Centre is that aspect of the Throat Chakra which expresses itself in the head. Its colour is turquoise green. It can be felt as a pulsation in the back of the head at the top of the spine, sometimes when we are speaking or singing and whenever we are creating from ourselves. It is the place where Intuition enters into brain consciousness. These Intuitions or Inner Tuitions come as pictures, sensings, feelings, as an inner voice, or they are translated directly into action or speech, sometimes described as channelling. Channellings may be attributed to our own being, some aspects of which we are aware and others which we are not, or to some other outside entities not currently in human form.

The Carotid Body is the outer physical expression of the Alta Major. It relates blood chemistry and pressures to respiration. Changes in the level of carbon dioxide, the waste product of respiration, in the blood are registered in the carotid body. The rate of breathing is altered to increase or decrease the amount of carbon dioxide we exhale and therefore the amount of oxygen and prana we inhale. We need prana or vital planetary fluid to live and to create.

The Alta Major governs the visual cortex at the back of the brain and many intuitions come as visual images, scenes and dreams, containing symbolic messages. It also governs the spinal cord, the junction between the spinal cord and the brain and the blood-brain barrier. Tension in the upper part of the neck which lead to headaches and migraines, are caused by excess or constricted energy in the Alta Major, which is not being given expression. When we don't follow our intuition and listen to our inner promptings our heads hurt.

In children this aspect of the Throat Chakra is naturally open and functioning and many children have intuitive, clairaudient, clairvoyant and other psychic faculties. These natural abilities are generally dismissed and denied expression in western cultures. When there is this huge discrepancy between what a child experiences and what everyone else around them seems to be saying (as in *The*

The Chakras

Emperor's New Clothes) then the energy in the Alta Major temporarily shuts down. The child's reality is denied which is very disturbing for the child, leading to a lack of self-confidence - the Self has been denied - and a lack of trust either in oneself or in other people.

When there is a strong soul impulse, the energy of the Alta Major can break through into expression in the form of coincidences, unexpected visions, revelatory dreams, unusual perceptions, sometimes under the influence of drugs or religious intoxication. However once the existence of the subtle faculties of perception are recognised the Alta Major begins to unfold and come into expression once more.

The unfolding of the connection between the two aspects of the Throat Chakra - the Throat Centre and the Alta Major, is a reflection in etheric matter of the building of the Antahkarana or Rainbow Bridge in mental matter. The Antahkarana connects the Spiritual Spiral of Manas, Buddhi and Atma to the person alive in the world. It is built by awakening and connecting the three head centres, and spans out through the Crown Chakra.

The Alta Major is one of the three major head centres. When it is awakened and connected with the Crown Chakra and Ajna Centre, the three physical head centres - the carotid body, the pineal and the pituitary glands, also awaken to spiritual energies. Circulation of energy through these three head centres causes the awakening of the Third Eye, located in the centre of the head (see later meditation and energy exercises).

The Ajna Chakra

The Ajna Chakra is the one chakra in the etheric body which is not usually depicted as a sphere, but is imaged as a rose pink heart with a golden wing on either side. This image is seen at the top of the Caduceus of Mercury (see previous illustration), which itself symbolises the raising of the Kundalini energy from the Base to the Ajna Centre via the Ida, Pingala and Sushumna - the dedication of the material life to the life of spirit. It is the symbol used by the Sufi order to represent the dedication of the personality to the inflowing energy of the spirit through the Crown Chakra. The Ajna Chakra is located between the eyebrows. Visualisation of its symbol or of light in this position will evoke a pulsation in the chakra.

The Ajna Chakra carries the energy of Buddhi, of love-wisdom and pure reason. It is the main synthesising centre for the integration of personality. Many people in incarnation at this time in first world cultures are focused on personality integration. This is reflected in the appearance of the *me* generation of the 1960's, 70's and 80's with its focus on individual development and expression. This is quite a new departure in our own culture and different from the rest of the world where there is more focus on the good of the whole community rather than of individuals. As healers we work to clear, balance and make whole any congestion in the Ajna Chakra.

The Ajna Chakra is a major synthesising centre in the etheric body. Here the many different qualities of the energy within the personality are accepted, integrated and made whole. With its unfoldment come visions, initially of colours and misty forms which become progressively distinct. The faculty of clairvoyance - clear seeing, begins to develop. Through the gradual expansion of vision in conjunction with the awakening of the Alta Major we begin to discriminate between illusion and reality. When awakened and linked to the Crown Chakra, the Ajna Chakra integrates our knowledge of ourselves as spiritual beings with our physical, emotional and mental lives on earth. We have the strength to act from that perspective.

The outer physical expression of the Ajna Chakra is the pituitary gland, which regulates all the other endocrine glands in the body. It has a biochemical and an electrical component and is the main regulatory connection between the chemical systems of the body, including hormone production and the blood system, and the electrical nervous system. The hormones produced by the pituitary body regulate the hormones produced by all the other endocrine glands, controlling the sexual cycle, the growth of the body, its maintenance and its death, lactation and skin colouring as well as excretion through the kidneys. Disease in any of these functions may be a reflection of disturbance in the Ajna Centre as well as directly in the chakra in the associated area of the body.

The awakening of the Heart Chakra also directly affects the pituitary gland via the blood stream and in a sense the Heart Chakra is represented in the head by the pituitary gland. There is a direct connection between the love expressed in the Heart and the love-wisdom of the Ajna Chakra.

The Ajna Centre governs the upper part of the face, the eyes, the nose and the ears. The most common minor illnesses caused by disturbances within the Ajna are colds, flu, blocked sinuses, ear infections, poor sight, etc.. Inability to perceive or understand clearly a particular emotional or mental problem are usually the cause of these common diseases. With a cold, we are crying on the inside rather than the outside, unable to express the emotions that we feel as tears. With earache we do not want to hear voices from either outside or from within.

More enduring disabilities associated with the senses such as blindness or deafness are caused at a deeper level in the psyche. They have a profound effect upon the way life is lived and the sufferer must adjust to a world designed for people with five functioning senses rather than four or less. Creatively such disabilities often lead to the development of intuition, of clairvoyance and clairaudience. Karmically we choose such diseases for the experiences that they bring to us and for the fulfilment of our life's purpose.

As the Ajna Centre is the synthesising centre for the personality in the etheric body, it has relationships with all the centres in the body. In particular it is related to the Sacral Centre. During sex, when the body, emotions and mind are in balance, Kundalini energy may awaken and be raised to the Ajna Centre and there blend with the energies of the Crown Chakra. Sex becomes an act of mystical and spiritual union as well as one of physical and emotional pleasure. This is a transformative experience of great power and is the basis of Tantric sex.

The Ajna Centre is closely related to the Crown Chakra. At a certain point in development when the synthesising function of the Ajna has awakened, the Ajna and Crown Chakras vibrate in unison. The linking of these two centres establishes a direct conscious alignment between our Soul, the mind and the brain, and we are able to contact our Soul energy at will. A magnetic field is created which embraces both the head centres and affects the pineal and pituitary glands. This magnetic field can be recognised in two ways. It is felt as an inner radiant sun in the head and as a dynamic energy centre through which the will and purpose of our being can make itself felt. The relating of the Ajna and Crown Chakras to the Alta Major and the circulation of energy through these three centres brings the energies of the Spiritual Triad into the etheric body.

Whenever we pursue our spiritual development there will be disturbances in the Ajna Centre. These will be experienced as minor diseases - headaches, eye strain, sinus problems, etc.. When we resist the transformative nature of the energy of this chakra these ailments may become more serious, but they are part of a process directed by our Soul which is, by its nature, hard to resist.

Crown Chakra

In its fullness the Crown Chakra is a centre of radiant light in which all the colours of the rainbow are visible. It is situated on top of the head towards the back. In babies the Crown can be seen physically beating in the depression between the soft bones of the skull, before they have met and joined up. During sleep the hair on a baby's Crown will often stand on end streaming with the energy moving through the chakra. The Crown Chakra carries the energy of Atma or Spiritual Will into physical manifestation. When the Crown Chakra is awakened we are able to come into resonance with the will and purpose of our being. It connects us to our strength and power as spiritual beings. It allows us to identify with the Spiritual/Atmic Sphere and to bring such contact back into brain consciousness. As a lotus the Crown Chakra is imaged as having thirty two crystal white petals.

The thread of our life, the Sutratma, enters the body through the Crown Chakra. The life thread has two aspects - Life and Consciousness. The life aspect constitutes the principle of coherence and integration holding us in form and anchors in the heart. The consciousness aspect which makes us Self-conscious, rational, Self-determining human beings anchors in the brain. The consciousness thread itself divides into three, anchoring into the three physical head centres - the pineal, the pituitary and carotid bodies. This particular process of anchoring begins at conception and is completed by the age of seven years when the child becomes truly Self-conscious.

In death both aspects of the sutratma are withdrawn from the body via one of the exits in the etheric body, producing loss of consciousness and disintegration of the body. (See Chapter Ten). In sleep the energy of the consciousness thread is withdrawn from the brain. We become unconscious to the physical world while our bodies remain alive with our consciousness focused elsewhere.

The sutratma is reflected in the three energy channels that run through the body from the Base Chakra to the Crown, and expressed in the spinal cord in the physical body. The three nerve channels are called the Ida, the Pingala and the central Sushumna. The red Ida carries the energy of feeling and ideas which are emotionally coloured. Although they are well-meaning, they lack the organised form that mental energy would give to them and on their own they lack force and peter out into insignificance. The yellow Pingala carries the energies of mind, activated by personal ambition, which can move too fast and burn themselves out. When these two energies are equilibrised they complement each other. Then the energies of Being can ascend and descend via the central blue Sushumna, passing easily through the chakras and outwards into manifestation. The Soul can then express its energies on earth.

The Crown Chakra expresses itself physically through the pineal gland - a small pea-like body attached to the back of the third ventricle of the brain. The pineal gland produces melatonin, a light-sensitive pigment. As the Crown Chakra awakens the pineal gland begins to function as an organ of illumination and spiritual perception.

Through the Crown chakra we build the Antahkarana which connects the three chakras in the head to the three aspects of the Spiritual Triad. The pineal gland connects to Atma or spiritual will, the pituitary gland connects to Buddhi or love-wisdom and the carotid body connects to Manas or mind. We build the antahkarana slowly over time through our experiences of life, and consciously through meditation and the directed use of energy. The conscious circulation of energy through the three head centres creates the opening of the Third Eye in the centre of the head. The Third Eye is a doorway to perception of the energies of the Spiritual Triad. It is perceived as a blank screen on which subtle energies appear as moving images of colour, light and sound, like watching scenes on a movie screen. The awakening of the Third Eye allows the development of the faculty of direct perception.

The Crown Chakra governs the brain and central nervous system. The nervous system is the physical expression of consciousness, while the blood system is the expression of the life energy. All diseases of the nervous system are related to the condition of the Crown Chakra and the anchoring of the sutratma into the brain. Where this anchoring is incomplete in children there will be mental and physical retardation and in adulthood there will be emotional and mental disorders such as schizophrenia, a name which covers a multitude of little understood symptoms.

One of the most common diseases in the head is the headache, caused by a constriction of the energy of being as it flows into or out of the Crown, Ajna or Alta Major Chakras. Tension builds between the brain and the skull which finds no release through the closed head centres. We feel this pressure as pain. Headaches respond readily to healing with the hands and through the aura. As soon as a flow of energy is created through the Crown, Ajna and Alta Major Chakras, the constriction is released and the headache passes away as the energy flows freely once again.

Whenever our spiritual life is developing and the Crown Chakra is in conscious unfoldment, there can also be quite startling changes in the size and shape of the head. Lumps and bumps appear and disappear in an alarming manner. These are the physical expressions of the energy changes occurring within the head centres and their reaction to energy stimulation. They are part of the process of the development of the head centres. They are not normally brain tumours though we may fear that they are. However, painful or persistent changes should be further investigated to ensure that they are not in themselves a sign of disease.

The Chakras

The Crown Chakra is related to the Base Chakra. Where the Base Chakra connects us to Mother Earth and is responsible for our most physical earthly experiences - being born, giving birth, being alive, the Crown Chakra connects us to the non-material spheres of Spirit. It is through the Crown Chakra that we may glimpse the Spark of life which we are. These two energies meet and blend in the Heart and release love into our lives.

The Minor Chakras

As well as the seven major chakras in the etheric body there are twenty-one minor Energy Centres. The minor centres are related to the functioning of individual organs and parts of the body and function under the direction of the nearest major chakra, excluding the Spleen Chakra. The Spleen Chakra is unique in the body in that it is a double chakra, which governs the spleen and also has connections to all the seven major chakras. The Spleen Chakra is responsible for the assimilation of planetary and solar prana from the air we breathe and from the radiations of the earth and the sun; and for its distribution throughout the etheric body. This function is vital for our health since prana gives life to the etheric and physical bodies. Without it we cannot live in physical form.

The positions of the minor chakras are given as follows :
one on the sole of each foot
one on the back of each knee
one at each side of the pelvis (associated with the reproductive organs)
one at the stomach
double chakra at the spleen
one at the liver
one at the diaphragm
one between the shoulder blades
one at the top of each breast
one on the palm of each hand
one at the top of the breastbone (parathyroid glands)
one behind each eye
one behind and above each ear.

There are also energy plexi in the body and in particular in the head which may have a transitional importance, e.g. there are several energy points between the Ajna and the Crown chakras that begin to function as the head centres awaken.

Energy moves in triangles. Circulation of energy through three points creates movement and hence restores imbalances, reduces stagnation and repression and creates health. When we are healing a diseased organ which is under the direct control of a minor chakra, we make energy connections between that minor chakra, its governing major chakra and another related minor or major chakra. We then circulate energy between the three chakras. For example, for a disease associated with the digestive functions of the liver, we would circulate energy through the minor liver chakra, the governing major Solar Plexus, and the minor stomach chakra. For a disease associated with the breakdown of amino acids and the formation of urea in the liver, we would circulate energy through the minor liver chakra, the Solar Plexus and the Base Chakra.

As healers who are attempting to work consciously with energy, the degree to which we are aware of the nature and condition of our own energy system, is the degree to which we can know the energy condition of others and so truly heal.

Positions of the Minor Chakras

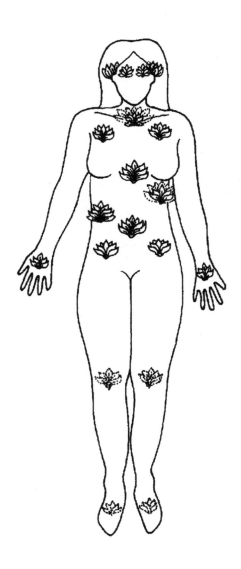

AMH

EXERCISES:
For the Unfoldment and Development of the Chakras

There are certain basic instructions that apply to all the exercises. They are as follows :

1. The Physical Body should be in as comfortable a position as possible while keeping the back upright and straight, so that the spine and the chakras are aligned. If we lie down we tend to fall asleep as we relax, leaving the body unconsciously. Our aim in these exercises is conscious self-exploration with a clear eye.

2. Imagination is recognised as the creative faculty in all these exercises. Energy follows thought and where we are able to clearly visualise the movement and direction of energy, there energy will follow. Imagination helps create the correct conditions for experiencing different energy states. The chakras may be imaged as being located on the front, the back or the middle of your body. Follow your intuition.

3. Breath is used consciously for the circulation of prana in the etheric body, and for vivifying and stimulating the chakras. On the in-breath we consciously draw prana into the etheric body. Holding the breath we circulate energy through the chakras and carry out the creative work of the imagination. On the outbreath prana, qualified by the energy of particular chakras, is distributed throughout the etheric and other vehicles.

4. At all times we listen to our Intuition and its instructions to us. This is particularly important in those exercises where we are raising our energy levels. We must dare to continue when we get scared, but we must know when to stop for our safety. It is our intuition which helps us ride the razor's edge.

Locating and Energising the Chakras

In this exercise we experience the location of each chakra and feel some of its qualities, by drawing the energy of the earth and the heavens into the physical/ etheric body.

1. Sit comfortably and for several minutes allow the thoughts and feelings of everyday to subside and slip away. Feel the floor or earth beneath you supporting your body. Listen to the sounds of human activity and of nature all around you then turn your attention to your own body.

2. Watch your breath as it flows in and out of the nostrils and feel it begin to slow down. Do not force it to slow but watch it slow. Take a deep breath in, hold the breath for as long as it feels comfortable and then breathe out. After the outbreath hold the breath for a moment, then breathe in again. Repeat the cycle until the pattern is established. Breathe in, hold the breath, breathe out, hold.

3. Take a deep breath in, hold the breath and imagine streams of light/

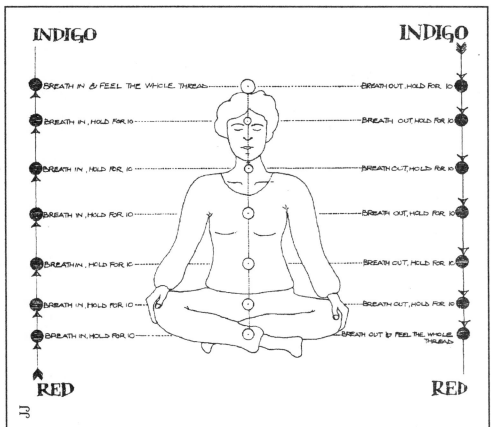

INDIGO   INDIGO

BREATH IN & FEEL THE WHOLE THREAD············   ············BREATH OUT, HOLD FOR 10

BREATH IN, HOLD FOR 10············   ············BREATH OUT, HOLD FOR 10

BREATH IN, HOLD FOR 10············   ············BREATH OUT, HOLD FOR 10

BREATH IN, HOLD FOR 10············   ············BREATH OUT, HOLD FOR 10

BREATH IN, HOLD FOR 10············   ············BREATH OUT, HOLD FOR 10

BREATH IN, HOLD FOR 10············   ············BREATH OUT, HOLD FOR 10

BREATH IN, HOLD FOR 10············   ············BREATH OUT & FEEL THE WHOLE THREAD

RED   RED

JJ

~LOCATING & ENERGIZING THE CHAKRAS~

energy flowing upwards from the centre of the earth, through the ground where you are sitting into your legs and the Base of the Spine Chakra. Locate the Base Chakra in women between the vulva and the anus and in men between the scrotum and the anus. Breathe out and hold the breath for a few seconds.

4. Take a deep breath in, hold the breath and imagine a pulse beating in the Base Chakra at about the rate of a heart beat...dub...dub...dub...dub... Once the pulse is established count the pulse for ten beats and feel it beating in your body. Breathe out and hold for a few seconds.

5. Take a deep breath in and as you breathe in, imagine that you are pulling the light energy up from the Base Chakra to the Sacral Centre located at the sacrum, the midpoint of the pelvis, or in the womb space. Hold the breath and locate the pulse in the Sacral Centre. Breathe out and hold for a few seconds.

6. Take a deep breath in, hold the breath and feel the pulse beating in the Sacral Centre for a count of ten. Breathe out and hold.

7. Take a deep breath in. As you breathe in imagine that you are pulling the energy up from the Sacral Centre to the Solar Plexus, located behind the tummy button. Hold the breath and feel the pulse in the Solar Plexus. Breathe out and hold.

8. Take a deep breath in. Feel the pulse in the Solar Plexus for a count of ten beats. Breathe out and hold.

9. Take a deep breath in and draw the energy upwards from the Solar Plexus to the Heart Chakra beside the physical heart in the centre of the body. Hold the breath and find the pulse in the Heart Chakra. Breathe out and hold.

10. Breathe in, hold the breath and count for ten in the Heart Chakra. Breathe out and hold.

11. Breathe in, draw the energy up from the Heart to the Throat Chakra at the neck. Hold the breath and feel the pulse in the Throat. Breathe out and hold.

12. Deep breath in, hold and count for ten in the Throat Chakra. Breathe out and hold.

13. Breathe in, draw the energy up from the Throat to the Ajna Chakra between the eyebrows. Hold and feel the pulse in the Ajna. Breathe out and hold.

14. Deep breath in, hold and count for ten in the Ajna. Breathe out and hold.

15. Breathe in and pull the energy up from the Ajna to the Crown Chakra. Hold the breath and feel the Crown pulse. Breathe out and hold.

16. Deep breath in, hold and count for ten in the Crown Chakra. Breathe out and hold the breath.

17. Breathe in, drawing the energy out from the Crown Chakra up into space reaching for the farthest star you can imagine. Breathe out and hold the breath.

18. Breathe in, hold the breath and feel the thread of energy moving through you from the centre of the earth outwards to the farthest star and feel the thread pulse for a count of ten through the body. Breathe out and hold the breath.

19. Repeat.

20. Breathe in, hold the breath and imagine the stream of energy reversing so that energy moves into the body through the Crown Chakra from the farthest star. Then breathing out through the mouth, let the jaw relax and the mouth hang open and feel the energy move into the Crown Chakra.

For the remainder of the exercise the emphasis shifts to the out breath rather than the inbreath and to holding the breath after the outbreath.

20. Breathe in, hold the breath and feel the pulse in the Crown Chakra for a count of ten. On the outbreath through the mouth, see the energy flowing like a waterfall of light and feeling from the Crown Chakra down to the Ajna Chakra. Hold the breath and feel the energy.

21. Breathe in, hold the breath and count for ten in the Ajna. On the out breath see energy flowing down from the Ajna to the Throat Chakra. Hold the breath and feel the Throat relax and expand.

22. Breathe in, hold and count for ten in the Throat Chakra. On the outbreath see the energy flowing from the Throat down to the Heart Chakra. Push the chest out, hold the breath and feel the Heart relax and fill with energy.

23. Breathe in, hold and count for ten in the Heart Chakra. On the outbreath see energy flowing down from the Heart to the Solar Plexus. Push the stomach muscles out as you breathe out. Hold the breath and feel heat fill your stomach.

24. Breathe in, hold the breath and feel the pulse for a count of ten in the

Solar Plexus. On the outbreath push the energy down from the Solar Plexus to the Sacral Centre. Push the abdominal muscles outwards. Hold and feel the Sacral Centre fill with energy.

25. Breathe in, hold the breath and feel the pulse for a count of ten in the Sacral Centre. On the outbreath push the energy down to the Base of the Spine, relaxing the pelvic floor muscles and the perineum. Hold and feel the Base Chakra fill with energy.

26. Breathe in, hold the breath and count ten beats in the Base Chakra. On the outbreath push the energy down from the Base Chakra through the legs into the earth. Hold the breath and feel the energy flow into the earth.

27. Breathe in, hold the breath and feel the energy pulse through the body, reaching from the farthest star down to the centre of the earth.

28. Continue to breathe deeply and evenly and feel the energy as it flows through the body. Feel what you are feeling in all parts of your physical/etheric body and any other qualities of energy entering the etheric body.

This exercise allows you to locate the chakras in the physical and etheric bodies, vivifying and balancing the whole etheric body.

Opening the Heart Chakra

This is an exercise which awakens the Heart Chakra and draws forth our essential Soul qualities of Love and Compassion. Through it we can experience our own deep nature, the wellspring of who we are, the place from which all healing proceeds. The Heart Chakra is that space where the energies of earth and spirit meet and mingle, releasing the energy of the soul, which is love. This exercise can be carried out on its own or in conjunction with the previous centring exercise.

1. Sit comfortably, let the arms relax and the expressions of the day ease away from your face. Let your cheeks and eyes relax and for a few minutes watch the breath as it flows in and out of the nostrils.

2. Bring your attention to your Heart Chakra and feel its pulse, its size, its shape, its colour.

3. Using your creative imagination, see your Heart being filled with all of the most beautiful colours that you can imagine. As much as you can, visualise actual colours and fill your heart until you can't put in any more colours.

4. When the Heart is full of colour, begin to fill your Heart with all the loveliest perfumes that you can imagine - the scents of honeysuckle, roses, jasmine, new-mown grass, rain, etc.. Continue until you can't think of any more to put in.

5. Begin to visualise all the places that you have ever really enjoyed visiting and being in and put these into your Heart Chakra.

6. Remember the experiences that you have had that have made you laugh and feel happy and put these into your heart.

7. Visualise all the animals that you have loved and put them in your heart.

8. See the people who you are close to and love and who love you and put them in your heart.

9. Feel your Heart Chakra swell and grow until it feels like it will burst with

OPENING the HEART CHAKRA

⋇IN BREATH⋇

colour, perfume, places, creatures, people and all the experiences which have brought you joy. Fill your heart until there is no more room.

10. Take a deep breath and become aware of the pulsing in your Heart Chakra and its colour, size and shape. Breathe deeply and evenly for several minutes and really feel the energy in your Heart.

11. Take a deep breath in, hold the breath, feel the energy and on the outbreath, sound an OM from the Heart. See all the good feelings and love in your Heart begin to move outwards through your body. See a wave of colour and energy move outwards to the tips of your toes and fingers and the ends of your hair.

12. Breathe in. Hold the breath and on the outbreath sound another OM and see the energy radiate outwards from your body filling up the space around you. Watch your good feelings fill up the room you're in or the place in nature, then expand to the whole building or the countryside around you.

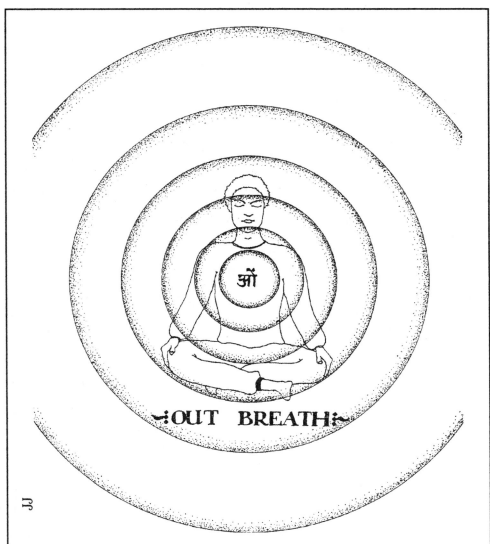

ॐ

:OUT BREATH:

JJ

13. Breathe in. Hold and on the outbreath sound an OM and see the energy radiate outwards to fill the street where you live, then the town or the landscape that surrounds you.

14. Breathe in, hold the breath, breathe out and sound an OM and radiate energy outwards from your heart to the whole country in which you live, then to the continent of which you are a part and on to the whole planet. Cosmic travellers can continue radiating to the planets the limits of the solar system, the galaxy and the ends of the universe.

15. Feel the feeling in your heart.

16. Slowly bring your consciousness back into your body noticing your breath as it moves in and out of the body. Become aware of the sounds of activity going on around you. When you are ready open your eyes. Place your hands palms down on the floor or the earth to ground yourself.

Centring in Being

The practice of Centring in Being, centring within the energy field of the Soul, is carried out at the beginning of any diagnostic or healing session. This ensures that the healer is radiating from their Soul and always remains positively polarised in relation to the patient and therefore cannot take on any of their patient's disease.

The energy of the soul can be experienced directly or by coming into resonance with its particular energy frequency. The soul's energy expresses itself in different forms, e.g. through the seven chakras or through the consciousness aspect of the sutratma which anchors into the brain. By focussing our attention on the chakras in the etheric body we can come into resonance with the soul's energy and are thereby able to shift dimensions and come into a direct experience of the soul.

The detailed instructions given here for Centring in Being are a guide for beginners. As the ability to focus attention at will and to visualise precisely improves, the energy contacts can be set up rapidly in a matter of moments. This exercise prepares us for all forms of energy work, healing, meditation, massage, other complementary therapies, or any creative activity such as singing, painting, thinking, etc.. This exercise also begins the process of learning to discriminate between different qualities of energy and protects us from taking on our patients' diseases.

1. Sit comfortably and allow the body to relax and let the cares of the everyday world slip away. Watch the breath as it flows in and out of the nostrils for a count of twenty breaths.

2. Take a deep breath in, filling the lungs and bring your attention to your heart. Hold the breath and see the electric blue Heart Chakra, located in the centre of the body near to where the physical heart is, beating in rhythm with the heart beat. Breathe out. Repeat three or four times.

3. Breathe in, hold the breath and visualise a thread of light moving from the Heart Chakra down through the body to Base or Secret Chakra which is coloured a dull red that grows brighter as energy moves through it. (The Base Chakra is located on the perineum between the vagina or scrotum and the anal sphincter.) Breathe out.

4. Breathe in, hold the breath and visualise the thread of light extending from the Base Chakra down through the floor you are sitting on into the earth. See it moving towards the magnetic energetic core of Planet Earth.. Visualise the earth in as much detail as you can from the earth at the surface through different layers of the rocky crust, through the red hot molten fiery body of the earth to the centre. Imagine its texture, weight and density as the thread of energy passes through it. Breathe out. Repeat breaths until this visualisation is stable.

5. Breathe in, hold the breath and feel the energy pulse as it moves from your Heart Chakra to the centre of the earth. Breathe out.

6. Breathe in, hold the breath and visualise energy returning from the centre of the earth through all its layers, coming up through the ground back into your

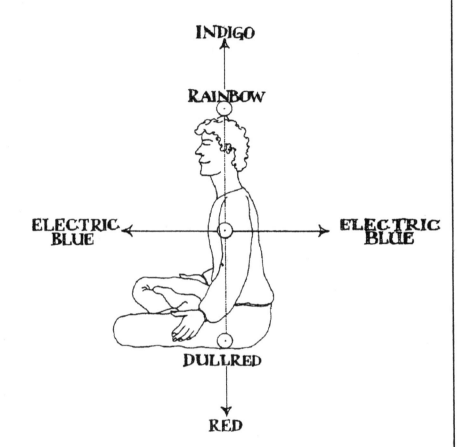

❧CENTRING in BEING❧

INDIGO

RAINBOW

ELECTRIC BLUE

ELECTRIC BLUE

DULLRED

RED

JJ

body via the Base Chakra and from there up through the body to the Heart Chakra. Breathe out.

7. Breathe in, hold the breath, and feel the energy of the earth moving up through the thread invigorating the Heart Chakra, opening it out. Breathe out.

8. Breathe in, hold the breath and visualise a thread of light moving from the Heart Chakra to the sparkling white/rainbow-coloured Crown Chakra on top of the head. Breathe out.

9. Breathe in, hold the breath and visualise the thread of light extending out of the Crown Chakra into the air above the head, up through the ceiling and out of the roof of the building you're in (if you are), up into the sky, through the atmosphere and the deep indigo blue of space, out across the solar system, then across the galaxy and the universe reaching to the farthest sparkling star you can imagine, your star. Breathe out. Repeat breaths until the image is stable.

10. Breathe in, hold the breath and see the energy pulse along the thread as it moves between the Heart Chakra and your star. Breathe out.

11. Breathe in, hold the breath and visualise sparkling energy returning back from the farthest star across the universe towards the solar system, past the planets into the earth's atmosphere, coming in through the roof of the building you are in, into the Crown Chakra on top of your head and down to the Heart Chakra. Breathe out.

12. Breathe in, hold the breath and feel this star energy invigorating your Heart, meeting and blending with the energy of the earth. Feel your Heart Chakra opening out and energy beginning to radiate outwards in all directions horizontally. Breathe out.

13. Breathe in, hold the breath and visualise yourself with your chakras like beads on a necklace of a thread of light which connects the centre of the earth to your star. Breathe out.

14. Breathe in, hold the breath and feel love and compassion, the energy of the Soul begin to pour through the electric blue Heart Chakra, radiating horizontally outwards in all directions. Breathe that energy outwards through the body.

15. Breathe in, hold the breath and stabilise the outward flowing Heart energy.

Once you are centred in your own Soul, put the set of energy connections which got you there to the back of your mind. You are now ready to safely begin healing or any other creative activity. You can continue with the visualisation, breathing loving compassionate energy out into the world around you, to your home and family, your village, town or city, to the continent on which you live and to the whole planet, healing all those who are in pain or suffering.

The purpose of this exercise is to allow you to experience what it feels like when the energy of the soul is pouring into the personality vehicles. Once you know what this energy feels like and you can begin to invoke it at will, then you can centre yourself in moments.

CHAPTER FOUR

The Causes, Nature and Diagnosis of Disease

All disease has its roots in the past and its branches into the future. Disease is an effect created out of our past as individuals, as part of a family, as members of different communities, as part of the human species, and as part of the expression of Gaia, the Planetary Logos of the Earth. How we deal with our disease has effects which continue on into our future. Healing which occurs in this moment *NOW* resolves these two forces from the past and future, changing our lives in the present.

Causes of Disease

All disease is the result of the inhibition of the free flow of Soul energy into and out of our mental, astral and etheric bodies into the physical body, interacting with physically and psychically harmful viruses, bacteria and poisons in our environment. Whenever the energy of our Being is restricted as it flows into or out of one of the seven major chakras in the etheric body, we become susceptible to environmental toxins and are likely to become ill - physically, emotionally, psychologically or spiritually. In this book of Esoteric Soul Healing our focus is upon what we can do for ourselves and others within our energy bodies, rather than on the vast topic of how to remove toxins from the environment which also needs urgent world attention.

There are two main reasons why our Soul's energy can become restricted resulting in two types of disease. Firstly there are those diseases which are caused by the resistance of the matter of the mental, astral and etheric/physical bodies to the impact of more subtle energies from the Soul and Spiritual Triad, i.e. when the matter of the Personality vehicles is not in harmony or resonance with the incoming energies. Secondly there are those diseases which are inherent within the matter of the planet as a whole and are due to the resistance of the planetary substance of the Earth to more subtle energies.

Included among the first category of diseases are all the non-infectious diseases, mental and emotional illnesses and certain cancers. Schizophrenia is an example of a disease which is the result of the impact of harmful astral energies upon the etheric/physical bodies, as they pass through *holes* in the normally complete protective etheric web. The holes in the etheric web may themselves be created by severe emotional trauma, that is, by the impact of astral energies vibrating at a frequency which is destructive to the etheric body. This can happen at birth or in childhood. Holes can also be created by the impact of etheric energies which are out of resonance with the matter of the etheric body such as emissions from TV, electrical and telephone transmitters. Certain substances also have this effect, in particular hallucinogenic drugs, a fact used by shamans for the conscious opening up of the etheric web.

Cancers are the response of the body to the impact of physical energies either in the form of specific carcinogenic substances or as radiations which are destructive to the human body. Some cancers are caused by daily exposure to a carcinogenic substance over a length of time, as with cigarette smoking, and others are caused by brief exposure, as in nuclear radiation. The difficulty in tracing the causes of cancer lies in the time delay between the initial exposure and the onset of the disease 20-30 years later. As yet we have very little protection against carcinogenic or nuclear substances although people have always lived and survived in parts of the world that are naturally radioactive.

The rise in the numbers of people suffering and dying from cancers of all types is directly related to our development as an industrial society and the pollutants placed haphazardly in the environement and the growth in the use of nuclear energy for the production of bombs and electricity. This development is a symbol of the unfoldment of consciousness within humanity as a whole. As yet we have not found a solution to the problem of cancers and only when we have realised as a whole species, that we have to change the way we live, will the true resolution of these diseases come about. When we realise that the human body cannot withstand the impact of such a large increase in the levels of carcinogens and background and specific radioactivity and do something to change our use of these substances, this will also mark an expansion in the consciousness of humanity as a whole. It will be a group initiation of major importance for our species, until then we are all dicing with death.

The second category of diseases are those which are inherent within the planetary substance itself. Like any other being Gaia is ever unfolding into herself through her expression the Earth and everything which lives and moves and is a part of her body and being. Bacteria, viruses, poisons and allergens are all part of this expression even though they may have an adverse effect upon other beings in nature. We are all subject to the diseases caused by these elements which includes infectious diseases - physical, emotional and mental, which pass between human beings, animals and plants. Everywhere there are germs we could *catch* at any moment, but normally we don't. Disease only comes at specific times and in specific forms.

The Nature of Disease : Energies and Forces

Human beings are essentially composed of energies and forces. A force is an energy which is anchored. A free energy is more subtle and potent than a force. However at any one time in our lives free energy may be less effective within us than an energy which is already anchored as a force. For example, the emotional energy of the Solar Plexus is often more potent in its effects upon our daily lives than the energy of the Heart Chakra, which swings slowly into action. This is so even though the free energy of the heart - the love and beauty of our Soul, is infinitely more potent than the anchored force of our emotions.

One way of looking at disease is to view it as an effect of inpouring energy upon existing forces. In human beings there are two main free energies - the Spark and the Soul. The Spark expresses itself through a vortex of forces - the Spiritual Triad, and the Soul expresses itself through another vortex of forces, the Personality. Throughout life the energies of essence and being unfold into expression through the agency of forces. The more that these energies and forces resonate in harmony with each other the more we can truly be ourselves on the earth. Disease is the result of conflict between energies and forces or between forces alone.

Conflict between energies and forces appears in the form of those diseases which are caused by the resistance of the mental, astral and etheric/physical bodies to the impact of Soul energy. Conflict between forces demonstrates as difficulties related to the interplay between the chakras in the etheric body. For example, we sometimes experience conflict between our heads and our hearts, i.e. between our Head and Heart Chakras; or between our Solar Plexus(emotion) and Sacral Centre(sexual attraction); or between sexual creativity and mental creativity - the Sacral and Throat Chakras. When the force expressed by any one chakra is repressed there will be compensatory adjustments in the energy flow of the other chakras, especially those to which it is particularly related.

Death is the result of a final conflict between forces. The area of conflict is the patient's etheric/physical body. Sometimes during a severe illness or when we have a traumatic accident, our Soul withdraws its energies from the physical body, leaving only forces behind. If the disease is potent the patient cannot bring energy into the body to combat the warring forces and the patient loses the will-to-live - the energy inherent in being and necessary for physical life. The magnetic power of the planetary life then reabsorbs the life within the atomic structure of the physical body via the Earth Thread anchored into the Base Chakra and the patient dies. As healers we recognise when the will-to-live has gone and the forces are at war. We apply our skill in helping the patient to die easily. (See Chapter Ten on Death and Conscious Dying)

Fire by Friction

Throughout our lives the lotus of our Soul is unfolding into expression in the physical ,astral and mental spheres. This unfoldment is expressed in the ever changing relationship between our Soul and Personality. There is always some degree of friction between the two as our different aspects come into play. Some days we are lost in thought, other days in emotion. Sometimes we are focused on our work or our relationships or our spiritual development. Sometimes we serve others and sometimes we are selfish. This constant shifting of attention gives us a sense of learning, changing, growing, stagnating, failing, becoming whole and expanding. All these states can be perceived as degrees of unfoldment within the lotus of an individual chakra and within the lotus of the Soul.

When a particular point of friction between Soul and Personality becomes fixed, for example when we get stuck in the repeating patterns of our emotions and thoughts, disease or *Fire by Friction* comes to return the relationship to one of free-flowing harmony. It is our Soul calling to its expression, the Personality, which creates the point of friction for its purposes. It is our Personality which then concentrates upon the point of friction leading to and sustaining disease.

Our aim as healers is to assist the patient in shifting their focus of attention away from the point of friction in the diseased area, back to their own Soul. The energy of the Soul allows the point of friction to be viewed from a different perspective thus helping resolve the conflict. As healers we need to be able to locate the point of friction within one of the Personality vehicles. We can do this by several different methods including clairvoyance and direct perception. Broadly speaking the majority of people are astrally focused and the point of friction will be within the astral body. Some people are mentally focused with points of friction in the mental body. Few people in incarnation are purely physically focused or focused in the Spiritual Triad although there are different degrees of personality integration and surrender to soul energy.

Focus of Attention and Types of Disease

The vast majority of human beings in incarnation today are astrally focused. We live and move and have our being in a vast sea of emotion, plummeting with its storms, cresting its waves and becoming still in its calm waters. This polarisation leads to certain categories of disease caused by points of friction within the astral body. These diseases are the result of the inhibition of the free flow of Soul energy both into and out of the Solar Plexus, the Sacral Centre and the Heart Chakra in particular. The following are a few examples of these types of disease and their causes in the emotional body:

Emotional suppression and constant introspection leads to liver diseases and gastric problems ranging from indigestion and heartburn to ulcers and cancers.

Dislikes, hatreds, constant irritations lead to diseases affecting the blood stream, including infectious diseases, boils, sores and skin complaints.

An irritable nature, bad temper and *unexpressed anger* lead to headaches and migraines.

A frustrated sex life through its repression or nonfulfilment leads to devitalisation and general ill health, also to unfulfilling sexual obsessions, sexual difficulties and diseases of the sexual and generative organs.

Self-pity and lack of self-confidence lead to indigestion, intestinal problems, catarrh, colds, bronchitis, poor teeth and ear problems.

The mentally polarised person is affected by those diseases related to the energy of the Head, Heart and Throat Chakras, which carry the energy qualities of the *Good*, the *Beautiful* and the *True*. Diseases related to the suppression of these three energies include the following :

Depression, inferiority complexes and a sense of failure are caused by resistance to the will-to-good as it enters the Crown Chakra. We feel bad about ourselves.

Good manifests through the interplay between the Crown and Base Chakras. Diseases related to the Base Chakra - in the legs or at the bottom of the spine, are engendered through the inability of the Base Chakra to respond to the energy of the Crown Chakra. We can't move in the right direction even when we know what it is. We can't make life happen for us.

Beauty manifests through the Heart Chakra. Heart and stomach diseases are caused by our inability to express the love energy of our Heart and Solar Plexus and through the inability of our emotions to respond to the beautiful.

Truth is expressed via the Throat Chakra. When our personality is unable to express or respond to truth and we are unable to live up to our own high ideals, the diseases created include rheumatism, arthritis and diseases affecting the bone structure of the body. There are also repercussions in the Sacral Centre with corresponding sexual disorders.

There are potent forces for transformation at work during any illness. Disease is the result of resistance to the flow of energy within the mental, astral or etheric/physical bodies creating points of friction. Esoteric Soul Healing can resolve the point of friction and bring transformation within these bodies. As healers we recognise that destiny or the design of our Soul is at work through the whole process of the disease and its healing, in order to bring about such a transformation.

Disease by its very nature alters our perspective on life. We feel ill, sick, awful. We have a headache, a pain. We feel depressed, low, tired, dull, not ourselves. Unless we are unlucky, this is not how we normally feel. An illness turns our attention inwards, away from the outer world to focus upon the disease and our suffering. The ways in which we experience our disease, what we understand of it and its causes, can change our perception of ourselves and the world in which we live, both now and in the future.

On the simplest level we all catch colds, coughs, flus, tummy bugs, etc.. We all experience the same sorts of feelings during these illnesses. Our human suffering is the same to greater or lesser degrees. The correct handling of these diseases can break down our sense of separation, isolation and loneliness, increasing our own compassion and love for other people in their suffering. We can come to really know and understand that we are one humanity experiencing the same feelings and difficulties. This can bring to us the first intimations of the oneness of our Soul.

Focus of Attention of the Patient, Points of Friction and the Approach of the Healer

The type of disease we attract at any particular time is determined by our focus of attention i.e. on the location of the point of friction between our Soul and Personality. We are not usually that conscious of our focus of attention but age and physical growth is a major factor in determining where it might be.

As new born babies we are attached to our physical bodies by the strong thread of the sutratma, which is anchored into the heart and brain, but has not yet extended and linked to the three head centres. This process takes another seven years after birth to complete. Throughout this time much of our attention is unconsciously focussed on the growth and the development of the physical body and our relationship to our immediate outer world. This focus is reflected in the pattern of physical development in the baby and young child as energy and strength move slowly down through the body from the head.

The new born baby has little muscular control apart from the ancestral reflexes which disappear within a few weeks of birth. We cannot immediately put our hands where we want them to go or hold our heads up, but within days and weeks, our muscles strengthen and coordination improves. We learn first to hold our heads erect and then as the energy focus moves down through the body and arms, we learn to lift ourselves off the floor with our arms as we lie on our tummies. Control over the arms and hands develops over the next few years becoming a fine dexterity that no other animal or machine can mimic. Energy and strength move down to the pelvis and legs and we begin crawling and later walking. At each stage development follows the focus of our attention. As children we suffer infectious diseases, such as measles, chicken pox, mumps, often the result of conflict between forces in the physical body when the point of friction is located in the physical/etheric body.

Some developments in our lives are progressive, such as physical growth, and others, such as the unfoldment of individual chakras are dependent upon the Soul purpose of the individual human being. At one time in our lives we may be completely focused in our emotions, expressed via our Sacral and Solar Plexus Chakras. This happens in adolescence and points of friction will normally be in the astral body. At another time our attention may be completely focused in the head centres, around say 26-29years of age when points of friction will be in the mental body. In our forties during the midlife crisis we may again become emotionally polarised but on a different turn of the spiral. Later in life our attention may shift into the Soul and Spiritual Triad and in old age as the physical body decays, we move back to a physical focus. Points of friction and therefore disease shift accordingly.

Life is a mystery. We are only ever living *Now* under the illusion of progressive time. We tend to see things as progressing from one state onwards to another, from the past into a future which gets better, moving towards a state of perfection that we will eventually reach. When we are perfect, i.e. not like we are now, everything will all be OK. But that is not really how it is. This progressive view of time does not take account of the obvious cyclic nature of the whole of creation, from birth, through growth, maturation and procreation, to decay and death, with many minor cycles of life, death and rebirth inbetween.

Our life is more adequately described as a gestalt - a rhythmical pattern picture in which different aspects of ourselves cycle into and out of focus at different times, all triggered by our inner life purpose and often mirrored by events in the outside world. We are conscious of some of these aspects and unconscious of others. Life is an ever-changing river in which perfection lies in this moment now, in the fullness and wholeness of its expression in many different forms, some exciting, some dull, some painful, some joyous. As Esoteric Soul Healers we view the healing of disease from within this broader perspective.

As healers we need to be able to locate the point of friction within the patient's mental, astral or etheric vehicles. The point of friction appears differently to each healer. For some it is a point or circle of fire, a spot of heightened colour or a mark in the aura. It can be a rip or tear, a dark stain. It can have a geometric form or be an irregular blob or it can merely be a knowing that it is there.

We need to learn how to perceive the degree of unfoldment within the patient's consciousness, which demonstrates as openness and energy within each of the chakras and within the lotus of the soul. This perception can indicate directly the point of friction. This perception is not a mental judgment but a direct *seeing* on the inner eye of the patient's energy condition.

In discerning the degree of soul unfoldment we in no way judge our patients for where we think they are. At any moment we can all move into another aspect of ourselves with a greater or lesser degree of awareness. No matter how sensitive we are as healers we cannot see and know everything or assume that we are *better* than our patients, because we see them at their weakest and most vulnerable point. Neither can we assume that what we perceive is ultimately *right* for our patients. The universe is full of many mysteries and only the individual her/himself can truly know their own destiny. As healers our focus is not on ourselves and our relative status, but on the removal of our patient's suffering.

Every patient needs to be approached in the way which is appropriate for where they are now. This includes the relationship between their current disease and their overall life purpose. Although each person is an individual with a unique energy gestalt there are certain generalisations which can be made about our approach as healers, depending on whether the patient is physically, astrally or mentally focused.

The *physically oriented patient* is aware only of the symptoms of the disease they are suffering and has no interest in its causes. These patients include children and animals. In approaching these patients we direct energy via our own consecrated personality expression, synthesised in the Ajna Chakra, to the patient's etheric body.

The *astrally oriented patient* is usually anxious, worried and fearful of their disease and of the healing experience. It is therefore necessary to help these patients to relax first of all, since a calm emotional body is necessary for the passage of healing energies in both the patient and the healer. When the source of the disease is in the astral body, we focus the energy of our Soul in our combined Ajna and Crown Chakras, but we direct energy via our own Solar Plexus. We use our Soul energy not for actual healing but to bring the corresponding chakra in the patient - their Solar Plexus - into resonance so that it can respond to the incoming energy of their own Soul. It is this energy which heals their disease.

The *mentally polarised patient* can be approached by working via the head centres. We work to bring their focus of attention from the head centres down into the Heart Chakra so that they can feel their own Soul's energy and bring their consciousness more fully into the physical body, opening a gateway to the chakras in the lower body.

Patients who are focused on integrating their personality vehicles and rendering them receptive to the energies of the Soul can be guided to direct energy within their etheric bodies. Such patients have a degree of awareness of their own inner processes and we gain their conscious cooperation in healing. We can talk with them about the causes of their disease and perceptions on their current energy state and their life patterns.

Preparation for Diagnosis

Disease usually speaks very plainly. The type of disease and its location in the body gives direct information as to the nature of the energy inhibition as well as the chakras involved. For example, a patient has a sore knee and is unable to walk without pain. The way in which we walk determines where we can go and how quickly we can get there. For this patient the disease relates to their direction in life or the lack of it and the speed at which they are going. They may be doing a job which gives them little satisfaction and the painful knee is a prompting from the unconscious about their dissatisfaction. The effect of the disease is to slow the person down so they have more time to notice and feel the frustration that is there within them. We would begin the healing session by working with the Base Chakra and the minor chakras behind the knees.

Another person may suffer from continual sore throats and laryngitis, which makes it difficult to swallow and to speak. This disease is related to what we are expected to swallow in our lives, how much truth we have to sit upon and keep hidden and what we would like to say, but are unable to voice. It can tell much about our honesty with ourselves and others and how much truth we are able to accept in our lives. Here healing would begin with the Throat Chakra.

A headache is an aching head, a brain which is under pressure and not balanced by the expression of feeling. We would work with the adjacent Head Centres and the Solar Plexus. Similarly a stomach-ache is the result of an aching Solar Plexus, caused by emotional pain, being unable to digest what is happening for us or to take in nourishment from our environment and those around us.

Disease sometimes comes after a particularly difficult time in life is over. While stress is occuring excess energy is often suppressed, pushed down or ignored so that we can cope with situations as they are happening. When the crisis is over the suppressed energy is often released as disease. Sometimes instead of letting go of stress and taking hold of the new, we cling on to the old and familiar and rework it over and over. Stress and fear of the new emerges as disease. These emotional energies need to be faced, allayed and redirected.

We can gain important insights into the nature of a particular disease through reading correctly what the disease is saying to us. This type of diagnosis requires a knowledge of human physiology and the relationships between the organs of the body. But the main faculty necessary is common sense and being able to read the obvious. Louise Hay's book *You Can Heal Your Life* gives details of many ailments in different parts of the body and their corresponding psychological meaning.

Diagnosis of Disease

Correct diagnosis of a disease and its underlying cause is a major part of the healing process. We train ourselves to know whether the patient is physically, emotionally or mentally polarised so that we can locate the point of friction. We can then relate the effect - the disease, to our perception of the underlying cause via the area of the body and the chakra in the etheric body controlling that area.

As well as asking the patient for details of their disease and its causes at the beginning of the session there are four methods of energetic diagnosis working from the effect of the disease to its cause. We can use these methods separately or in combination to locate the point of friction and the affected chakras accurately. This location can be described in terms of energy and placed in an emotional, mental or spiritual framework to assist the healing process in the patient.

For diagnosis and during practice session the patient can be standing, seated in a straight backed chair or lying down on a flat couch, a bed or a mattress on the floor, whichever is most convenient.

1. Sensing with the Hands

As well as being powerful transmitters of energy, the hands are also sensitive energy receivers and can be used to diagnose disease and disturbances in a person's energy field. The sensations felt in the hands can be strong and obvious or fleeting and subtle. You won't know which it is for you until you try.

Begin sensing the patient's aura with your hands on a level with the physical heart at the back if they are seated or standing, or at the front when they are lying down. When the patient is lying on their back all sensing is done at the front and sides of the body. Hold your hands with the palms facing towards the patient and notice the sensations that you feel with your hands. Become accustomed to the energy field in the space around the patient's Heart Chakra. Close your eyes if it helps you to concentrate more easily on the sensations in your hands. You may notice feelings of heat and cold, tingling, pins and needles, prickling, energy streaming, impressions of colours, shapes, feelings and other images. Note all sensations. Register the colours and condition of the Heart Chakra

Move your hands towards the patient's body and see how near you can get to the surface of the body or clothing before there is a definite sensation of pressure in the hands. This may be at one inch, at five inches or it may gradually fade out at a few feet. This impression gives you an idea of the openess of the Heart Chakra and therefore the degree of unfoldment of the patient's being - the more open the heart, the more unfolded the lotus of the Soul.

Slowly move the hands up through the space around the body to the shoulders and neck and the Throat Chakra. Again register all sensations that you feel with your hands. The aura and consequently the hands may dip inwards

Sensing the Aura with the Hands

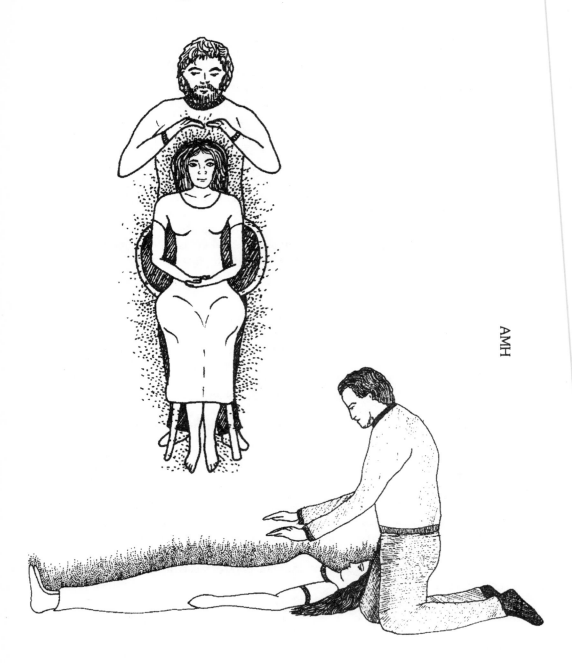

AMH

towards the neck showing perhaps how the patient separates their head from the rest of their body, or bulge outwards over the shoulders showing the weight they carry. Note all impressions however fleeting.

Move the hands up around the head and notice the sensations that you feel around the head chakras - at the Alta Major, the Crown and the Ajna. When the patient is seated bring the hands over the top of the patient's head and then down the front of the body noticing any sensations in the hands. Move the hands down the body over the Heart, Solar Plexus, Sacral and Base Chakras noticing sensations as you go. Move down the legs to the feet and then up the sides and backs of the legs and up the sides or back of the body to the level of the heart, sensing the condition of the chakras from the back as well as the front of the body.

In some patients the aura will seem to be distorted in certain places. It may bulge or it may feel constricted. There may be bright colour in some areas and dark spots in others or lack of colour altogether. Some chakras may be bright and others appear dim or not there at all. Use your intuition to help you interpret the sensations felt in your hands. Trust that what comes immediately to your mind is correct. Don't think about interpreting the information, listen for and sense the interpretation. Be prepared to be wrong and to make some mistakes. Dare to be right, and wrong.

Sensing with the hands can be carried out rapidly in a matter of minutes to gain an impression of the state of the aura and chakras and the energies which the person is expressing or repressing. All impressions no matter how fleeting and ludicrous they may appear, should be noticed.

When used carefully, sensing with the hands helps us become more attuned to intuition. Intuition is the key to the accurate diagnosis of the causes of a disease and from there its healing.

2. Clairvoyance

Clairvoyance is the ability to see or sense colours and images within a person's aura through the agency of the awakened Ajna Chakra. This faculty may be consciously developed or may be a natural faculty we have had since childhood. Through this sense we can locate the point of friction in the personality vehicles.

The colours that we see in the aura are one of the ways in which we register the presence of different qualities of energy. Which colours we see varies according to our own personal point of view and can include physical, etheric, astral, mental and soul colours, which are all different.

Physical colour we all know about but even here there is a vast difference in the ways in which we see colours depending on the condition of our eyes and in part on how many names we have for them.

Etheric colours are similar to physical colours but have a shimmering quality like the effect of a heat haze on a summer's day. Etheric energy underlies the physical body and as prana is constantly flowing through the physical/etheric body. It is this energy which is visible on Kirlian photographs. The different colours and energy flows give an indication as to the state of our energy field and our health. Similarly when viewed clairvoyantly the health aura can be seen in the area adjacent to the skin.

A healthy person will have a bright aura. When they walk into a room we can see etheric energy flowing out through the aura quite easily. They glow with health. When a person is ill, our first impression of them is one of dullness, lack of vigour and energy. The aura looks grey or brown or darkened as the flow of etheric energy is inhibited and diverted to the site of the disease. This impression is etheric. It is not just due to subliminal cues of poor skin colour and the way in which the body is held, but can be perceived in a sick person who is viewed from behind.

Emotional or astral colours are vivid and strong. They are the brilliant colours of dreams and of certain forms of meditation where we move out of the physical into the astral sphere. These are the colours that sometimes flash in the chakras - electric red and purple, etc..

A particular emotion can colour the aura very strongly and appears as either a spot of colour, an undulation or a blaze of colour stretching out from the aura for several feet. There are certain classic emotional colours seen in the aura, e.g. anger - seeing red, green - with envy, yellow - with fear, black - with hate, sunny - with laughter, and golden - for joy. Although these are the classic colours they may not be the ones which you see. It is only by looking at people in different emotional states and judging for yourself which colours represent which emotions, that it becomes possible to know at a glance what someone is feeling or suppressing. When an emotion is suppressed its colour is often darkened, muddied or turned into its complimentary colour e.g. red into green.

Where emotions are repressed or excited they show up in the aura in specific areas related to individual chakras. They show where an emotional trauma has left its scars in the physical/etheric body, either as a colour, image or feeling. For example the physical and emotional scars of an accident can remain in the aura for many years. These can be seen by the sensitive clairvoyant.

The emotional threads of our relationships are visible too within the aura. The emotional relationship between a mother and her newborn baby is normally strong so that each includes the other within their aura. This can be easily seen and felt. As the baby grows this inclusive relationship loosens, becoming a bridge between the two auras, centred on the Solar Plexus, and gradually diminishing through time and experience until it becomes a thread.

Similarly we establish emotional threads with lovers, following well-known routes. At first we are in love and the experience is all-consuming and exclusive. We are in each other's aura, we can't bear to be away from each other for a moment. Gradually this inclusion diminishes to a thread between our two astral bodies, anchored in the Solar Plexus or the Heart, where it is nourished and maintained, dies away or is abruptly cut to leave a raw sore place. These threads are visible to the clairvoyant healer.

Mental colours though more potent in one sense are less easy to see clairvoyantly, having a pale, luminous, pastel quality. Mental energies can extend to great distances from the body and are responsible for the phenomenon of telepathy, telekinesis, etc.. There is a constant interchange between the aggregation of mental energies that make up the mental set of the individual and the thoughtforms that condition the whole of life on the planet. Thoughtforms are agglomerations of mental and emotional matter fuelled by the energy of many minds or any one particularly focused mind. Imbued with desire they are held in form by the will of the beings from whom they emanate. Huge thoughtforms condition our life on this planet and directly influence the way in which we all experience our lives. Our individual thoughts and ideas are constantly changed by and changing the thoughts of everyone around us. Unconsciously we are in contact and able to influence each other - a thought which gives us hope for the future.

Soul energies are seen in the aura as the degree of radiance, brightness, expansiveness and presence. The more the Soul's energy is in manifestation then the greater the depth of our colouring, the brighter we appear to be. Radiance is a quality that comes from within, emanating from a bright centre.

The colours in the aura can give a lot of information on the general and specific health of the patient and their pattern of unfoldment. In those people in whom the faculty is well-developed clairvoyance can give detailed images and information on the condition of the patient and their disease, and the position of the point of friction in the etheric, astral or mental bodies. We need to look for the point of friction and see where it is, and believe what we see.

3. Registration in the Healer's Body

Many untrained healers are able to diagnosis disease by registering the illness in their own bodies. Once they tune into the patient they feel the patient's pain in their stomach or head, or wherever. This is often extremely uncomfortable and such healers have to learn to either reduce the strength of the sensation or to redirect it into another method of diagnosis. This sympathetic reaction can leave the healer feeling tired and debilitated as they feel all that their patients feel, which is not helpful when healing.

The way to avoid being overwhelmed by other people's experience is to focus our attention as healers within our own Soul and to make registration of the disease conscious. By Centring in Being, in our Soul, as described in the Exercises on the Chakras, we become positively polarised in relation to the patient and act, not as mere receivers of sensation, but as mirrors to the processes going on within the patient. As mirrors we reflect sensation but do not absorb it. During the diagnostic and healing process our attention is drawn to particular parts of our own body, which reflect the stronger sensations and feelings experienced by the patient. We can register in our own bodies where the point of friction is in the patient because our attention is drawn there.

When we are directing healing energies we use the sensations that we feel in our own bodies to tell us what is happening within our patient's energy bodies. The energy connections established at the beginning of a healing session ensure that we are positively polarised in relation to the patient and we can therefore know that these sensations are not our own.

For example, when working with a patient's Solar Plexus, we can usually feel any energy distortion within their Solar Plexus as a slight tension or knotting in our stomach muscles. When an energy change takes place and the distortion is resolved in the patient's Solar Plexus, there is a simultaneous release of tension in our own stomach muscles with a feeling of relief. During a healing session as we work to balance and heal distortions in our patient's energy fields and they become more and more relaxed, we register the healing changes as feeling more and more relaxation within our own bodies. As a result we should end any healing session feeling completely relaxed ourselves. We may be tired but we should not feel drained.

It takes experience to trust that the energy changes which we feel in our own bodies during the healing process have actually occurred for our patients as well - that our bodies can act as mirrors to other human bodies. This is repeatedly confirmed by our patients who describe their relaxed state. Trusting that what we feel and sense is true and real is one of the most important aspects of healing.

4. Direct Perception

Direct Perception of the energy condition of the patient's chakras, of their pattern of unfoldment and the location of the point of friction, is the most accurate method of diagnosis. Direct perception involves the ability to concentrate the mind and see/feel energy on the *Third Eye*. The Third Eye is the energy centre created in the centre of the head by linking the Crown, Ajna and Alta Major centres, so that they revolve upon themselves into other dimensions of reality. See the exercises at the end of this chapter for the Awakening of the Third Eye.

The Third Eye acts as a screen on which we can view directly the patient's energy field. For the diagnosis of disease we focus our attention on the Third Eye in the centre of our head. Once we are concentrated we then focus our attention on whichever part of the patient's energy field interests us - the whole aura, the chakras, the etheric, astral or mental bodies or the Soul itself. We can then perceive the degree of conscious contact which the patient has with their own Soul and the relationship between their Soul and Personality and the point of friction creating the disease. We can if we choose look into their past and also possible futures. The amount we can perceive and its accuracy depends on the depth of our own awareness.

As with all other forms of diagnosis and with actual healing we have to learn to trust absolutely the perceptions that we have about our patients and their conditions. Often the most pertinent perceptions for the patient are those which we have the strongest doubts about communicating to them. They involve us personally in the process of healing while focused in our Souls. Tears which come to our patient's eyes come to our eyes also and their fears are ours. In reality we are both transformed by the experience. As the patient resolves their disease, we develop as healers by walking the razor edge of our intuition and by communicating our inner perceptions.

The process of diagnosis takes place at the beginning and also during the healing session. As we work with the patient's energy field and begin to balance energies within it and in the chakras, we also check on the energy condition of the other chakras which may change as a result of the healing work that we do. We continue to gather information throughout the healing process using any of these forms of diagnosis.

EXERCISES:
Improving Diagnostic Techniques

Sensing the condition of the Chakras using the hands

The condition of the seven major chakras can be sensed using the hands by focusing our attention on their particular locations in the physical/etheric body.

1. Begin by standing in front of the person and with both hands held palms outward on a level with the Heart Chakra. Sense the energy coming from the Heart Chakra as light, colour and sensation. This impression gives you an idea of the openness of the Heart Chakra and therefore the degree of unfoldment of the patient's soul - the more open the heart, the more unfolded the lotus of the soul.

2. Move the hands up to the Throat Chakra and feel its condition - colour, shape, size and radiance, with the hands.

3, Move the hands up around the head and notice the sensations that you feel at each of the head chakras - at the Ajna, the Crown and moving to the back of the body, the Alta Major.

4. At the back of the body sense the energy in all the chakras moving down the spine from the Heart Chakra down through the Solar Plexus and Sacral centres to the Base Chakra. See if there are differences between sensations at the front of the body and at the back.

5. Move around to the front of the body to the Base Chakra and then come up the front of the body via the Sacral Centre and Solar Plexus to the Heart Chakra, again sensing the condition of the chakras.

6. Gather the information you have received from your hands and report to the person telling them what you think your findings mean e.g. disturbance in the Solar Plexus indicates emotional disturbance, etc.. Listen to their feedback.

Practice sensing the aura and the chakras with the hands with lots of different people in varying states of health.

Developing the Clairvoyant Faculty

Clairvoyance is a subtle faculty which we all possess. It exists on the periphery of normal vision allowing us to see etheric forms and colours. Often we are unaware of its existence, putting peculiarities in our vision down to dust in our eyes, or just something seen out of the corner of our eye that disappears when we look at it directly, etc.. As children we are often naturally clairvoyant and see the auras of people, animals and objects with their different colours. As we grow up we are told that what we see is not real. Many people who are short-sighted are also clairvoyant, but unfocused. The fuzziness which can be seen is the borderline of etheric vision. So take off your spectacles and look at the world in a different way. Instead of screwing up your eyes in the attempt to see clearly, examine the areas around bodies and objects for colour and imagery.

The main way to develop clairvoyance is to *look* at people and objects and to allow your imagination to be free. Again be prepared to make mistakes. Place a friend against a light wall and standing a few feet away carefully examine the inch or so next to the person's skin or clothing all round the body. Let your imagination open and don't define what you are allowed to see before you have looked. Register all the colours, feelings and sensations that you experience in your friend's aura and tell them what you notice. Listen to any feedback from them about how they feel and where they are at. Learn to equate colours and sensations with feelings and thoughts. Try the experiment with different people. With people that you know well relate what you see to their general well-being.

Look at people that you don't know at all - its an interesting way to spend a train journey or that time in the office when you need a break. Look at animals, birds, trees and plants, at rocks, precious stones, water, air and fire. Everything that exists carries energy and has an aura. The way to see it is by looking, sensing and trusting that what you see is real.

Development of the Three Head Chakras and the Opening of the Third Eye

Contrary to popular opinion the centre between the eyebrows, the Ajna Chakra, is not the *Third Eye*. The awakened Ajna Chakra allows the faculty of clairvoyance to develop - the ability to see in the etheric and astral realms. The *Third Eye* however is an energy space in the centre of the head which comes into activity only when the three major chakras in the head - the Ajna, Crown and Alta Major, are awakened, functioning and related to each other.

The functioning Third Eye allows direct perception of energy states in people and places, contact with the Spiritual Triad and the ability to see through to a causal level - that of the causal body or Soul. It also allows us to read what is usually known as the Akashic records - the memory of all past and future events *written* in the Light of the Eternal. The awakening and relating of these three head centres is one of the first steps in this process.

1. Sit comfortably and centre yourself in your Heart using the centring exercise given earlier or your own method.

2. When your Heart Chakra is open shift your attention to the Ajna Chakra, the centre between the eyebrows, and feel its pulse, its colour, size and shape.

3. When you can hold this centre in your consciousness and feel it vibrating, visualise a thread of light moving from the Ajna to the Crown Chakra. Transfer your attention to the Crown Chakra and feel its pulse, colour, size and shape.

4. When you can hold the Crown Chakra in your awareness and feel it

vibrating, visualise a thread of light moving from the Crown Chakra through the back of the head to the Alta Major at the base of the skull. Transfer your attention to the Alta Major. Feel its pulse, colour, size and shape.

5. When you are able to hold the Alta Major in your consciousness and feel it vibrating, visualise the thread of light returning to the Ajna. In your imagination see the thread of light passing through the brain just above the roof of the mouth and back of the nose to the Ajna.

6. Visualise the thread of light circulating through the triangle of the three head centres from the Ajna to the Crown, to the Alta Major and back to the Ajna again and so on.

7. Watch the light as it begins to move more quickly between the chakras. Shift your attention more and more rapidly from one chakra to the next moving your mind nimbly and accurately from one space to the next.

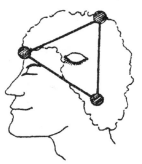

8. Continue to move the energy through the three centres until a triangle of moving light is firmly established. Then speed the circulation even more, so that the triangle itself begins to rotate in the head.

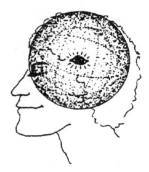

33

9. Using your imagination watch the rotating triangle begin to spin so that it becomes three-dimensional, creating a sphere of light spinning in your head. Fill your whole head with this ball of light.

10. When you can see this sphere clearly in your head, focus your attention on the space in the centre of the sphere and feel that space. Each time your attention wanders bring it back to this space. As your attention becomes focussed and you are able to hold your mind steady in the centre of the sphere, the Third Eye opens. This is an energy state within the body which allows access to other dimensions of reality which are free from the material world. It may be seen as an eye, but more deeply felt as a black velvet space into which images and perceptions project themselves.

The practice of this exercise increases concentration and improves the ability to focus the attention at will and to move energy in the etheric vehicle. These activities are all part of the unfoldment of the three head centres. When practised regularly it may accompanied by changes in the shape of the head which are due to pressure changes between the chakras, the brain and the skull. These are part of the process of unfoldment.

CHAPTER FIVE

The Practice of
Esoteric Soul Healing

There are two main forms of Esoteric Soul Healing - *Magnetic Healing* and *Radiatory Healing.* In Magnetic Healing we use our hands to direct *Prana* or *Active Radiatory Heat* as a healing energy. In Radiatory Healing we use the energy of our own Being to call forth *Soul energy* within the patient's etheric body which then effects a cure.

In Magnetic Healing we place our hands either in contact with the patient's aura and etheric body or directly on the patient's physical body. In Radiatory Healing we use the radiatory energy of the Soul moving out from our own centre through the aura to evoke the patient's Soul presence within their personality vehicles. Here physical or etheric contact is unnecessary if we are able to focus our attention at will on the patient's non-physical vehicles. With Radiatory Healing we can heal at a distance as well as in close proximity.

Principles of Healing

All healing is based on three principles. The first is that in reality there is no separation between people or between objects - we are all One. The planetary etheric body is whole, unbroken and continuous and the patient and healer are integral and intrinsic parts of that etheric body.

Secondly the continuous relationship between the patient's etheric body and the healer's etheric body can be used, once conscious contact is established between the two, for the definite circulation of healing energy.

Thirdly, the threads of relationship can be used as conductors for different types of energy transmitted by the healer to the patient.

In these three principles lies the hope of healing and the possible danger to the healer of becoming receptive to the patient's disease. For this reason as healers, we must always remain positively polarised in relation to our patients. No part of our etheric or physical bodies is allowed to become negatively polarised. We establish this positive polarisation by centring ourselves in being at the beginning of any healing session.

In Magnetic Healing we use both hands positively although each can be used to direct energy into the patient's etheric body or to draw it off. In Radiatory

93

Healing we focus ourselves in Being so that we are automatically positively polarised in relation to our own personality as well as to that of the patient.

The Healing Space

Most healers find that it is important to create their own healing space which is especially set aside for healing, meditation, prayer and other calm and focused activities. This is not strictly necessary for healing to take place but can be an aid to the learner as well as the professional healer, since a consecrated space maintains and holds healing vibrations. Such a psychic framework allows the healer to focus their attention quickly and to generate healing energies easily. The healing space should have two chairs of equal height which can be placed facing each other for the introductory part of the healing session. There should be comfortable seating, a couch or massage table, or a day bed or mattress for the patient to sit or lie on during the session. Pillows and a light blanket can be available for patients who require them. Keep the room itself warm since the patient's body temperature decreases while they are lying still and relaxed. The healer will usually feel warm from all the energy work.

The healing space should be clean and have a clear vibration. A healing atmosphere can be created by having a lighted candle in the room perhaps on a special healing altar dedicated to your personal healing deities and guides. Ensure that the room smells pleasant by burning incense or aromatherapy oils before the healing session begins. It is best not to have incense burning during a session as some people are allergic to it. Before your patient arrives cleanse the space psychically either with incense, smudging all the corners of the room as well as the healing couch, and/or by sounding several OMs or by ringing small bells which harmonise the sound and unseen vibrations in a room.

Preparation for Diagnosis and Healing

All Esoteric Soul Healing sessions begin with a face to face meeting between healer and patient seated if possible directly opposite each other so that eye contact is established. This is the first step in the diagnostic and healing process when you welcome the patient and help them feel safe and cared for. It is very important to develop a *good bedside manner* which shows that you empathise with the patient and wish to help relieve their distress.

Ask the patient for a short account of the physical, emotional, mental and spiritual symptoms of their disease and its history. In particular note what was going on in the patient's life prior to the onset of their disease, such as relationship breakdown, death of a loved one, changes at work, etc. There are often one or more experiences which trigger the appearance of the disease and tracing these events gives a direct clue to its causes. This conversation will immediately give you some idea as to whether your patient is physically, astrally or mentally polarised, their degree of soul contact and the possible site of the point of friction.

This information is not strictly necessary for the Esoteric Soul Healer who works with the energy vehicles and can perceive directly the energy condition of the chakras during diagnosis. It is possible to work with the information received directly from the energy vehicles alone, translating it later if necessary, into life story. Verbal information will however tell us about which chakras need our attention and often the location of the point of friction. While we are learning the skill of healing it is also very helpful to confirm energy impressions with material realities. When a healing session is complete it also helps the patient if we can translate the healing experience into terms they can apply in their everyday lives. The patient can then see how emotions, attitudes and thoughtforms condition their life experience and help create their disease.

At the beginning of a healing session we establish as clearly and quickly as possible the main components of the patient's disease. When we have listened to the details of their illness we ask the patient what they hope will be the outcome of the healing session and we affirm their desire for healing. This begins the process of releasing resistance and of welcoming healing and transformation in the present.

It is at this stage that we ask the patient if there are any unseen beings who they would like to be present to help with the healing process. These may be personal angels, guides, goddesses or gods, family members, people who are important to the patient, etc.. For further information on this part of the healing session see Chapter Six on Devas, Elementals, Angels and Sound.

We also describe to the patient the form of the healing session, whether they will be lying down or sitting on a chair, how long it is likely to take - 20-30 minutes, and that they may find themselves relaxing deeply and sometimes falling asleep and that this is good.

Position of the Patient during Energetic Diagnosis and Healing

After the introductory stage we either seat the patient in a straight backed chair or ask them to lie down on a flat couch, such as a massage table, or on a comfortable bed or mattress on the floor. There are advantages and disadvantages in each position. In some situations it is more convenient to use a chair rather than a couch, daybed or the floor and this can be particularly so for older people and those who find it hard to bend their bodies to lie down. However when seated the patient may be unable to completely relax and it can be difficult for the healer to reach or touch as necessary some parts of the body, such as the back, when it is resting against a chair or the lower chakras at the front of the body. In Magnetic Healing in which we use our hands to transmit healing energy sometimes we want to physically touch the body as well as the aura, and may need to use a low backed chair or at least one with an open back.

When the patient is lying down on their back we work with the chakras located at the front of the body, unless we have a couch with a face hole or there are cushions so that the patient can comfortably lie face down. How the patient lies depends on what is most comfortable for the patient and where the disease is located in the physical body. The more physically relaxed they can become during the session the greater the healing which can occur. Placing a pillow beneath the head and beneath to knees also relaxes the body. Since we are working primarily with the patient's energy field we may like to cover them with a light blanket, so that they feel warm and comfortable. Whether the patient is seated or lying down the healer needs to be able to move freely as necessary around all sides of the patient's body and head, so it is best to position the patient in the middle of an open area.

Before we begin the energy work of the healing session we make the patient comfortable either seated or lying down. When the patient is seated the healer begins by standing behind the patient. When the patient is lying down the healer stands or sits at the side of the patient. The healer works with their own spine in an upright aligned position.

Ask the patient to close their eyes and to allow themselves to relax as much as they can, to let their everyday thoughts and cares slip away and if they want to they can fall asleep. Many patients will fall into a light doze.

Centring in Being for the Healer

At the beginning of any diagnostic or healing session energy connections are established by the healer within their own vehicles and an energy rapport is set up between the healer and the patient for the easy transfer of healing energies between the two.

Begin by centring yourself within the energy field of your own Being as described in detail earlier. Focus in the Heart Chakra and connect from there both to the centre of earth and to the farthest star you can imagine in the heavens. Allow the Heart Chakra to fill with these energies and with your Soul's energy, ensuring that you are positively polarised in relation to your patient..

Many trainee healers ask about ways to prevent themselves taking on their patients' diseases and symptoms. The best way to protect yourself while healing is to always maintain a positive energy field in relation to the patient. Centring in Being renders the healer's own energy field positive in relation to that of the patient so nothing negative can enter it. This open heart stance is maintained throughout the healing session.

When you have difficulty establishing these connections you may take on the patient's disease. This transference is unnecessary and is an illusion on the part of the healer. It usually means that you have become preoccupied with the patient's need. Your anxiety for the patient means that you become temporarily negatively polarised and unprotected. The cure for this is to always work with a radiating Heart Chakra as well as with the Head Centres, so that a steady flow of love is always moving out from you towards the patient.

Once the Heart Chakra is open and radiating energy outwards from your Being, put this set of internal energy connections to the back of your mind, literally by placing the image at the back of your skull at the Alta Major centre.

Connecting to your inner Healing Group

As human beings each of us is part of a larger Soul Grouping, some of whom are in incarnation and some of whom are out of incarnation. This soul group may be connected by a particular ray energy, say a 7th ray soul group, or may be a karmic grouping connected so that they can experience and contribute to particular activities at a particular time, for example, to bring certain changes in consciousness at the beginning of the new millennium which will affect the experience of the mass of humanity. Soul groups sometimes incarnate generationally, at the same time, and also may incarnate across time and space. Souls within such groups are usually recognisable to each other, having a deep sense of familiarity and a natural love for each other. The larger soul group can be contacted by coming into resonance with their energy field for many purposes including healing.

In esoteric soul healing once you have centred in Being and your heart is radiating energy, then consciously link from your heart to your Soul Group, seeing yourself as part of a large circle of healers, who are here to help in the healing process, enhancing your personal healing abilities.

Prayers for Healing, Calling the Angels

Once you have set up your personal energy connections it is time to say out loud any prayers for healing you wish to make, calling firstly upon your own particular healing angels, guides and deities to be present to assist you in the healing process (See Chapter Six) and then on those beings to whom the patient is particularly connected. This is a short simple prayer said out loud, asking for help in healing and connecting both healer and patient to the source of all healing.

Personally I like to work with goddesses and feminine energies in the healing process and there are particular healing beings to whom I feel connected. Since I live in Glastonbury upon the Isle of Avalon, I ask the holy beings of the Isle of Avalon who guard all rites of passage and healing to be present to help. I also invoke (call to be present) Bridie, goddess of healing and at times the Nine Morgens who rule Avalon, and Ariadne or Arianrhod, goddess of transformation in the labrynth. I am also happy to call in masculine energies as requested.

The following is an example of such a healing prayer:

"I call upon the Holy Beings of the Isle of Avalon,
I call upon Bridie, Goddess of Healing,
I ask that you come and be present at this time
Bringing your blessings of healing,
And that everything which happens shall be
For ....(the patient's) greatest good."

If the patient is seated this prayer can be said when standing behind the patient with the hands resting gently on the patient's shoulders. When the patient is lying down prayers are usually said without physical contact.

Connecting Healer and Patient

The next step is to set up threads of connectedness between yourself and your patient and to centre the patient within their own Being. This is done whether the patient is usually able centre themselves when well or not.

1. Using your creative imagination focus in your own Heart Chakra and visualise a thread of light moving from your Heart Chakra to the patient's Heart Chakra, creating a simple figure of eight connection between the two Heart Chakras.

AMH

2. When this image is established focus your attention in your Base Chakra and visualise a thread of light moving in a figure of eight from your Base Chakra to the patient's Base Chakra connecting you together. Then focusing your attention in your Crown Chakra see a thread of light moving in a figure of eight from your Crown to your patient's Crown Chakra. See yourself connected at the Base, Heart and Crown Chakras.

When setting up these connections it is usually easier to visualise the patient in a similar physical position to your own, that is, seated or standing with an straight spine. The patient may in actual fact be lying down. However the energy connections are being made in dimensions other than the physical and do not necessarily have the same form. This exercise stretches the imagination in its attempt to visualise connections in more than the usual three dimensions and prepares us for working in the non-physical dimensions of reality.

3. Return your attention to the patient's Heart Chakra and visualise a thread of energy moving from their Heart Chakra down to their Base Chakra and from there continuing down into the ground, moving towards the centre of the earth. Visualise energy returning from the centre of the earth back into their Base Chakra and from there back to the Heart Chakra, invigorating the Heart..

4. Focus on their Heart Chakra and see a thread of energy moving from their Heart Chakra up through their body to their Crown Chakra and continuing out through the Crown upwards into space to the farthest star. Visualise energy returning from the farthest star back into their Crown Chakra and back down to the Heart Chakra, invigorating the Heart.

5. Focus your attention on the patient's Heart Chakra and visualise the energy of their Being flowing out in all directions from their Heart Chakra.

This process anchors the patient's Being if only temporarily, into their etheric body. It also connects the energy bodies of the patient and healer for the

Patient and Healer connected at Head, Heart + Base Chakras

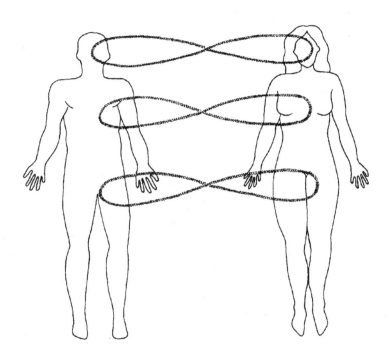

AMH

easy flow of healing energies. While you are learning to be a conscious healer this whole process of centring and connecting to the patient may take several minutes to complete depending on your ability to concentrate and visualise. With experience the establishment of these connections can take place in seconds.

Soul to Soul connection

Healer and patient are now connected to each other energetically and centred in Being via their Heart Chakras. Now is the time to form a definite connection between your two Souls which are in essence one and the same.

Focus your attention in the centre of your head and using your imagination visualise a triangle of energy linking you, the healer in physical form with your Soul and with the patient's Soul. As you will realise the Soul itself does not have a physical location, it is an energetic space. For imaginative purposes however you can give it a physical location if you want to, such as in the space above the Crown Chakra, or within the Heart Chakra, or in front of your body or behind your body, anywhere you choose. You can also locate the Soul as an energetic space in your imagination.

99

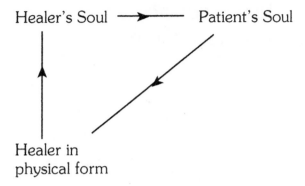

Healer's Soul ⟶ Patient's Soul

Healer in
physical form

As we see it in our imagination so it is. The creation of this triangular relationship will be felt as a definite change in atmosphere, a deepening or an expansion, within the healing space. A certain stillness appears which both the healer and the patient can feel. The patient begins to relax and feel less anxious about the healing process.

Once this triangle is set up the patient's Soul can be brought further into their etheric body by sounding the note of your own Soul. This is a silent sounding of the healer's Soul within the Heart Chakra (see Chapter Six on Using Sound in Healing), which produces a complementary response within the patient increasing the flow of life energy to their Heart Chakra. This is a gentle sounding done with care so that the inflow of life energy is not too sudden and therefore destructive.

Once this soul relationship between the healer and patient is established, you are ready to make your energetic diagnosis of disease. When written down this process of creating energy connections to the patient seems quite long but in practice and with experience takes only a few minutes.

Energetic Diagnosis

Use one or more of the four methods described in the previous chapter to make your energetic diagnosis of the patient's condition. Sense the condition of the patient's aura, energy field and chakras using either your hands, clairvoyance, registration in your body or through direct perception using the Third Eye. Begin by noting the general condition of the aura - its colour, luminosity and shape around the body. Examine each of the seven major chakras in turn beginning with the Heart Chakra and moving up the body to the Crown Chakra and then down through the lower chakras to the Base Chakra.

In particular focus your attention on the Chakra or Chakras connected to the patient's disease. This will have been made clear to you during your introductory conversation with the patient. For example, the patient tells you they have a sore throat - you know that the Throat Chakra needs attention, or they have an emotional problem - go to the Solar Plexus, or they have sexual difficulties - look at the Sacral Centre, etc.. Note the colours or qualities of the chakras and sense whether there is too much or too little energy in each chakra. Try to see if there is constriction on the energy moving into or out of the chakra.

Examine all the other chakras too to find hidden complaints which the patient may not know about or which they have not disclosed to you. Often patients will come with one ailment when they are actually worried about something else but are afraid to say.

Locate the point of friction within the mental, astral or etheric bodies. See the point of friction using your imagination. If you don't see it immediately imagine where it might be and locate it within the patient's aura. Trust your imagination.

When you have completed your diagnosis you are ready to begin healing using either Magnetic or Radiatory Healing. Throughout the healing process continue to check the condition of the chakras and the ways in which they respond to the flow of healing energy.

Magnetic Healing

In *Magnetic Healing* we use *Prana* also known as *Active Radiatory Heat* or *Vital Planetary Fluid*, flowing through our hands as a healing force. We consciously accumulate and circulate Prana by linking our Soul, Heart Chakra, brain and hands.

Prana enters the body via the skin and with the breath and circulates through the etheric body via the nadis or energy channels which make up the etheric body. It is stored in the double Spleen Chakra, which has direct connections to the seven major chakras. In Magnetic Healing the Heart Chakra, Soul and brain are connected, creating an energy triangle through which Prana can circulate and be amplified. From this triangle energy is directed via the Ajna Centre into the arms and hands. At times it is also necessary to withdraw excess energy into this triangle rather than stimulate an already overexcited chakra.

Energy Connections for the Healer

Begin by focusing your attention in your Heart Chakra and becoming conscious of your connection to that deep part of your nature which is your Soul, the infinite source of loving energy which lies within the centre of your Heart. Again the Soul does not actually have a physical location but you visualise it as if it does. One of the easiest ways I have found for this purpose, is to imagine that the Soul is located a couple of feet behind the physical body on a level with the heart or just above. Draw the Soul's energy from behind into your Heart Chakra.

Using your creative imagination see the energy of Being moving as a stream of loving light from the Heart Chakra to the pituitary gland in the centre of the brain, focusing it there using the Ajna Chakra as a distributing point. From the brain see the flow of energy move back to your Soul, creating a triangle of energy - Soul to Heart to brain to Soul. Move energy through these three points.

When you begin it can often be difficult to visualise energy relationships

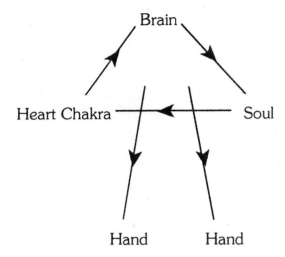

between physical and abstract constructs, e.g. between the brain and Soul. This process becomes easier with practice as we free our imagination. These are energyrelationships not physical relationships and though they are described as triangular, it is in the sense of having three points rather than being two or three-dimensional.

Once the triangle is set up circulate energy through the three points, moving energy through them faster and faster until the three points themselves begin to move, creating first a circle of connection and then a sphere of energy. This process generates and amplifies the energy in the Etheric body and Prana is drawn into the triangle/sphere from the Spleen Chakra and with the breath. Breathing naturally slows and deepens to take in more Prana. This happens automatically and is not something you have to think about. You can usually feel this pranic energy in your body as warmth and stillness.

With focused intent direct this energy down your arms and into your hands and fingers.

Using the Hands

Our hands are very sensitive instruments. Physically they are the most sensitive parts of our bodies apart from the tongue. They react to touch, heat, cold, texture and sometimes light and colour. Etherically they can transmit and receive energy from another person's etheric body or from animals, plants, liquids, crystals and stones. They have an intelligence of their own which we learn to register and trust. In energetic diagnosis we use them to receive information and in healing we use them to transmit healing energies.

The palms of the hands are normally used to transmit or receive general energy and information to and from the chakras or the whole energy field. Used as transmitters energy can be focused through the palms onto large or smaller

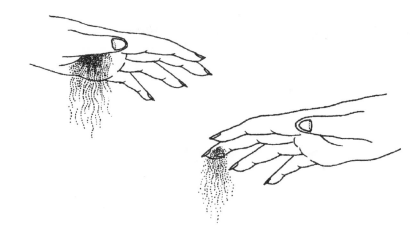

AMH

spots in the etheric or other vehicles. The tips of the fingers are used for more precise inputs of energy or withdrawals and for working on small areas, such as pressure points or nodes on acupuncture meridians.

In Magnetic Healing the hands are used in two ways. The hands can be laid directly onto the physical body usually through clothing, although skin to skin contact can be more comforting on painful parts of the body. Hands can also be laid on the auric/etheric body at a distance of a few inches from the surface of the physical body in the aura. A combination of both methods can be used as directed by intuition.

When there is physical pain or discomfort I usually lay my hands lightly onto the physical body, so that pranic heat can bring rapid physical as well as etheric relief. Other people prefer to heal without touching the physical body at all, just touching the auric body. I also use flowing hand movements in the aura to clear energies away and to smooth and balance the aura. Experiment with your hands on and off the physical body and find how you work best. Ask friends you practice with which feels good.

Laying Hands on the Physical Body

The patient may be sitting or lying down and adjustments need to be made accordingly. Lay one hand on the chakra governing the diseased area either on the spine or at the front of the body. Lay your other hand on the part of the body in which the patient complains of pain or distress or if there is no physical symptom where you have diagnosed the physical/etheric location of the point of friction. Hold your hands there in position, feeling prana circulating through the hands and through the patient's body, until you feel a definite change in the quality of the energy circulating. This change may be felt as an evening out of tension, a smoothing, a lightening, a feeling of peace and relaxation, which often results in the disappearance of physical pain or tension. It can also be just a sense that its

103

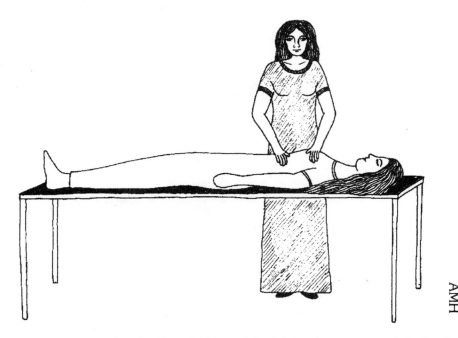

AMH

time to move your hands. This change will be felt by the patient and the healer and when it has occurred the energy imbalance is resolved. The disease eases.

This initial process of working with the diseased chakra may take anything from a few minutes for say, a headache to 15 minutes for a deeper disease. Stay with your hands on the diseased chakra until you feel its energy condition change. By laying the hands on the physical body Prana flows back and forth through the diseased area, burning up the disease through Fire and absorbing *forces* without penetrating the healer's body.

Laying Hands on the Etheric Body

When the patient is seated begin by placing one hand at the back of the patient's body over the chakra governing the diseased area. Place the other hand at the front of the body over the same chakra. Circulate prana through the chakra governing the diseased area, gently moving your hands, drawing energy through the chakra. This movement can be from the front to the back of the body or from the back to the front depending on your intuition's instructions. Continue this process until it feels right to stop.

When the patient is lying down place one hand over the diseased organ or part of the body and slowly withdraw the hand towards your own body. Follow this action rapidly with your other hand. Alternate your hands in drawing energy out of the chakra. Drop any idea you may have learned elsewhere that one hand is positive and one is negative. At no time do you allow any part of your physical/etheric body to become negatively polarised in relation to the patient. Use both hands positively and radiate love from the Heart Chakra.

AMH

In this form of Magnetic Healing the warring *forces* creating the disease are withdrawn by the action of *energy* passing through your hands in a regular time sequence. These *forces* pass through the hands but are unable to focus there because of the concentration of healing energies in the hands.

Another practice is to place one hand over one diseased chakra or area and the other over a related chakra with yourself as the third point of the energy triangle. For example in releasing a headache place one hand over the Ajna and the other over the Alta Major and circulate energy through yourself and the two chakras until there is an easing of discomfort.

According to Alice Bailey healers with second, third and fifth ray souls naturally heal by laying their hands on the physical body. First, fourth and seventh ray healers naturally heal by laying their hands on the etheric body. Sixth ray souls naturally use both methods. It is advisable once the natural method is perfected to develop the second method for times when it is needed.

Balancing out the Other Chakras

Continue to draw energy through the diseased area and its governing chakra until you feel a definite shift in the quality of energy circulating. Once this change has occurred check through the remaining major chakras for any other related imbalances. For example, a sore throat can be due to excess energy within the Throat Chakra - the mental creative centre. This may be caused by a point of friction within the mental body. When the energy in the Throat is in excess, there can often be a reciprocal inhibition in the energy of the Sacral Centre, the physical creative centre. Therefore check out the Sacral Centre with your hands for any imbalance, listening to what your hands tell you is happening. If necessary repeat the healing process with the Sacral Centre.

Begin healing with the chakra governing the diseased area and then check out the related chakras. When you have completed your energetic diagnosis and healing there check through the remaining chakras to give an overall balancing of the etheric body. Essentially allow your hands to move where they want to go and follow what they tell you to do.

Whether your hands are in contact with the patient's physical or etheric body, once your work with the chakras is complete, gently smooth the aura by passing the hands over the whole length of the patient's auric body. Here you may find ripples in the energetic flow surrounding the body as a consequence of your work with the chakras and your action here is to smooth these ripples out until the aura feels smooth and whole.

Visualisation

As with all forms of healing the ability to visualise greatly aids the healing process. Energy follows thought and imagination, bringing healing in its wake. Visualisation is carried out by the healer on behalf of their patient and by the patient who has conscious soul contact. Visualisation has been found to be very effective in enhancing self healing in even the most dire diseases, such as cancers and heart disease.

Visualise energy moving in the triangle of Soul, Heart and brain, through your hands and through the chakras. See colours and pressures change in the chakras with the release of constriction. In as much detail as possible imagine the devic forces at work in repairing damage in the etheric body. (See Chapter Six). Imagine the healing process at work in the physical body repairing damaged tissues and restoring health. These physiological processes include seeing increased blood flow to diseased tissues bringing white blood corpuscles to remove damaged or unhealthy cells. The blood stream also brings food and energy for the building of new healthy tissues. This visualisation requires some knowledge of the body's auto-immune systems.

Closing the Healing Session

Giving healing may last ten minutes or an hour. At its close withdraw the pranic energy in your hands to the Ajna Chakra and from there by an act of will return the energy to your Soul. This withdrawal usually happens automatically without conscious thought, once healing is complete. You will feel it as a change in energy or in the way your attention shifts quite suddenly away from full concentration upon the patient back to the outer world. Always check that this process has taken place so that you are energetically protected outside the healing situation.

While giving healing it is not actually necessary to speak to the patient at all. All your concentration can then be focused on holding the energy threads clearly. Talking can also prevent the patient from relaxing deeply and distract them from the subtle changes occurring within their bodies, and from an energy experience which they may never have had before. This experience can be extremely powerful for someone who has never really felt energy move inside their bodies. It can have a profound effect on their view of reality, particularly if they are materially focused. It is one of the effects of disease which is causal into the future.

Sometimes the patient will speak to you of their experiences as they are happening. It is good to listen to the essential information they give you while encouraging them to move more deeply into their inner experience, into the space where there are no words, only feelings, images and sensations. The karmic knots which create disease in later life are held in wordless space. The patient can report what has happened to them later on at the end of the healing session.

When you feel that healing is complete give thanks out loud to those unseen beings who have been present and helped in the healing process. Speaking aloud also alerts the patient to the fact that the healing is over, although they will often register this as a change in energy and will spontaneously open their eyes. If the patient is seated you may like to place your hands on their shoulders for a few moments to ground their energy. If the patient is lying down go to the foot of the couch and placing your hands on their feet, hold the feet for a few moments to ground them into their physical body. If the patient is asleep touch them lightly on the arm to wake them. It may take them several moments to bring their consciousness fully back into the body and you should make sure that they take their time and move slowly into an upright position. Do not leave the patient on their own as this breaks your empathetic connections to them. This type of healing is unlike other forms of complementary therapy where the therapist may leave the patient alone to collect themselves at the end of the session.

Throughout this part of the healing session maintain your energy connections to the patient. Centred in Being, hold the figure of eight connections at the Base, Heart and Crown chakras, stayed connected on a Soul level and continue to radiate love from the heart. When the patient has returned to waking consciousness encourage them to tell you about their experience during the healing and listen to them with full attention. This is a time when causes of disease which may have been hidden from view can rise to the surface of consciousness, sometimes with tears of release and relief. Maintaining an open-hearted empathetic stance gives your patient the space to speak their truths to you.

Describing experience also helps anchor into the patient's brain consciousness subtle experiences they might otherwise dismiss or forget. This feedback also gives you, the healer, confirmation of your energetic work. Talk to the patient about any insights and perceptions they or you have had during the healing process on the cause and nature of their disease. This may be on the location of the point of friction and its meaning in emotional and psychological terms. These perceptions may come as images, words or phrases to be discussed with the patient. This part of the session can be extremely important for a full realisation of the cause of the disease and its complete healing.

Before the patient leaves the healing space withdraw all energy connections from them by an act of will, seeing all energy streams and figure of eight threads returning to your own chakras. Make sure your patient is fully grounded before they leave the healing space.

When the patient has left the room clear the healing space energetically by sounding OMs or bells or by smudging with incense to remove any disturbed energy which may otherwise linger in the room.

RADIATORY HEALING

In Radiatory Healing the healing agent is the Radiatory Energy of the Soul flowing out through the healer's aura. An energy field is created by linking Soul, brain and Heart Chakra via the Sutratma, and circulating energy through these three points. In this way we create a radiatory energy field which evokes the patient's own Soul energy and stimulates the patient's personality vehicles. Radiatory Healing is given to patients who have some channel of conscious contact between their Soul and personality.

There are two main differences between Magnetic and Radiatory Healing. The first is that with Radiatory Healing contact between healer and patient is subtle and not tangible - there is no physical contact of any kind with the patient. The second is that the order in which we set up the Soul, brain, Heart triangle to generate healing energy is different.

All the preparatory steps in the Radiatory Healing session are carried as for Magnetic Healing including welcoming the patient, talking about symptoms, making them comfortable, centring in being, offering prayers for healing, connecting healer and patient energetically, centring the patient, linking souls, and making an energetic diagnosis, which in the case of Radiatory Healing is always done vusing direct perception.

It is more beneficial during Radiatory Healing if the patient is lying comfortably on their back on a couch, a bed or flat cushions, since they can relax more easily. If necessary cover their body with a light blanket to keep them warm as the body often cools down as it lies still. The healer sits to the side of the patient where the disease is located, also in a comfortable position but with an upright spine. Where the disease is psychological it may be effective to sit at the patient's head. There is no need to touch the patient's body at all during the healing session although it can feel good to have a hand to hold or a person to hug when the session is complete.

Energy Connections for the Radiatory Healer

Having set up the initial energy connections within yourself and to and for the patient make your diagnosis of the patient's energetic condition using direct perception on the Third Eye (see Chapter Four). Note the condition of the chakra governing the diseased area of the body as well as the condition of the other major centres.

Begin the healing process by focusing your attention in your Heart Chakra. Feel your Heart Chakra opening and its energy radiating outwards. Using your creative imagination visualise a thread of energy moving from your Heart Chakra to your Soul. For this purpose imagine the Soul as being located above the top of the head, though in reality the Soul is everywhere in all things. Let yourself feel the energy of your Soul which is love.

Next visualise a thread of energy moving from your Soul, via the sutratma which enters the body through the Crown Chakra, to your brain, anchoring in the physical head centre of the pituitary gland. From here return the thread of energy to the Heart Chakra.

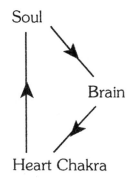

Circulate energy through the three points of the Heart, Soul and brain by shifting your attention from Heart Chakra to Soul to brain to Heart, until you can clearly sense the triangle of energies. Once this triangle is easily felt/seen, watch it begin to rotate upon itself until it is moving so quickly that it appears to be a disc of light. Visualise this disc rotating upon itself until it becomes a sphere of light from which energy begins to radiate in all directions out through your aura. This is the Radiating Energy of Being.

The energy of Being energises the healer's three personality vehicles and the aura, via the threads of connection set up at the beginning of the session. The presence of your Soul within your personality vehicles invokes the presence of the patient's Soul, bringing the patient into direct contact with the energy of their own Being. It is this Soul energy which can heal them if the time is right. In addition the patient's mental attitude is strengthened and clarified by a clear mental emanation from the healer's aura and their emotional body is helped to attain quiet and dispassion through contact with the healer's calm emotional body. The healer's radiating etheric and health auras have corresponding effects on the patient's aura.

By mingling the two auras, both responsive to Soul contact, the energy of Being is automatically directed to the point of friction in the patient's physical/ etheric, astral or mental body, which is the seat of the disease. This contact has a tremendous effect upon the diseased area and the chakra governing that area becomes energised and blockages are released, leading to healing of the point of friction. Throughout this process the healer has little else to do other than maintain conscious Soul alignment and keep their personality vehicles in a calm and quiet state. Healing takes place because all Souls are one.

We all begin as healers from wherever we are and not all of us have total and consistent Soul contact at will. I am including the following suggestions for additional healing visualisation which can be carried out by the healer who is learning how to hold themselves in conscious Soul alignment. This energetic visioning helps focus the mind and develops concentration as well as complementing the healing process.

Linking Chakras

Focus your attention in the centre of your head and using your imagination set up an energy link between the chakra governing the diseased area in the patient's body and the corresponding chakra in your own body.

Link the two chakras with a figure of eight thread of light. By synchronising with the patient's disturbed chakra, the same chakra in the healer's body acts as a magnet drawing forth a response from the patient's chakra. This response illuminates the point of friction so that it becomes visible. Look for it.

Once the disturbed chakra is in rapport with the healer's chakra, sense whether the patient's chakra is under or overstimulated - whether Soul energy is inhibited as it flows into or out of the chakra. If the chakra is overstimulated it will look and feel more intensely coloured than usual with flashes of other colours. It may also appear enlarged and distorted. If this is the case increase the potency of your own chakra by increasing the amount of Soul energy flowing through it, and using your focused imagination abstract excess energy from the patient's centre.

If the centre in need is understimulated it will look/feel small, pale, dark and on occasions may seem to disappear altogether. In this case send a ray of your own soul energy into the patient's chakra as a stimulating point of energy, which evokes the patient's own energy restoring health.

An alternative to both these actions is to hold the two parallel chakras in your own and the patient's body en rapport and to let nature take its course as the energies balance out through time. As healer you need to hold the situation steady and give the patient confidence.

This link also acts as a mirror in your own body for what is happening within the patient's body. As in magnetic healing you can feel the changes occurring in the patient's body within your own body. When the inhibition into or out of the chakra in the patient's body is released, you can feel this release as a pressure change within your own parallel chakra.

Once you have linked chakras in this way you wait, holding your personality vehicles aligned to the energy of your soul. Remain calm, allow the space to deepen, since a tranquil emotional and mental body are necessary for the passage of the healing energies of the Soul. Listen and watch for information on the patient's condition. The major part of your work is complete. From this point it is your intuition which directs all further proceedings and which if required will give you information via imagery and words on the causes of the disease.

Using your Intuition

When you have balanced out the chakra in need, intuition may direct you to focus your attention on other chakras. Repeat the same process there. Intuition may guide you to focus on particular parts of the patient's physical/etheric, astral and mental bodies, neutralising and blending colours, adding or removing energy from the chakras and balancing energies as described.

Intuition is your channel of direct knowledge about the way things are, for yourself and your patient. By linking Souls, you come into contact with the patient's purpose and destiny. Intuition enables you to experience and know a little of this and therefore of the causes of their disease. In healing as in everything else, the instructions of intuition are your way of knowing the correct course you should take for the healing and wholeness of your patient. By implementing the directives of your intuition healing will be in line with the purpose of the patient's Soul.

This absolute trust in the directions of intuition comes with experience. You may receive confirmation of its truth immediately when the patient tells you of their experience, as pain disappears and healing occurs, or this confirmation may only come weeks later after the event, in a chance conversation with the patient.

Additional Energy Experiences for the Patient During Radiatory Healing

Disease and its healing are part of the unfoldment of human consciousness and major factors in our becoming aware of our true nature as human energy Beings. In addition to the procedures given so far there are several energy experiences which reinforce and amplify the healing process and anchor into brain consciousness our true nature. The following are such exercises:

Washing the Etheric Vehicle and Chakras with Colour

After balancing the chakra governing the diseased area and any other related chakras, you can wash the patient's whole aura and energy field with colour to remove distortions and heal minor imbalances.

Using your creative imagination see a wave of colour pass through the patient's etheric body, moving from below their feet through the body and head and out above the head. The colour used is determined by intuition in the moment the decision is made to carry out this exercise. It is not planned beforehand.

As the colour wave passes through the body see it removing all minor distortions and flashes of extraneous colour within the aura, as if they are ripples in the wave. Allow the colour to flow through wave upon wave, changing colour if so guided by intuition. There are colours which have a definite healing effect upon the whole etheric/physical body. Among these are green - the colour of nature, of plants and trees, often used in hospitals because of its recognised healing qualities; blue - the colour of the heart which heals; and magenta - the healing ray of the planet at this time. However, all colours of the rainbow can be used effectively at one time or another. Choose your colour according to your immediate knowing.

Particular colours excite individual chakras. For example, washing a chakra with its own colour will cleanse its energy and enhance its vibration. Complementary colours can be used to remove excess energy by neutralising it. For example, using a wave of green to neutralise an excess of red in the Base Chakra or red flashes in the Solar Plexus has an effect similar to taking a walk in nature.

Energising the Patient's Chakras and Aura

This is a general toning exercise for the etheric body which cleanses and energises the chakras and gives the patient the sensation of floating free from their physical body (if they are not asleep). It also gives a direct experience of being focused in Being.

As you sit beside the patient, visualise the whole of their etheric body as a body of energy and light lying in front of you in the same shape and form as their physical bodies. Next visualise two streams or cones of energy entering their body at both ends, through the Base and Crown Chakras. These streams can be seen as a red stream of light entering the Base and a white stream entering the Crown Chakra, moving inwards towards each other.

Visualise the two streams of energy moving towards each other at the same speed in a parallel movement through the chakras, so that they are paired as follows :

red light in the Base Chakra	white light in the Crown Chakra
red light in the Sacral Centre	white light in the Ajna Chakra
red light in the Solar Plexus	white light in the Throat Chakra
red light in the Heart Chakra	white light in the Heart Chakra

As the two cones of energy meet and blend with each other in the Heart Chakra, they form a hexagonal shape, which allows energy to be released from within the chakra. This energy is golden in colour and radiates outwards in all directions horizontally from the chakra. Visualising this energy encourages its unfoldment from within the chakra.

Imagine the two energy streams moving on through the chakras, the white stream moving down from the Crown towards the Base Chakra and the red stream moving upwards through the chakras to the Crown, in a parallel movement:

red light in the Throat Chakra   white light in the Solar Plexus

red light in the Ajna Chakra   white light in the Sacral Centre
red light in the Crown Chakra   white light in the Base Chakra

The two streams finally move out through opposite ends of the body.

red light out of the Crown   white light below the Base Chakra

Each time the two streams of coloured light meet in a chakra, golden light is released from the hexagonal shape that is created. This golden light represents the energy of the Soul being released into the etheric vehicle. As each chakra bursts into golden activity, golden light radiates outwards horizontally in all directions and a third golden stream of energy is released running parallel to the white and red. This golden thread moves through the body and out through the Base and Crown Chakras, so that there are now three threads of energy moving through the patient's etheric body.

See the patient in their etheric body begin to slowly revolve upon these three energy strands, as if their chakras are a set of pearls strung on a spiralling thread of white, red and gold, which links the earth and the heavens.

Hold the patient in this experience for as long as possible with the aid of your focused imagination. The patient will feel very relaxed, as if they are floating far out in space. They are able to experience the energy of their Soul and its reality in and out of time and space.

You can also use this visualisation for yourself to enhance your own experience of your chakras, Soul energy and to energise and heal your own body.

Patient's Experience of Radiatory Healing

The patient will usually relax automatically once the healer-patient energy connections are established and will experience a great sense of well-Being. If there is any difficulty in setting up this rapport, return to your own energy system and radiate energy from your Heart Chakra. Consciously still your own emotional centre and allow your Solar Plexus to relax. You will know your patient has relaxed too when all sense of tightness or inhibition is released from your own Solar Plexus centre.

During the session the patient's relaxation may deepen into sleep or may be experienced as a sensation of floating in or above the physical body, as the etheric web between the patient's etheric and astral bodies is temporarily transcended. If the patient does fall asleep they should be allowed to sleep for as long as they need to. During this sleep the Soul's energy directly resolves any imbalances within the astral or mental body, absorbing the point of friction causing the disease.

During the patient's sleep you may find that you also feel suddenly sleepy too. This is not just fatigue. Your consciousness is moving out of the physical into the astral sphere to complete the healing process. Ultimately you are attempting to move consciously out onto the astral, rather than unconsciously and your aim

113

is to stay awake as this happens. Once the point of friction within the patient's astral body has been resolved, this feeling of sleepiness disappears from the healer. The patient will sleep until the Soul's healing energies have moved through all their personality vehicles. They usually awaken feeling very relaxed and replenished.

Where the patient remains awake for all or part of the session, they will have certain energy experiences, depending on their sensitivity to energy and degree of Soul contact. These experiences may include numbness in parts of the body, heat, cold, energy rushes up and down the body and in specific parts, seeing bright colours in various chakras, having visions and hearing voices and sounds. Long forgotten memories may emerge from childhood and past life experiences may be remembered.

Closing the Healing Session

As with Magnetic Healing, a session of Radiatory Healing usually comes to a close in its own natural timing. You will find that your concentration has shifted away from the patient and your Soul energy automatically withdraws into itself, as the patient's own energy field invigorated by their Soul becomes strong enough to take over. Once this end is reached the patient will usually open their eyes or awaken if they have been asleep. On some occasions the patient may continue to sleep as the energies work their way through their personality vehicles. This is even though the healer's energies are withdrawn and the healer may physically move away from the patient. Do not however leave them on their own in the healing space as this severs all energy connections between healer and patient which is not a good thing to do at this point since the healing process is not yet complete. Again give thanks for the presence and assistance of any beings who have helped in the healing process.

When the patient wakes give them time to adjust to being back in their physical bodies before talking with them about their experiences. Ask them how they are feeling and what they have experienced. Assist them in verbalising their experience. Correlate their replies with your own experiences. As with Magnetic Healing this is an important part of the healing session when subtle experiences are anchored into the patient's brain consciousness and reinforced.

Often during the healing experience you may have specific insights into the physical, psychological and spiritual causes and nature of their disease and it is at this time that you talk with your patient about them. These insights come as images, sounds and words, which may be related to particular events in the patient's past or may provide a key to the future. Some of this information may at first seem foolish or irrelevant, but you need to dare to be wrong and speak the truth that you see. The razor's edge is to completely trust your intuition.

Before the patient leaves the room by an act of will withdraw all energetic connections between yourself and the patient returning your own energies back to your chakras. Again make sure that the patient is grounded back in their physical body before they leave the healing space. After Radiatory Healing it is a good idea to suggest to patients that they are gentle with themselves for the next few hours, not rushing back into a hectic life but giving themselves time and tranquillity to fully absorb their experience.

Clear the healing space by sounding several OMs or bells or smudging with incense.

Follow Up Action

At the end of the healing session some healers like to offer suggestions for follow up activity by the patient. They may advise the patient to return for another healing session, or to have other complementary therapies. Some healers offer additional distant healing using Radiatory techniques. These are all ways of assuring the patient of your continuing support in their healing process, but are not strictly necessary.

Time taken for Healing to Occur

Sometimes healing is instantaneous - the pain disappears, the lame walk - miracles do occur. But often there is a time delay as the Soul energies move through the personality vehicles to the physical body creating change. If the disease is mental or emotional the patient will often feel much better immediately after the healing session. On the following day they may feel a little low in spirits and then on the second day, if healing has occurred, they begin to feel much better. They begin to experience something of the true nature of their Soul's energy in everyday life.

If the patient has a physical disease, they usually feel slightly better after the healing session, but a real change in the disease may not appear until 24 hours after the session. During this time the patient may wonder if there has been any healing and what was that energy movement all about. When the change does take place a day or so later they may not connect the two events. You need to advise the patient that there may be a time delay in healing.

No matter how much we want to heal and remove suffering, we are restricted by our own limitations as healers and by the will and purpose of the patient's Soul. It is their Being which for its own purposes has created this disease for the experiences which it brings to the patient both now and in the future. We should not feel too dispirited if we cannot heal everyone or even if we can only heal a few. We can only do our best and we all begin where we are.

Which Kind of Healing to Use?

Which kind of healing is used for any disease depends on three things - the abilities and degree of unfoldment of the healer, the point of awakening and conscious soul contact within the patient and the nature of the illness.

As healers we are all at different stages of Soul unfoldment with different natural abilities. When you start learning about healing it is best to begin with Magnetic Healing and move into using Radiatory Healing as you begin to develop the ability to visualise, to establish conscious Soul contact, concentration and discrimination between different kinds of energies.

There are many different kinds of healers depending on our natural abilities and inherent ray energies. Some use Magnetic Healing alone or Radiatory Healing alone or a combination of both. Some healers are able to work effectively with certain diseases, e.g. cancers, while others cover a whole range of ailments.

I use a combination of the two methods. Sometimes I will use Magnetic Healing so that Pranic Heat can be felt by the patient and at other times I don't use my hands at all. Sometimes I use Magnetic principles at the beginning of a session and Radiatory at the end. Sometimes I use Radiatory principles alone. I follow my intuition as to which method I should use at any given time.

The principles of both forms of healing can be used in combination with all other kinds of healing therapies including allopathic and homeopathic medicine, massage, counselling, psychotherapeutic techniques and all forms of complementary health care.

The degree of conscious soul contact in the patient, assessed during diagnosis, also affects the type of healing given. Where there is little Self awareness, we use Magnetic Healing to work directly with the disease in the patient's etheric body. Where there is conscious soul contact, we can use Radiatory Healing and work with the patient on the conscious direction of energy in all the vehicles. We can use Radiatory Healing for requested absent healing.

The nature of the disease also determines the type of healing given. Where there is pain, soreness or stiffness, Magnetic Healing with the hands can provide almost instant relief for the physical body. The Active Radiatory Heat of Prana allows tense muscles to relax and pain to ease away - tension or resistance to energy is the main cause of pain. This relaxation hastens the healing process. At other times the physical body may be in such extreme pain that it can't bear to be touched at all, even etherically and the patient needs to relax into the energy field of their own Soul, shifting attention away from the disease and their physical body to experience their natural energy state.

Keeping Records

If you are planning to become a professional or part time healer it is a good idea to keep an accurate record of your sessions with your patients. Under the Data Protection Act these must be kept in a safe and secure place and not disclosed to anyone who does not have authority to see them.

These records should include the name, address, telephone number, date of birth, date of session, name and address of doctor, major life diseases, presenting symptoms, energetic diagnosis, type of healing given and energetic activity, healer's experience, patient's experience and any recommendations given for follow up activity.

This ensures that when patients return for further consultations you know who they are and their story and can check on the results of your healing activity.

Developing Qualities of the Healer

Anyone who is attempting to heal consciously with energy will be concerned in developing the following abilities :

The ability to establish immediate rapport with all kinds of people. This is an energy rapport which requires us to be open and vulnerable to the patient as well as them being open to us.

The ability to create rapid alignments at will between Soul, the mind, the head centres, the physical brain and the Heart Chakra.

Using the mind illumined by the light of the Soul to discern the psychological causes of disease.

The ability to establish a relationship of cooperation between ourselves and our patients which allows us to enter the patient's energy field with ease.

The art of diagnosis, so that we know the location of the point of friction and which of the major centres we are treating for any disease.

The ability to determine the patient's degree of conscious Soul contact which determines the predominating energy in their etheric body, whether they are astrally or mentally polarised and the likely location of the point of friction.

The art of listening to and cooperating with the patient's Soul so that all inflowing energies into the patient's etheric body will be focused on bringing relief to the diseased area.

Being able to protect ourselves against the transference of disease from the patient by maintaining a positive radiatory stance throughout the healing session, if necessary radiating purely from the heart chakra.

The ability to withdraw the healing energy field when the patient's own energy field is strong enough to take over.

This may seem like an awesome range of talents and abilities to develop, but again we all begin somewhere. In addition most would be healers have some previous life experiences as healers and much of our learning is a process of remembering what we already know.

CHAPTER SIX

Devas, Elementals, Angels and Sound

Hydrogen is the simplest atom in the physical universe. It is composed of one positively charged proton and one negatively charged electron. The proton and electron are held in relationship to each other by a force of attraction between them. In esoteric terms this force of attraction is known as a *Deva*. Two protons or two electrons are held apart from each other by a force of repulsion, which is also composed of devic substance. The former belongs to a class of devas known as the *Building Devas* and the latter to the *Destroyer Devas*.

All atoms and molecules in the physical universe are held in form and in relationship to each other by a combination of building and destroyer devas. Some of these devas are minute, like those in the physical atom and others are enormous, such as those which hold the constellations in place.

Devas are not confined to the physical sphere of existence only, but are found wherever matter of any quality is built into a form. Human beings are particularly connected with the devas of the mental, astral, etheric and physical spheres. Healers are primarily concerned with the activities of the building devas rather than the destroyers, as much of our work involves the rebuilding of damaged and diseased tissues. The one destroyer deva we may come into contact with is the Angel of Death.

The building devas are separated into two categories of activity. There are firstly those devas whose function is to build matter of the different spheres into form. These devas are usually described as the Builders or as Angels, e.g. Solar Angel, Healing Angel, Archangel which have long been described in religious material. The second group are those devas which are built into form and are known as Elementals.

There are four groups of builders and four groups of elementals who are normally accessible to human beings:

Builders or Angels

builders of the mental sphere	- the gaseous
builders of the astral sphere	- the liquid
builders of the etheric world	- the etheric
builders of the dense physical sphere	- the dense physical

Devas, Elementals, Angels and Sound

Elementals

of air	- sylphs
of fire	- salamanders
of water	- sprites and undines
of earth	- gnomes, elves and fairies

Devas appear in many different forms which are not normally apparent to the human eye. They can be seen etherically by those whose Ajna Chakra is awakened and who are clairvoyant, and by those who have direct perception. They have a presence which can be perceived in some way by the sensitive person.

The form in which we see devas depends to a large extent upon our cultural background. In Britain and Europe there are strong folk traditions of fairies, gnomes, elves, trolls and the little people, which have been illustrated in fairy tales

In the Christian, Jewish and Muslim religions there are angels, cherubim and seraphim, and archangels with wings and shining robes. In the east devas are part of the vast pantheon of gods and goddesses of the Hindu and Buddhist traditions. We can see devas in any of these forms.

We can also experience devas as pure forces without form. They can be seen and felt as intense spots of activity and/or colour and as the matrix intrinsic in every pebble and crystal, every flower and tree and in all the forms we create as human beings from motor cars to symphonies, poetry to homes. (For further information on devas read *Devas, Fairies and Angels* by William Bloom, Gothic Image, and *Nature Spirits and Elemental Beings* by Marko Pogacnik, Findhorn Press.)

Devas and Consciousness

Devas move in a parallel evolutionary stream to that of consciousness or Being, ranging from the tiniest forces - the elementals to the angelic hosts which allow the great galaxies of the universe to manifest themselves. This is the devic stream. The evolutionary stream of Being includes mineral, vegetable, animal and human beings, and planetary, solar and galactic logoi.

The two evolutionary streams are intimately linked together with one major difference between them. All Beings are in process of expressing their unique quality, which is consciousness - the principle of coherence and self-determination - in the worlds of form. Devas are in process of incorporating consciousness into their lives. Beings are able to express themselves through the agency of devic forces, and devas become conscious through the agency of individual and group being, in particular through human beings.

Human beings are Self conscious. We have free will which we can use or not. We choose our behaviour consciously or unconsciously and are able to express our unique consciousness as we will. Devas have no such free will. They are automatically responsive to the creative will of other beings, such as human beings, planetary and solar logoi. This is an energy response caused by a synchronous vibration.

Our needs as human beings are inextricably linked to those of the devic stream of evolution. We cannot express ourselves in the physical realm, we cannot create the good, the beautiful and the true without the agency of devic forces. Devas cannot follow their path to Self consciousness without our creative inspiration.. The more conscious we humans are of this relationship the more we can help each other. As we begin to express our true Self in the physical sphere we attract to ourselves individualising devic energy which is in process of becoming Self conscious.

Each human being is associated with an individualising deva. This deva builds the causal body, the vehicle of consciousness, of the Soul and is known by various names - as our Guardian Angel, Solar Angel and the Angel of the Presence. Sometimes we are able to sense our Guardian Angel almost as a separate identity within our awareness, overseeing and protecting us as we go through life. As our Guardian Angel is evolving into Self consciousness this sense of individuality and separateness is a true reflection of how things are.

In esoteric traditions the processes of Initiation involve successive confrontations between the forces of the personality, known as the Dweller on the Threshold, and the Angel of the Presence who carries the energies of the Soul. In the fourth initiation the causal body is destroyed and the individualised angel is set free. The Presence of the Spark can then express itself directly through the personality vehicles as it chooses. Not many human beings in incarnation are at this point of evolution.

All living beings have a deva associated with them. Just as our physical body is created from billions of individual cells, so this deva is the sum total of the forces of attraction and repulsion holding the energy of Being in form. In the case of the being who ensouls our planet, this deva is known as the Spirit of the Earth. Similarly every rock, plant and animal has a deva associated with it, whose needs and capabilities are inherently matched by those of the individual rock, plant and animal. The birds of the air have a special relationship with the devas since they too have the ability to fly like angels.

Devas and Sound

Devas are swept into activity through the agency of *Sound*. This sound can be physical or more often is soundless - a sound which is only heard in the Silence. When we close our eyes and look within, moving beyond the sounds of the outer world, we can hear the silence and the sounds of the world of being. Whenever a clear note is sounded devas of a synchronous vibration automatically respond to that note building and destroying forms through attraction and repulsion.

Sound is recognised by most religious and esoteric traditions as the creative agent in the universe. *"In the beginning was the Word and the Word was with God and the Word was God"*, is an idea fundamental to Jewish and Christian teachings. In western esoteric tradition the Logos, which means the Word, is the name given to Beings who ensoul planets and solar systems. In eastern teachings the AUM or OM is the sound which is said to encompass the whole of creation. The A brought the universe into existence, the U continues it and when the last

121

echo of the M has faded away our universe will have disappeared returning to its source.

All beings from a solar logos to a human being to a rose manifest themselves through the sounding of their own unique note and through the automatic response of the devic realms to that note. We humans manifest ourselves in the physical world through the agency of the devas of the mental, astral and etheric/physical spheres, who cause the matter of these spheres to coalesce and form vehicles of our expression.

As we become more conscious of our Soul, its note is sounded ever more clearly in our everyday lives, automatically attracting to ourselves devic energy which responds to that coherent, inclusive, love vibration. We are then able to create new forms in the physical world which are attuned to that note of being and can express the good, the beautiful and the true.

In terms of healing the delight of this relationship between human beings and devas is that a clear note sounded from a vision of wholeness and health, held in the mind of a human being, automatically calls in devic forces to create that health in actuality. This vision of health is built initially in mental matter with the aid of the building devas of the mental sphere. Once this thoughtform is created and the impelling energy of being continues to move through it, it is then expressed in emotional matter with the help of the building devas of the astral sphere, and precipitates into the physical sphere through the agency of the devas and elementals, bringing health to the physical body.

The automatic response of devas to sound does not depend on the motivation of the being who is sounding the note, on whether their motivation is positive or negative. The response is dependent on the clarity and strength of the note sounded. There are people who can work extremely clearly in mental matter, but who have no connection with the energy of their own Soul. Without this connection the forms which they create in the world may be inherently wrong or *evil*, for example, people who manufacture and sell weapons of destruction, or who traffic in death dealing drugs. The extreme of this can be seen in Hitler's ideals for Germany, which had powerful impact because of the potency and clarity of the originating note, but with no connection to soul energy.

What we create depends on our motivation. Our ability to heal and make whole depends on our connection with our own Soul and its presence in our daily lives.

Devas and Healing

Certain devas are specifically attuned to healing energies. These include the individualising devas who respond to the note of our Soul and those devas who respond to the magenta and green healing rays of the planet.

Many healers work in cooperation with a healing angel - a deva specifically attuned to healing energies. By sounding the note of the Soul with power and clarity at the beginning of any healing session, we automatically invoke the presence of a healing angel who is able to work with us at the appropriate frequency. This angel assists in stabilising all the energy connections and radiatory fields we create and helps rebuild damaged and diseased tissues.

Specific healing angels are attached to healers for the purpose of mutual exchange and growth. They are not something which we can decide with our minds that we want to assist us. They are purely responsive to the note we sound and our own purpose in being. A healing angel comes to us rather than us demanding to have one, although the intention to heal harmlessly helps to create the correct conditions.

At the beginning of a healing session, as we set up our energy connections and centre ourselves in being, we can sense the entry of a healing angel into our energy field, as a distinct change within the energy field and as a definite other presence. This angel may have a form which we register with our inner vision, appearing as an angel, as a colour or as formless. For its development the angel needs our acknowledgement of its presence. This is one of the reasons why we pray out loud at the beginning of a healing session, for assistance from healing angels and other helpful presences.

The healing angel assists us in setting up energy connections and stabilising the energy field. We can assume that once we have set up these connections and put them to the back of our minds, they will be held in form by the angel until the healing session is over and we have withdrawn our energy connections by an act of will.

The healing angel who assists us is at a parallel point in evolution to ourselves, able to work with the devas of the etheric, astral and mental bodies, to the degree that we are conscious of their workings. This healing angel works with the elementals to rebuild the etheric body, which underlies diseased physical tissue. Conscious healing with a healing angel is more effective since all energy connections are held stable throughout the energy session and we have greater freedom to move in the flow of our intuition.

A healing angel will not appear if we attempt to heal patients for whom there is no possibility of healing, especially the dying. The Angel of Death is a destroyer angel whose energy is repulsive to that of healing angels.

Certain healers have a special relationship with the Spirit of the Earth, the deva for the whole planet. These healers work with the results of major epidemics and natural catastrophes. They are often nurses, doctors and rescue workers who are not consciously aware of their healing skills. This is a specific form of service.

Visualisation of the Activity of the Healing Devas

The process of healing involves the rebuilding, harmonising and transforming of the matter of the etheric/physical, astral and mental bodies. It is the activity of the devic forces which allows this rebuilding to take place. By recognising and visualising their presence and activity, we assist their work as builders and their evolution.

We can visualise them in any form that we choose. Building devas of the mental body are usually seen as yellow, those of the astral body are green and those of the etheric body are violet. Once we have determined the location of the point of friction within the patient's vehicles, we visualise building devas of appropriate hue flowing into the disturbed vehicle and transforming the matter of that vehicle.

For example, in a patient with viral hepatitis, where part of the liver is destroyed by viral infection, we locate the point of friction, perhaps in the patient's mental body. We visualise the patient's mental body with its pale luminous colours as say, surrounding the patient's physical body. We see the point of friction within the mental body, however it appears to us to be. It may be as a dark spot, a hole, an intensity of colour, a fire, an absence. We visualise the yellow building devas of the mental body moving into activity, bringing light and colour, removing darkness, filling the hole, reducing intensity, putting out the fire or closing the gap. We hold the devas in our imagination until their activity is complete and the point of friction is transformed.

In our imagination we move to the astral body, seeing its vibrant colours and the corresponding reflection of the point of friction within the astral body. We repeat the process here calling in the green astral building devas. When that is finished we move on to the etheric body and see the violet etheric building devas rebuilding and transforming the etheric structure which underlies the physical liver. We see the etheric web of golden light reforming and as it does so healthy cells and tissues begin to aggregate upon the complete etheric body. We maintain this visualisation for as long as our intuition tells us that it is necessary.

The Use of Sound in Healing

It is through sound that we express our creative will as energy beings. This sound is not physical, although physical sounds, in particular in music, can invoke the presence of devas and feelings of transcendence and bliss. The note of our Soul calls into activity the devas of the spheres who build matter into form, so that we can express ourselves in the world. Soundless sound is a creative agent used in healing.

When we come into contact with the energy of our own Soul, its note is automatically sounded throughout our vehicles. It is a sound which can be heard with the inner ear by ourselves and others. This note of the Soul is evocative - it calls forth the presence of being within the listener. This is what we are doing in healing when we centre ourselves in being at the beginning of a session automatically sounding our Soul's note.

As well as the sound generated by our Soul, each of the major chakras has its own note, which vibrates in resonance with the basic note of the informing being. During a healing session, once we have set up our energy connections and have linked the needed chakra to our own parallel chakra, we sound the note of that chakra in our own body. This sounding evokes Soul energy within the chakra governing the diseased area in the patient, clearing any congestion.

The sounding of the note in the healer's chakra happens automatically when we focus our attention upon it. We can increase the power and effectiveness of this process by making it conscious, by creating a triangle of energies. The

note we sound can be soundless or sounded physically.
We do this as follows :

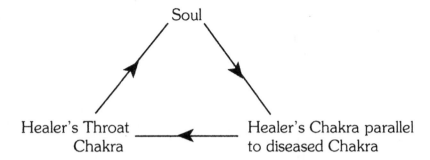

We link our Soul to the chakra in our etheric body which lies parallel to the chakra governing the diseased area in the patient's body and thence to our throat chakra. We circulate energy through this triangle in the direction shown. We relax our physical throats allowing energy to flow through the throat chakra. We sound this note soundlessly.

We can also sound this note physically so that the transformative energy of being is anchored physically into the body. We set up the same triangle of energies as before directing the energy out of the Throat Chakra into the voice. We relax our throats, open our mouths and let the sound that is there come out.

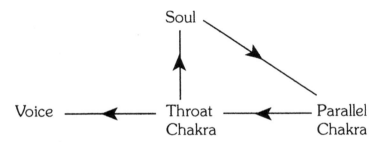

This physical sounding requires confidence in your ability to express the energy of the Soul through your voice and the ability to hold the threads of energy still and unbroken. This is possible with practice and is very effective as a healing force, since it calls not only on the healing devas of the subtle worlds, but also those of the physical body, speeding the process of healing.

Outer physical sound is a reflection of an inner sound, which is taken up by the sylphs, the elementals of the air, and built into the sounds we hear with our ears. Our highly developed human communication skills are based upon sound in the form of words, without which our minds would not have developed their creative reasoning and imaginative faculties. In allopathic medicine high frequency ultrasound is passed through objects and translated into pictures. It is used to see inside the human body, e.g. to look at the developing foetus in the womb. Sound is also used to help heal broken bones more quickly since the cells, via the devas, are encouraged to repair themselves more rapidly. There are also low frequency sounds which can damage and kill.

Certain types of music have a direct effect upon the chakras and can be used to stimulate or quieten individual chakras. Much of classical music resonates with the centres in the Head and the Heart Chakras. Popular music tends to stimulate the Solar Plexus, Sacral and Base Chakras, as well as the Throat and Heart Chakras. Some modern music synchronises with the Crown and Ajna Chakras. Different combinations of sound allow different qualities of energy and hence devic forms to come together, blend and transform. Today's electronic instruments create sounds which have never before existed and with them come new devas. This is part of devic evolution which humans are helping to create.

We can also use physical sound in healing as an anchoring force. The sounding of the OM is useful since it implies wholeness and completion. It can be used at any point during the healing session to anchor in particular energy threads or changes, and can be sounded to close the session and to clear the healing space of any disturbed energies. The pitch and tone are determined by our intuition, we open our mouths and let the sound come out. We can also sound the OM soundlessly.

EXERCISES:
Recognising Devic Forces

Just like human beings devas respond when their presence is recognised. The best way to learn about devas is to allow the possibility of their existence and to encourage their visible and invisible presence.

Devas appear not only as the fairies of our childhood story books, but in much more commonplace forms that we have seen many times and dismissed as *nothing*. The movements which we see in the corner of our eyes, the brilliant spots of colour and light that flash momentarily before our eyes, are not merely figments of our imagination or dust particles on our eyeballs. They are often devas and they have a reality and actuality all their own.

There are now several books available on devas and their nature, in particular those suggested earlier and others published by the Findhorn Foundation. Here are some suggestions on developing contact and communication with devas.

Seeing Devas

On a clear blue sky day or when there is uniform cloud cover without rain, lie outside on your back on the ground and look up at the sky with open eyes. Allow your eyes to adjust to the light of the sky and let your depth of focus change, moving from the surface of the eyeball out to infinity.

At first you will probably notice the movements of tiny particles of dust, hairs and tears on the surface of the eyeball. Then focus a few inches away from the eye and look to see the etheric structure of the air as it moves. This etheric structure appears as moving whorls and eddies, faint and light against the background of sky or cloud, and as millions of tiny dots moving very fast.

Look higher into the sky holding the eyes steady and focused until spots of white and coloured light begin to appear. These are the free-flowing devas of the air - the sylphs. Sylphs can be more easily in some places than others, such as places where nature itself is strong and wild, or in places where landscape energy lines meet and mingle.

Nature Spirits

Being with nature in stillness gives us and the devas space in which to appear within our consciousness. Few people feel that they can afford the time to stop and just be in nature for a few hours, but it is one of the most healing experiences we can give ourselves. By stopping our busyness we have the chance to hear the sound of our own Soul and we can also experience the healing qualities of nature spirits.

Sit in any natural place - on a mountain, by the sea, in a wood and let your body, mind and emotions relax for a few hours or more. As you slow down the peace of your own soul nature comes slowly to you and so will the devas, called by the silent sounding of your soul note. Try sitting under a tree for a few hours and listen to the wisdom of the tree allowing the possibility that its spirit will come to you. (Who knows what the bodhi tree spirit said to Buddha). Allow the voice you hear within to be the voice of the tree spirit and not just of your own mind.

Nature spirits abound. They are everywhere in all places waiting for recognition and waiting to communicate with you. People who spend their lives in nature - farmers, gardeners, foresters, often have an unconscious special relationship with the nature spirits. They sound a note to which devas and therefore plants and animals automatically respond. Such people are said to have green fingers, plants flourish in their care.

Bringing these unconscious relationships into consciousness allows us to communicate with the devas and therefore to work more effectively with them. This is a particular initiation into the mysteries of the earth which opens the doors to perception and other realities.

Tree and Landscape Devas

On a clear day at sunrise when the landscape colours are turning from grey to golden, or near sunset when the shadows are beginning to lengthen, look at trees against a skyline. This can be a single tree in a garden or park or a group of trees in a wood. Look at the tree from a distance where you can comfortably view the whole tree. Look at the edge of the tree, the outline of the leaves and branches and notice the pale shimmering aura and etheric body of the tree. This can usually be seen as a narrow band of pale blue or violet light around the edge of the tree.

Look again at the tree and then in the air five to twenty feet around the tree. If necessary move back from it so that you can see above and to the sides of the tree. Here it is possible to see the faint colour of the deva of the tree against the sky, often two or three times the size of the physical tree. Tree devas are pink, violet or blue in colour depending on the type of tree and this colour can be seen quite definitely shimmering against a background.

Certain trees have a very powerful presence and their deva can be clearly seen and felt. This is often so with very old trees and those which have had long human contact. They may act as guardians for gardens and homes and whole valleys in nature. Put your arms round such a tree and listen to its secrets.

In any natural landscape there are greater and lesser devic presences. The greater presences are often associated with particular Mother Trees or with landscape features, such as rocky outcrops, hills and valleys. These landscape devas govern whole areas of land - whole valleys or mountains. In many traditions these spirits of the land are regarded as goddesses and gods not only of the surrounding areas but for the whole planet. Mount Kailash in western Tibet is the home of Shiva, creator god in the Hindu pantheon. Mount Everest is home to a goddess. We can communicate with these spirits in meditation and prayer.

Music Devas

Wherever musical instruments are played, whenever voices sing, sylphs, devas of the air and ethers automatically appear in colours of every shade and hue. Music becomes beautiful when it calls to the devas to build matter of pure quality into forms which are resonant with the energy of being. When we play and sing from our hearts then the devas of the air who respond to that loving energy will build the forms which brings that energy to our listeners. Some pieces of music and some performances, even singing in the bath, have a profound effect upon us for this reason. The form communicates its essence through sound and the agency of the devas.

When music is being played in a room look, using the Ajna Chakra and the Third Eye to see the devas of the air and ethers as they build the forms which carry the music. They will be there with their many colours and shapes building upon each other in the same way that an oscilloscope shows visually the shapes of sounds. Watch the great choirs and orchestras as they perform.

Sounding Exercise for the Healer

This exercise is designed to help the healer practice soundless or physical sounding.

1. Sit comfortably and watch your breath as it moves in and out of the nostrils for twenty whole breaths.

2. Focus your attention and link your Soul, the Base Chakra and the Throat Chakra with a thread of light energy.

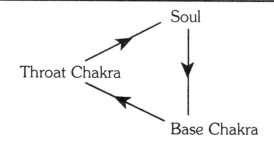

3. Circulate energy through the three points of the triangle.

4. Take a deep breath in and focus your attention in the Base Chakra. On the outbreath sound the note that comes to you, either physically with the voice or nonphysically in the Throat Chakra :

Dooooo.....   or Ahhhhh..... or Hummmm.....   or OM.....

5. Circulate the energy through the three points of Soul, Base Chakra and Throat Chakra and repeat the process two more times, sounding the note of the Base Chakra three times in all.

6. Shift your attention to the Sacral Centre and repeat the process, setting up a triangle of energies between the Soul, Sacral Centre and Throat Chakra. Take a deep breath in and sound the note that comes to you on the outbreath physically or nonphysically :

Reeee..... or Ahhhhh.....   or Hummmm..... or OM.....

Repeat three times sounding the note of the Sacral Centre.

7. Repeat the whole process in each of the major chakras :

		or Ahhhh	or Hummmm	or OM
Base Chakra	Do	or Ahhhh	or Hummmm	or OM
Sacral Centre	Re	..	..	..
Solar Plexus	Me	..	..	..
Heart Chakra	Fa	..	..	..
Throat Chakra	So	..	..	..
Ajna Centre	La	..	..	..
Crown Chakra	Te	..	..	..
Above head	Do	..	..	..

This exercise can also be used during a healing session as part of the healing/energising experience for the patient, establishing first of all an energy link between the chakra in the healer's etheric body and the parallel chakra in the patient's etheric body.

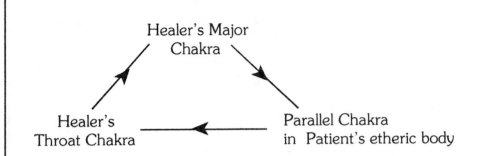

Sound the note in each of the major chakras three times, linking each time with the parallel chakra in the patient's etheric body.

CHAPTER SEVEN

Healing in the Emotional Body through Regression

Many human beings in incarnation today are astrally polarised, acting and reacting from our emotions. In this chapter we examine particularly the way in which our emotional conditioning is set up in life and ways to integrate these powerful energies into our wholeness.

As energy beings we choose the circumstances into which we incarnate in order to fulfil our Soul's purpose. From a vast range of possibilities we are magnetically attracted to two human parents, who will provide the conditions necessary for our growth and development so that we can fulfil our Soul's purpose in time and space. We may incarnate into a slum, a palace, a desert, a loving family or a family at war or we may be abandoned at birth. We choose our parents for the way that they are. We choose our conception, our time in our mother's womb and the actual way in which we are born, whether we are plucked from the womb by Caesarean section or emerge naturally in peace and grace. This choice is usually completely unconscious.

The whole process of birth is an initiation into the mysteries of physically manifested life. It has powerful effects which reverberate throughout our lives. From the moment we are conceived we not only begin to grow physically we also begin to sow the seeds for our future emotional, psychological and psychic development. These seeds anchor into our unconscious through the experiences we synchronistically have primarily with our mothers, during our conception and our time in her womb. They are cliched in the way in which we are born into the world and how we are received by that world during the first months of our lives.

These seeds are what is described in religious literature as Karma. Karma in this sense is not simply the debts which we have to pay for behaving badly or the fruits of behaving well. It is a magnetic choice by which we pattern our future experience, in order to fulfil ourselves within the particular place and time span into which we incarnate. It is created in the present as much from our future as our past.

Seeds of karma are carried from life to life within the subtle causal vehicle of the soul and are expressed via the genetic inheritance from our parents, from which our physical bodies are created. They ripen through interaction with the world. This karma is not only personal it is also collective. We are all subject to the karma of being a part at any one time, of a particular grouping of human

Healing in the Emotional Body

beings - a tribe such as the Kogi or the Navajo, or a race of people, such as the Jews or the Palestinians, Serbs or Croats. We are also subject to the karma of being a human being on a planet which is rapidly being destroyed by the activities of human beings.

Through childhood and into adulthood karmic seeds ripen and mature, forming the basis of our personality and the habits and structures of the character by which we become known in the world. What begins as a small but significant experience at birth generalises into a statement about how life is for us which we repeat in many permutations and which determines our behaviour sometimes for the rest of our lives.

As an example - when we are wanted by our parents, when our conception is planned and achieved in loving orgasmic union, the seeds of that experience develop within us as an inner knowing that we are desired and desirable. We are secure in the knowledge that our presence on the earth is wanted and we carry that inner security with us for the whole of our lives. When either or both of our parents does not really want us, we experience their lack of desire as we are incarnating. This seed develops into an underlying feeling of insecurity, of not really being wanted by the world, of being undesirable. This lack of security surfaces later in our lives in different sorts of situations, in our work, in our relationships, etc.. We spend a lot of time searching for security in other people, in material possessions, work, etc., but none of these can overcome the fundamental feeling of insecurity for more than a short time. This is the life dilemma which we will spend much of our lives dealing with and trying to resolve.

From the very beginning we have a role in creating our own reality. We magnetically choose the way we are born and that choice determines the way in which we experience life on earth. However this choice is unconscious - it is made before consciousness has developed, but it is directed according to the purpose of our Soul for its own fulfilment. If it were a choice over which we had any conscious control, who would ever choose to incarnate as a child into a war zone or starvation or into any place of suffering. As we grow in life particular character traits develop in response to external conditions, which mirror the internal unconscious seeds laid down at birth.

Some of these traits are harmonious and acceptable to us allowing us to express ourselves freely. Others through time become problems, limitations - our relationships fail, we feel alone, scared of relating, unable to express ourselves, we don't know where we are going or what to do. Underlying these traits are life statements, established during our time in our mother's womb and at birth, which represent in words the energy of the seeds of our karma. These life statements are unconscious until they are revealed to us. They have a creative or limiting effect upon our experience, depending on their nature. They are the things we hear ourselves saying about ourselves and our lives in unguarded moments and which we repeat often through life.

The following are some examples of common life statements :

I am loved	no-one loves me
I am wanted	no-one wants me

life is easy	life is hard
the world is wonderful	the world is hostile
people care for me	people hurt me
I can breathe easily	it hurts to breathe
I can move easily	I am stuck
I am safe and protected	I am unsafe and vulnerable

We choose to experience the karmic effects of particular life statements within our unconscious emotional minds because of the experiences that they bring to us. For our own inner purposes we have a need to know what it is like to feel loved or unloved, wanted or unwanted, to feel that life is easy or to find it all a struggle, etc.. We experience life in these ways over and over again until the patterns become conscious; or until the significance of those experiences for us are realised - what love is, what desire is, etc.; or until we reach a point where we no longer want or need to go on experiencing those same old patterns of emotion and thought, and consciously choose to behave differently. We want to be released from responding automatically to events and instead want to act from our authentic selves - from our Souls. To do this we need to make the unconscious patterns and their seed causes conscious.

One of our purposes in being alive is the resolution of these seeds of our karma. By making them conscious, by choosing and realising them, we can stand free from karma. We are then able to change our experience of life and make it better for ourselves and for others. Every day we face new situations and challenges which throw light on the nature of our unconscious motivations, which bring these karmic seeds into our awareness. Most of the time we take no notice. When we want to we can tackle these seeds directly by returning to the initiatory experience of our birth where the process began.

Early Physical and Emotional Patterning

As the baby leaves her mother's womb, she remains attached to her mother through the placenta. As the baby takes in her first breath of air into her lungs, the placenta continues to provide the baby with oxygen and energy through the umbilical cord, ensuring that the transition from a watery existence into the dry world is as safe, easy and untraumatic as possible.

For many of us in western technological society, where *safety* and science has assumed control over the mystery of the birth initiation, our birth is not like this. The umbilical cord is cut before we have even taken our first breath, before independent breathing has become established or before the cord itself ceases to beat. As we struggle to take our first breath through the amniotic fluid which still fills our lungs, our source of energy via the umbilical cord is cut off. We become momentarily oxygen starved and feel as if we are dying. At the gateway to life it seems like we are going to die. For us the attempt to breathe becomes synonymous with near death and results in an inborn fear of dying.

In western society cutting the umbilical cord too quickly has become automatic in many hospitals with consequent effects upon millions of people.

135

Healing in the Emotional Body

The seed laid down in the unconscious mind is that if we fill our lungs with air it feel like we are going to die. From that moment on in order to avoid this possibility we try to stop ourselves from breathing too deeply. We restrict our breathing so that it becomes shallow and minimal, and as a result we restrict the amount of energy, both physical and pranic, flowing into our bodies. Our fear of dying at the beginning of our lives means we are afraid to live fully, often for the rest of our lives.

Another fashion in birthing techniques in the last 30-40 years has been to give mothers copious amounts of drugs to relieve the pains of labour. These drugs pass through the placenta and into the baby's body. The automatic learned response of the baby is that drugs relieve stress and numb the fear of both living and dying. The result of this use of drugs in nearly all hospital births (and most western births are now in hospitals), has been a massive expansion in the numbers of teenage and adult drug users, who are only repeating what they learned as new born babies. When you feel stress, either your own or someone close to you, or when you feel joy (at being born), take a drug. The best way to reduce the problems of drug abuse would be the development of non-pharmaceutical methods of pain relief for mothers in the birth chamber. However it will then take another 20-30 years for the problem to decline significantly until present generations of babies have grown up.

As newborn babies even if our first breath has not been traumatic, we learn very quickly that the way to prevent ourselves from experiencing emotions that are too powerful, painful, blissful or frightening is to hold our breath. When we hold our breath we cut down the flow of oxygen and prana in our bodies, emotional as well as physical, and feelings become less intense. Smoking cigarettes induces the same effect. Many of us already learned how to control our feelings while we were in the womb. We learned to restrict the flow of blood and hence oxygen and energy into our bodies via the umbilical cord and were therefore able to prevent ourselves from feeling anything we couldn't cope with, including anything painful our mothers were experiencing.

As a result of holding the breath our focus of attention shifts out of the physical and emotional bodies into our thoughts. We learn to think our way out of strong feelings. In pranayama (breath control) and meditation this holding of the breath is used as a technique for subduing the emotions in order to explore the subtle worlds of the mind and spirit. It is however, no good for solving emotional/ physical problems. In order to resolve emotional difficulties we need to experience them consciously both emotionally and physically, and to do this we have to breathe - fully and deeply.

In addition to holding the breath we also learn early in life that if we clench our muscles, we can restrict the flow of blood and hence energy and oxygen and feeling in our bodies. When this process becomes habitual our bodies assume particular patterns of emotional defence or armouring. We develop hunched shoulders, a slight limp, a squint, a bad back, or one side of the body feels weaker than the other. Often these characteristics run in families and have genetic as well as conditioned components.

Different types of armouring characterise different types of emotional repression and are built on particular weaknesses experienced during birth. For example, the shoulder which gets stuck and/or dislocated as we are being born is the shoulder which later in life is always raised higher than the other. The muscles in the shoulder hold tension as we attempt to protect ourselves from a hostile world that has caused us pain. Raise one shoulder and feel what it feels like. The physical body holds the memory of traumatic events long after the event has passed and holds the body in postures which are comfortingly familiar, while actually being extremely uncomfortable.

Our bodies also assume characteristic shapes according to how we withhold or release our energy. We lay down fat in our bodies in very particular places. We grow tall and thin, we stay short and solid, we have pear shaped bodies, or we are top heavy, etc.. These bodily characteristics tend to run in families but they are not just genetically determined from our parents. They are also the result of being nurtured within our mother's emotional as well as physical body and growing within both our parent's auras. There is an emotional as well as physical inheritance.

Building on this early patterning, whenever we don't want to feel a strong physical sensation or a powerful emotion, which can be anything from pain to grief to joy, we automatically hold our breath, clench our muscles and often remove our consciousness out of the body altogether. When this condition is habitual, our normal rate of breathing is shallow and our bodies show characteristic patterns of armouring.

When we don't breathe properly our bodies are literally oxygen starved and adapt to a lower level of activity than their natural capacity. We feel tired, lethargic, depressed - we don't have any energy. We take less energy into our etheric bodies, which become devitalised and unable to carry the full power of solar, mental and emotional energies. We become vulnerable to disease in all spheres.

Regression - Returning to Birth

There are several methods of returning to birth and childhood experiences, including regression catalysed by massage, breathing, recalling memories, Reichian therapies, primal scream, rebirthing and conscious connected breathing. Each method emphasises a slightly different aspect of the process but they all tend to lead to the same experiences. They are all powerful bodily experiences in which we allow ourselves to feel again the sensations and emotions which we felt or suppressed in childhood, in the womb and as we were being born - feelings of fear, joy, pain, sorrow, rage and excitement at being born into a new world. It is these feelings and the life statements associated with them which are still held in our physical bodies and unconscious minds, which shape our attitudes, expectations and ways of coping with adult life.

Our aim in returning to the birth experience is to make this earliest initiation conscious, so that we can take responsibility for the way in which we have set up our lives. Instead of seeing ourselves as the passive victims of circumstances which are beyond our control, we are able to realise that while those circumstances have made us what we are, we chose the circumstances. By allowing ourselves to consciously re-experience our feelings as we were being born we are able to complete them. We no longer need to go on repeating the same experiences again and again often in our most intimate relationships in the unconscious attempt to make those early experiences whole.

As a result of being reborn we open ourselves to the power of our life. We release into ourselves new streams of physical, emotional, psychic and spiritual energy. We are free to choose a spontaneous, Self-created way of living.

There are several ways of triggering the emotional and physical memories of our birth, including using the sounds of the womb, colours, massage and warm water. One of the simplest and safest methods is through conscious connected breathing.

Most of us restrict our breathing and therefore our emotions to some degree. In conscious connected breathing we allow ourselves to breathe fully, sometimes for the first time in our lives, taking oxygen and prana into the body in a continuous breath through the mouth. We breathe in and out evenly without holding the breath at either end of the cycle.

In the initial stages this continuous breath can result in hyperventilation. Our bodies become oxygen enriched, something we are not usually used to and we feel dizzy, faint or nauseous. Parts of the body go numb, tingle, get pins and needles and streams of energy rush up and down. Sometimes we become paralysed for a few moments. As we continue to breathe, energy begins to flow once again through muscles and tissues, releasing long held tensions and emotions. Some of these sensations are purely physical and others are felt as pure emotion. As we continue to breathe we are able to let these feelings go and express them as tears, anger, grief, laughter, etc..

Images and memories from the long buried past also rise to the surface of consciousness. We remember in detail events which until now have been forgotten. These memories do not necessarily follow a linear time sequence back to birth, but are grouped in families around a core seed laid down at birth. The memory moves from an event in the recent past further and further back in time until it finds this seed. All we have to do is to allow that whatever arises out of our own unconscious mind has its own reality and truth. This mind will continue to blot out what it does not wish to see or feel. Clues can lie in the fact that those events which we most hotly deny are often the ones which contain our truth.

As we continue to breathe consciously and in rhythm we are able to return in memory to the experience of our birth, our time in our mother's womb and our conception. These stages are preverbal and each is characterised by sets of body movements which are cues as to the stage which has been reached in the process of rebirth. As we relive our birth in bodily memory we also register consciously in words the life statements that resulted from the psycho-emotional karmic seeds which have until now controlled our lives.

One particular form of conscious connected breathing which became fashionable in the 1970's and 80's is known as rebirthing. It has been fully developed by Leonard Orr and a description of the process is given in *Rebirthing in the New Age* by Leonard Orr and Sondra Ray, and a summary is given in *Loving Relationships* by Sondra Ray (Celestial Arts, Millbrae, California).

In order to be with someone in their return to birth, we need ourselves to have experienced the process of regression and being reborn. It is not an experience that can be known by reading about it or thinking about it. We need ourselves to have felt the ways in which we block our own energy and emotions and to have felt that energy begin to move once again in our bodies. It is an extremely strong, integrative, emotional and bodily experience. If you are drawn to this type of healing in the emotional body, find a regression therapist who your intuition tells you can help you heal your emotional self.

Emotional Regression as Healing

The aim of returning to birth through any regression technique is to fully remember how we felt in our mother's womb and the actual physical and emotional processes of how we were born, while remaining conscious. In this way we complete the experience of birth and bring to light the karmic seeds which have brought us to this point in our lives. We are then able to recognise the benefits as well as the disadvantages which have resulted from the seeds of karma and can realise their purpose within our psyche. Their meaning in terms of our whole life becomes clear. Through this experience we are often able to come into contact with our soul's direction and purpose and to expand our creativity and experience as human beings.

For many people emotional regression and rebirth is an end in itself resolving many unconscious emotional dilemmas. Its completion allows us to be free from the constraints we have imposed upon ourselves in the guise of external events which have happened to us. For others it is the beginning of a recognition of the Soul that acts before and beyond our current emotional focus. Through rebirth we are newly initiated into the mysteries of life. We touch the life energy which is our Source and are jolted into the presence of the Self. As a result the energies within our personalities realign themselves and healing takes place. This is a powerful and effective method of healing in the emotional body.

An Emotional Regression Session

As healers working consciously with energy we can use connected breathing to trigger the process of regression, but we begin from a different perspective than that of a traditional rebirther. As in Magnetic and Radiatory Healing at the beginning of the session we consciously establish the usual energy connections between ourselves as healers and the regressee.

For the patient emotional regression is a process of allowing - allowing ourselves to firstly feel and then to express sensations and emotions which we may not have allowed ourselves to feel for practically the whole of our lives. Some of these feelings are painful, frightening or sad, while others are blissful, ecstatic and joyful. Some people find this process of self expression quite easy once they've got the hang of it, while other people, especially those who have devalued emotion, can find it difficult.

Healing in the Emotional Body

Healing regression takes place in an environment in which we feel safe and supported. The room should be warm and comfortable with cushions and mattresses on the floor, and also private, soundproof if possible and free from extraneous noises which may disrupt the session. There needs to be trust between the regressee and the healer so that the regressee can focus her/himself on internal rather than projected external fears.

The session begins with the regressee lying comfortably on their back with knees bent to loosen the pelvis, where tension is often stored. The healer sits on the floor to one side of the regressee. There should be enough room for free and safe movement without restriction. The regressee may at times move their body quite vigorously and may need to be protected by using cushions from accidentally hurting themselves. The healer needs to be ready to move in closely to the regressee's body when necessary or to move away to give them space.

As in any healing session we begin by centring ourselves in our Heart Chakra. We make energy connections to the earth and to the heavens and returning our attention to our Hearts, we feel the energy of Being fill our Heart Chakra and radiate out through our bodies and aura.

Once these energy connections are set up in our own bodies we set up similar connections for the regressee by linking the appropriate chakras in our own body to those in the regressee's body. We link the Base, Heart and Crown Chakras and visualise energy moving within the regressee's etheric body from the earth and the heavens to their Heart Chakra. We see the energy of their Being fill their Heart and radiate out through their bodies. We create a triangle of energies between our two Souls and the healer in physical form. During the regression we focus our attention on the illumination of the seeds of karma within the causal vehicle and the points of friction within the emotional body.

Once these energy connections are established we assume that from then on everything which happens during the session is symptomatic of the regressee's original birth patterning. Every movement of the body, every feeling felt or suppressed, every thought spoken or unspoken is relevant to the original process of birth. All the information about the birth is present in the here and now and available to the regressee if they can let themselves feel what they really feel and hear what they say. As healers we are there to assist the regressee in recognising what they are feeling, thinking, suppressing, saying and experiencing of their original birth.

As in Magnetic and Radiatory healing once we are connected to the regressee we use our own chakras as a balance and mirror to the regressee's experience. In particular we create a figure of eight connection between our Solar Plexus and the regressee's Solar Plexus which allows us to see points of friction within the astral body so that they can be brought into the light of consciousness and healed.

Throughout the session we give our complete attention to the regressee acting as a focusing agent for them. As they breath they return to the preverbal experiences of birth becoming less and less able to describe what is happening to them in words, although they can express emotion directly as sound. As healers we use physical and intuitive cues to help release feelings. We notice the sensations and feelings in our mirroring etheric bodies as well as receiving direct information from our intuition.

Sometimes a person will mask an experience which is too painful or frightening and will divert attention from one part of their body to another in the attempt to avoid an experience they don't want to feel. Our job is to assist them to return to an experience which we sense intuitively is there, when the time is right and they are able to cope with it. We need to trust our intuition and perception of events without imposing them upon the regressee.

Where necessary we can establish energy triangles to assist in bringing memories to the surface as they are laid down in different parts of the body, for example between the Solar Plexus, Throat and Heart chakras, or between a painful place in the body, its governing major Chakra and the Solar Plexus. These can involve any of the major or minor chakras.

At certain times during a session, when the regressee is nearing recognition of a particular emotional seed laid down at birth, we shift our attention out of our bodies and into the astral sphere. We do this by visualising our consciousness as moving out of the etheric body through a point of exit located on top of the head towards the front. We focus our attention on this point of exit and feel our awareness moving out through it into the astral sphere. Soul energy then flows directly to our astral bodies while we remain conscious. Initially we may feel as if we are falling asleep, but our aim is to be conscious and awake while in our astral bodies.

From here we establish a connection directly between our two Souls, astral bodies and physical bodies.

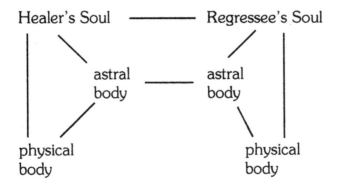

By setting up these energy connections consciously, when we intuitively sense that the regressee is nearing the cause of their experience, we not only ensure that the trauma long held in the physical body is brought to the surface, but that the karmic seeds reflected in the astral body are also illuminated by the powerful light of Soul. They can be recognised and their nature and purpose brought into conscious realisation.

Breathing

After establishing our initial energy connections the regression begins by asking the regressee to take several deep breaths, filling their lungs with air and as they breathe out, to let go of any tension that they may be feeling in their bodies. We ask them to become aware of where in their bodies they can feel tension and those parts where they don't feel anything. In everyday life most of us are unaware of our bodily sensations, except when we are in pain or ill. Our attention is focused elsewhere. In regression we turn our attention to the body and listen to what it tells us about ourselves.

We then ask the regressee to begin breathing continuously and evenly through the mouth into the lungs. The in-breath is light and even without strain, and on the outbreath we just let the air go. There is no attempt to control the intake of air or to hold the breath at either end of the cycle. We breathe through the mouth since a lot of tension is held in the jaw. This is one of the main places in the body where we hold on to what we are feeling and what we would like to express to the world.

From here on the session takes its own course as the regressee continues to breathe. The healer is there to prompt the regressee to breathe whenever breathing slows or stops, to hear the expression of emotion, to listen to remembered experiences and to support the regressee in the experiences they are having. At certain times it is appropriate for the regressee to stop breathing e.g. if they are remembering a traumatic loss of air during birth, but action here is directed by intuition. In the present the physical body will not stop breathing altogether as the breathing reflex will take over if necessary.

At certain times during a session, the regressee or our intuition will tell us to use our hands to direct Magnetic Healing energy to particular parts of the physical or etheric body. This energy assists in releasing tension within the muscles and joints and brings locked in body memories to the surface. Deep and surface massage are also helpful.

During the initial stage of connected breathing the regressee will usually hyperventilate and needs to be reassured that any odd physical sensations will pass, as they do, if they continue to breathe. One of the remarkable things about using the breath is the realisation that all feelings pass with the breath. We are so used to preventing ourselves from feeling painful experiences by holding the breath that it usually takes some time to realise that if instead we continue to breathe, painful events will pass and resolve themselves, losing their traumatic impact.

Stages of Development, associated Traumas and consequent Life Statements

During the process of regression and rebirth the physical body assumes certain characteristic positions which are connected to particular stages of physical development and to experiences in the womb and during and after birth. For example, there is the characteristic curled up foetal position, originally experienced during the early months of pregnancy. In this position we usually feel safe, secure and protected.

Also associated with different stages of development and experience in the birth process, are life statements which accurately reflect our actual physical and emotional experience. These original experiences are preverbal, but they produce an imprint in mental, emotional and physical matter, which is later verbalised in statements which underlie a person's character. In adult life whenever we hear ourselves saying "I always....." or "I never......" , we have a clue to some of our earliest experiences.

The following is a description of the various stages of development which we all have as we incarnate into the world, the possible traumas associated with those experiences, and the resulting life statements we carry with us into adult life. The traumatic possibilities given are the extremes and many of us do not have these experiences - our pregnancies are happy and whole events. However we seem to develop life statements from apparently minor experiences.

If we are able to talk with our mothers about what our birth was like often they will not remember much about it or will describe the experience from their own point of view, which is very different to the baby's point of view. A quick easy birth for the mother can be an intense, explosive and frightening experience for the child.

The following is not a complete exposition but gives an overall idea of the process. Not everyone needs or wants to re-experience all these stages, but some will be relevant. They are also not usually recalled to memory in the sequence given below but in the reverse order. Later memories cover earlier ones and some will be remembered before others depending on the family of memories to which they belong and the karmic seed around which they are aggregated.

Preconception

Some people are able to go back to a time before conception when they experience themselves as free energy beings in a universe of energy. This is usually a great and expansive experience for the regressee. They re-experience the way in which they chose their parents and their feelings about their choice. Certain people are also able to remember experiences that appear to be from their last incarnation on earth or of several previous incarnations. It is suggested by some healers that the process of birth into this life mirrors the manner of death in the last earth life. Whatever the experience is for the regressee is what is valid.

Possible life statements which arise from this stage include :

I don't want to incarnate
I chose the right/wrong mother
I chose the right/wrong father
This is (I am) a mistake.
I make the right choices

Conception

Individual physical life anchors at the moment of conception. Some people are able to return to this moment and re-experience themselves as either the sperm or egg and sometimes as both. This shows itself in characteristic body movements. When identified with the sperm the hands are held at the sides of the body and the feet move together in a swimming motion like a tail. A lot of physical activity is focused at the top of the head and is felt like a band around the head. This experience develops into a feeling of always having to break into something - originally the egg, in order to survive. The regressee, who may be a man or a woman, becomes identified with dynamic pro-active energy.

The experience of being the egg is on the other hand one of containment and then opening to allow something in, originally the sperm. We become psychologically identified with the dynamic receptive energy. The body movement here involves a sensation of roundness and rolling as the egg bursts out of the egg follicle and rolls down the Fallopian tube, and then of opening to the sperm.

We may also experience ourselves as both the egg and the sperm, which allows us to know both the dynamic active and receptive aspects of our nature necessary for physical manifestation.

The circumstances in which we are conceived have effects that continue throughout our lives. The amount of trauma associated with conception depends on how much we were wanted by both parents and the love in their union. We are called in by the quality of their love. The life statements on which we build our lives include :

I am wanted
I am loved
My parents want me

If our conception was an accident, a mistake, the result of rape or being unwanted by either or both parents we build our lives on statements such as the following :

I am not wanted
I am not loved
No-one wants me
Life is violent

Once conception has taken place, many people report a feeling of absolute bliss during the first week before the fertilised ovum has implanted in the wall of the mother's uterus, resulting in the life statements :

I am one with the universe
I am one with the divine....

Implantation

The fertilised egg implants into the wall of the womb about the seventh day after conception. Many fertilised eggs fail to implant and are naturally aborted either by arriving too early at the implantation site or through rejection by the lining of the mother's womb. A woman who is in contact with her own body can control her fertility at this point by inhibiting the process of implantation, either by sending white corpuscles to resist the fertilised egg as a foreign body or by secreting chemicals which abort the implanted egg.

During regression the person's energy becomes focused on one spot on their body usually the forehead, which searches for somewhere to attach itself to, often onto the healer's body or the regressee bends onto her knees and put her heads down onto a cushion or the floor. Where there was resistance to implantation, either from the mother who did not want a child or by the fertilised egg itself, this shows itself in a resistance in the body to becoming attached at the forehead.

Possible traumas depend on whether the mother wanted the child or not, leading to:

I am wanted

I am not wanted

and on the will of the fertilised egg to implant :

I will stay here

It is at this point that stubbornness and the battles of wills with parents and the world begins.

Living in the Womb

During our time in our mother's womb we are influenced by two basic sets of conditions. One is our own physical development within the womb and the other is the result of our being inside our mother's womb. We build our bodies within our mother's physical/etheric, astral and mental vehicles and we are subject to the happenings of her life. Often we take upon ourselves feelings, emotions and thoughts, including her unconscious life statements, which are not our own and rightfully belong to our mother. This is one of the beauties and tragedies of familial inheritance that is very hard to escape from. In this sense we are very much our mother's children rather than our father's. During regression it is possible to re-experience those life statements which are our own and those which truly belong to our mothers.

Traumatic experiences in the mother's life can have a traumatic effect upon the developing foetus, in particular, death or loss of the father of the child, or death of a close relative or friend. The general welfare and health of the mother is important - happy mothers make happy babies, a depressed mother sows the seeds of depression in her child. Another major traumatic experience for the

145

foetus is when there is a threat of abortion or loss of life at any time during the pregnancy.

The nine month pregnancy can be divided into three three-month long trimesters. During the first trimester most regressees report feeling wonderful, as we float freely in a warm, safe environment where all our needs are met. This develops in the second trimester into an absolute joy in rhythmic movement and an awareness of ourselves as the focus of our mother's happiness and her preparations for our birth. We develop a sense of value and self worth. The umbilical cord and placenta are experienced as love objects, friends and siblings. The resulting life statements include:

I am worthy of my mother's (and other people's) love
I have value
I have a friend (placenta)
I am loved
I am not alone

Trauma may come for the foetus during the first trimester when the mother discovers that she is pregnant. A hostile emotional reaction to the pregnancy and the real threat of abortion affects the foetus directly. It is here that fear and paranoia begin:

My mother doesn't want me
I have no value
I am not worthy

If the pregnancy continues this may develop into an emotional battle between the foetus and the placenta/mother, and the foetus begins to attack itself or the mother. This mutual hostility may develop into a feeling for the growing foetus of being overwhelmed by the blood which comes down the cord, which is seen to be bad. There is no way to prevent this badness coming in and the foetus attempts to tear at the umbilical cord to cut it off.

I am bad
I am being overwhelmed by badness from outside
I am better off without you
I don't want you

It is here that the foetus learns to survive by leaving its physical body when it feels overwhelmed by physical or emotional stress. It is here that real despair is felt.

During the third trimester in a happily accepted pregnancy as the foetus grows larger, the blissful floating feelings of the second trimester develop into a sensation of being held by the enclosing walls of the womb, safe and nurtured, leading to:
I love being held

I feel safe

Towards the end of the pregnancy these feelings may become oppressive if the foetus is large and/or the mother is small. The regressee may express this restriction in an inability to move their body although they may want to, as if they are being forcefully held. As the head engages in the mother's pelvis, the foetus may experience physical discomfort and restriction, all of which may be expressed later as life statements:

I am too big
I feel claustrophobic
Its time to get out of here (whenever there is any pressure)
I have to get out.

Labour and Birth

The process of labour is initiated by the foetus when it is ready to leave the womb through the production of a hormone directly into the amniotic fluid and through the placenta to the mother. Rhythmic contractions of the womb begin which lead to the dilation of the mother's cervix. The foetus has the experience of being squeezed on all sides, with as yet no means of escape. This can be a comforting experience or a more traumatic one of pressure, pain and panic, and a fear of being squeezed to death, leading to:

I've got to get out of this (pressure, pain)
I can't bear it
I hate being hugged (it might kill me)

In a normal delivery the regressee experiences intense pressure around the head and shoulders while the legs move in a rhythmical, pushing motion. The physical body assumes the exact position of the baby's body during labour and birth, with every pressure and dislocation experienced once again. The source of past injuries becomes apparent.

The baby's head may be presenting normally to the cervix or it may be at a difficult angle, or the baby may even be breech - feet first. Any of these situations can affect the baby's experience of birth making it more or less easy or painful with related life statements. The regressee's body will assume the appropriate positions.

During the second stage of labour when the cervix has dilated, the baby begins its descent through the cervix and vaginal canal out into the world. For many babies birth is a liberating experience, positively enjoyable, giving a sense of achievement, of moving through constraint to freedom. For some there is a shared sexual experience with the mother. For many babies in western culture, birth is traumatic, *assisted* as it is by doctors and drugs which accelerate or deny the true experience of being born. The traumas vary according to many different factors including :

147

whether the mother wanted and planned the pregnancy
the degree of cooperation between mother and foetus
the age of the mother and the foetus
whether its a first or subsequent birth for the mother
the size of the mother and her relaxation, fear and panic
the size of the baby's head and shoulders
the position of the baby during birth
the medical intervention and drugs given to the mother and
            therefore the baby during birth

One of the most traumatic experiences for the baby occurs if the umbilical cord is twisted around its neck. If the baby pushes forward and follows its natural instinct to leave the womb, it cuts off its first breath of air, leading to:

If I move I'll die
To try to live is to die
I can't trust my instincts
I can't trust my self
Life, freedom is death

There are other traumas that come with birth if the birth is particularly difficult for the mother, including the fear of tearing her apart, killing her or being killed by her resulting in:

I am a killer
She will kill me
She wants me to die
To live is to destroy

Here lies one of the roots of psychotic behaviour.
A large head and a narrow birth canal or a breech birth where the legs are born first and the head and shoulders may become stuck leads to :

I'm stuck
I can't get out of this on my own
I can't get out without someone's help
I'm going to die in here
Help !

Later in life the feeling of stuckness amplifies into any kind of claustrophobic experience from traffic jams to fear of travelling in lifts, as well as to the tendency in any stressful situation to feel stuck and unable to move forward.
Caesarean sections which are increasingly used in the name of safety result in beautiful, unsquashed babies, who have no knowledge of how to come through difficulties to something better. Later problems of life may completely floor them as they have not experienced that there is a way out through a dark tunnel. They

are good at beginning things but need help in finishing them off. Their body movements indicate the way they were born.

Entering the world

Leaving the womb is not the end of birth trauma. Babies can be born into a world of bright light that blinds their sensitive eyes. Their lungs can be filled with mucus that does not clear and sounds which were always muted by the mother's insulating body suddenly becomes very loud. For the Spock generations of children a baby's first experience was of being gripped tightly by the heels and slapped on the back and society wonders why there seems to be more child abuse these days. The experience can be so intense it naturally leads to:

I don't belong here
I don't belong on this planet
I come from somewhere else
People are strange
There's been a mistake
I shouldn't be here

Thankfully there is now some recognition by Leboyer and others of the need for a safe, dark, quiet place to give birth. For millennia this was how women naturally had their babies. Again technology and man's intervention in this natural initiation has effects for generations to come.

Cutting the cord

As described earlier the cord is often cut before it has ceased beating, leading to pain and shock as the baby desperately tries to breathe without its backup supply of energy and oxygen. This shock becomes associated with breathing:

I'm dying !
If I breathe I'm going to die
It hurts if I breathe (live)
To live equals pain

The regressee re-experiences this trauma usually as pain in the navel and gasping for breath. They feel as if they are going to die and become very frightened, often going pale and blue. Breathing returns once this trauma is relived. It is here that chronic breathing difficulties, such as asthma, begin and also where they can be healed.

The cutting of the cord and the loss of the placenta which has accompanied the foetus throughout its time in the womb may be experienced as the loss of a friend or sibling or part of the self, with accompanying grief.

149

When I was born I lost part of myself
To live is to lose

Bonding and breast feeding

Bonding between mother and child takes place during the first hours after birth and is essential for the secure emotional development of the child. It is characterised by eye contact between mother and child, skin contact, smell, the familiar sound of the mother's voice and synchronised head movements. When mother and child are given the space and time to bond and to establish breast feeding the baby feels secure and loved and welcome in the world. The baby smiles.

I am loved
I am welcome
The world is a blissful place
I've made it here

Often however the baby is removed swiftly from the mother to clean it, examine it, make it hygienic, and is handled in a way that is anything but gentle and loving. The world is unfamiliar, rough, harsh and the baby feels alone.

I am alone
The world is a frightening place
Touch is painful
I want to get back in the womb
I want to die
No-one loves me
I feel desperate

The baby cries long and hard or retreats into silence and non-communication with the world. The world is too awful to bear.

When breast feeding too is abandoned by the mother as too difficult or she is told *bottle is best*, the baby misses not only vital antibodies and the best food nature can provide, but also the delicious warmth, smell and comfort of mother. Many people spend the rest of their lives trying to find this missing experience in food or in other people. After being reborn the regressee will often make sucking movements with the mouth or search for a nipple or substitute to suck.

There are many variations in the life statements which are created during our time in our mother's womb and during and after birth. They depend on the exact physical, emotional and psychic experiences that we have. They may appear to be complex and exaggerated but can be clearly seen and felt during the process of returning to birth.

Completing Regression

A regression ends when there is a distinct change in the energy field surrounding the regressee. Energy connections between regressee and healer automatically disconnect. This may be when the regressee has re-experienced actually being born and is lying awake or asleep, curled up like a little baby; or their experience may be only one facet of the birth process. Different families of emotion centred on one seed or related seeds of experience are explored with each regression. We do not usually experience the whole birth process at one time. A regression can last anything from one to several hours depending on the regressee's resistance to feeling and expression and on the skill of the healer and on whether the time is right for emotional resolution. It can take anything from 5 to 50 sessions to encompass the whole of the birth process.

Once the regressee has returned to present consciousness, we ask them to describe their feelings and experience. This brings the experience fully into brain consciousness and completes the healing process in all bodies. We assist the regressee in connecting the life statements associated with particular traumatic and non-traumatic events during the birth process. We help them to see how those life statements have shaped their behaviour and experience from the moment they occurred until now. We help them to create positive life statements to change conditioned responses.

By experiencing these seed thoughts physically and emotionally and by making them conscious, the regressee is then for the first time free to choose whether to go on repeating a particular pattern of behaviour over and over again, or to change it. Since the seed has been made conscious and re-experienced in consciousness it becomes possible to make a choice. Until now because it was unconscious there was no choice but to go on repeating patterns without really knowing why. Now when a familiar pattern arises we can see it clearly for what it is and decide to react in a completely new and authentic way. This is a wonderful freedom.

Healing regression and returning to birth is a powerful and effective method of healing deep scars in the emotional body. It allows us to transform our past and our future behaviour and become more fully ourselves.

CHAPTER EIGHT

Psychic Reading
Healing the Mental Body

All energy, whether it is physical, emotional, mental, psychic or spiritual carries information. As human energy beings every moment of our lives we are radiating, absorbing, transmitting and receiving energy in one form or another. To extract information from energy we need first of all to be able to register the energy and secondly to understand the language in which it is written.

Physically we have receptors in our bodies which register different qualities of energy. We *see* light and colour with our eyes, we *hear* with our ears, we *smell* with our noses, we *touch* with our skin, and we *taste* with our tongues. Each of these senses has its own innate language which develops through our interaction with the world around us, giving us information about the physical world in which we live. If any of these senses is missing our experience of the world is diminished..

We register emotional energies in our emotional bodies. We learn through experience to discriminate between such diverse emotions as anger, joy, pain, rage, happiness, grief, sadness and excitement. We see these emotions in the expressions on each other's faces and through body language, as well as sensing them with our Solar Plexus, Sacral and Heart Chakras.

We register mental energies via the Head Centres and by using our minds, the language of which is pictorial, symbolic and imaginative. Thus we are able to *make sense* of the world around us.

Similarly we have psychic faculties which allow us to register psychic non-physical energies, such as those of the Soul and the Spiritual Triad. We can learn to recognise these psychic energies, not just as an anonymous jumble, but as having distinct qualities. Each of these psychic energies has its own language, which we can register with our psychic faculties - clairvoyance, clairaudience, clairsentience, telepathy and direct perception.

Psychic Reading is a method of registering the energy which is carried in a person's energy field or aura and extracting information from that energy field. The human energy field is composed of etheric, emotional, mental and soul energies, each of which carries information about the individual concerned. This information is accessible and can be read if we know the language in which it is written. It includes a person's current etheric, emotional and mental condition, detailed memories of past experiences, the nature of any imbalances within the psyche and their cause. It also includes probable futures, alternate realities, the reincarnational past and future, current difficulties viewed from the perspective of the whole lifetime and the direction and purpose of the Soul.

In Magnetic and Radiatory Healing our focus is upon healing energy imbalances within the chakras. Healing takes place through the energy resources of the Soul. It is not strictly necessary to look for or to provide factual information in order to heal disease. However we often need to understand our disease in terms of the unconscious patterns which motivate our lives, their origins, causes and purpose in our lives. Psychic reading is a means of obtaining this information using our psychic faculties.

Psychic reading is essentially a very simple process, once we are able to focus our attention wholly upon another person's energy field and are able to trust that what we see/feel/sense within our own psyche is true.

As with any healing session in psychic reading we centre ourselves and establish energy connections between ourselves and the inquirer. Once these connections are set up we focus our awareness on the Third Eye, and direct our attention towards the client's energy field. We ask direct questions of their energy field and Soul and trust absolutely that what comes to us in reply, in the form of images, stories, feelings and words, no matter how ordinary or bizarre, is relevant to the inquirer.

In order to do this successfully we must be able to remain focused upon the inquirer's energy field and be able to discriminate between information which is relevant to the inquirer and information which may be about ourselves if our attention strays. We follow the movement of any set of images that appear upon the Third Eye and report each image and answer to the inquirer. We ask questions of each image about their meaning and purpose within the person's life, probing ever deeper until there is a sense of resolution and completion. Healing takes place within the subtle bodies, in particular in the mental body.

The inquirer will only show us what they want us to see, consciously or unconsciously, and this choice is under the direction of their Soul. The inquirer can block information which they do not wish to reveal, but then there would be little point in having a psychic reading.

For the reader, psychic reading is a challenging exercise in trusting the inner voice and intuition. A reading can last from twenty minutes to an hour without necessarily receiving any comment from the inquirer on the validity of the information we are able to read within their aura. The inquirer listens without any need to comment on what they are hearing unless they want to. We could be completely wrong in what we are saying about the inquirer's past and present challenges. We have to be prepared to be wrong and to fail before we are free of our own pride in being right. It is only then that we may be able to see clearly and walk the razor's edge of our psychic abilities.

Psychic reading is usually carried out separately from Magnetic and Radiatory Healing. It is used to give an overall perspective on a current problem or life crisis, to illuminate causes, to show a way through a situation and to indicate possible future directions of personal and psychic exploration. On some occasions healing energies naturally flow in during a psychic reading or can be consciously asked for by invoking silently or aloud the presence of healing devas and beings. Initially it is advisable to separate the two experiences until each process is clear to the healer, although some information will naturally arise during a healing session it is not usually in the detail given in a psychic reading.

We can read for other people and for ourselves, although as with many of these skills it is usually easier to read and find solutions for other people's problems than our own. It is more difficult to remain detached from our own energy field. The degree to which we are able to explore another person's psyche depends on the development of our own consciousness and how far we have plumbed our own depths.

Procedure for Psychic Reading

Welcome the client to the healing/reading space and make them comfortable. Often they will be nervous and may need reassurance. Make yourself comfortable too so that you can concentrate on the reading when it begins. Sit face to face so that there is direct eye contact between reader and inquirer at the beginning and end of the session. Ask the inquirer if they have any particular problem they would like investigating. They may have one or more questions they would like answered or after describing their situation may prefer to ask nothing at all. It is not necessary for the reader to know anything about the inquirer before the reading as challenges will reveal themselves during the reading. However stating any problems often allows the inquirer to relax and feel more open to the reading.

Ask the client if there are any healing presences, guides or ancestors who they would like to be present during the reading. Suggest to the client that during the session they close their eyes to concentrate on what is being said and also on how they are feeling in their physical and emotional bodies. They should listen receptively to what is said during the reading, absorbing what feels right and discarding what doesn't sound true to them. They should allow themselves to feel their emotions and notice the ways their minds react. If they want to speak or interrupt the reader's flow of information they are free to do so.

As with any healing session begin by closing your eyes and centring yourself in Being. Connect from your Heart Chakra first to the centre of the earth and then to the farthest star. Radiate energy horizontally in all directions from the Heart. Set up energy connections for the inquirer, linking their Base, Heart and Crown Chakras to your own and connecting them to the earth and the farthest star. The inquirer usually has a problem of some kind which means they are not focused in their Heart in the present but upon a point of friction. The energy connections assist in bringing in the Soul's energy to illuminate the nature and causes of their current discomfort. Set up a triangular connection between your Soul, the inquirer's Soul and yourself in physical form.

The inquirer is often nervous before a psychic reading, especially if the process is unknown to them. Centring and establishing energy connections helps them to relax. Once centred ask the inquirer to say their name out loud, which helps anchor their awareness in their bodies. From here on there is no need for the inquirer to speak at all unless they want to. The reader asks questions of the inquirer's energy field and *reads back* the answers they receive to the inquirer.

Psychic Reading

At this point call in any healing presences that you or the inquirer may wish to be present to aid in the reading, asking that all that takes place shall be for the inquirer's greatest good.

Next connect your three head centres with threads of energy and rotate the triangle created to form a sphere of energy. Focus your attention in the centre of your head. Here is the blank screen of the Third Eye on which images, words and ideas are reflected. From here look out with closed eyes to the inquirer's aura. Ask aloud what the inquirer would like to show you, along the lines of :

"I'm looking at your aura (to focus your attention on the aura) *and asking what you would like to show me."*

In reply an image, a word, a phrase or a feeling, will come immediately into the space in the centre of our head, on the Third Eye. Take the first thing which comes no matter how odd or fleeting it may appear to be. Tell the inquirer exactly what you see/feel/hear. Follow the image, sound, etc., and see how it develops. Describe to the inquirer what you see. Sometimes the imagery will be obvious - you can see the inquirer doing something, walking along a street, seated in a house, etc.. Describe the emotions connected to the scene. Watch a story unfold as if you are watching a movie. When a sequence of images seems to have ended ask the inquirer's aura what that scene means to the inquirer in the present. Speak the answer that comes to your mind.

Sometimes the imagery flows easily and meanings are obvious. At other times the image is slow or can get stuck. It can be a closed door, or a blob or a locked box. Ask the image what it is saying to the inquirer and what it means for them. Tell the inquirer what comes to you in reply. Watch the image begin to unfold, the door to open so that you can see through it, the blob to take form and define itself, the box to open and reveal its contents. Its a question of trusting what you see/feel in the centre of your head and speaking what you sense/hear.

At each stage move deeper into the meaning of what you see, asking aloud the *what, how* and *why* of what you are perceiving. You may see the inquirer in a specific situation in the present or in the past as a teenager or in childhood. Assume that the central figure who appears in the story is the inquirer perhaps at an earlier age, sometimes as a child. A story may unfold of another time and space, a past, future or parallel reality in which the inquirer plays a major role. These characters may be women or men, regardless of the subject's present gender. Regardless of whether you or the inquirer believes in reincarnation say what you see. The stories provide an allegorical or reincarnational perspective upon the inquirer's present dilemma, revealing karmic threads. Speak all that you see or hear and ask for the relevance of the information to the inquirer in the present and say what you hear out loud.

Other beings may present themselves to the inquirer, who have things they want to say or feelings they want share. These beings may be seen/felt by the reader alone, but usually they are also recognised by the inquirer. They may be currently in or out of physical incarnation and usually have an important part to play in the inquirer's life. Often they are specific healing and devic presences who pour in healing energy to augment a psychic change as it is occurring in the subtle bodies. Their healing energy is felt by the inquirer and often results in an outpouring of emotion and tears. Sometimes deceased relatives may appear who have something they wish to communicate to the inquirer which can heal old wounds. Sometimes they want to ask for forgiveness.

There may be inflows of light, colour and energy and all are reported to the inquirer who may or may not experience them. Many of these effects are felt subliminally by the inquirer, who may never have noticed such experiences before. By saying aloud what is happening on an energy level, you affirm these experiences and bring them into brain consciousness for the inquirer as well as yourself.

Psychic reading is a healing experience as it lays open the psychological causes of disease. You can focus your attention either on the whole aura, reading the energy and information it gives as it naturally arises or you can work through the chakras, beginning at the Base and moving up through each one to the Crown Chakra. If there is an actual disease in the physical body as well, concentrate upon the chakra governing the diseased area and other chakras related to it.

Often the information within the aura is about previous life experiences and how these have carried over into present relationships with family members, lovers, authority figures, etc.. There are often links to a person's spiritual path through other lives and their spiritual direction in this life. These are common reasons for seeking psychic readings.

A reading lasts as long as the energy within the inquirer's aura is available to the reader. This can be 10 minutes, 30 minutes or an hour - as long as there is something important which is there to be read. The energy connections between the reader and inquirer are usually released automatically as the aura closes. The reading ends with thanks being given for the information received and to any healing presences who may have been invoked. After the reading, reader and inquirer discuss what has happened and again further emotions may be released at this stage of the session. It is at this time that the reader finds out how relevant their words may have been to the inquirer and if they have been able to translate their imagery into meaningful and relevant ideas for the inquirer.

It is a good idea to tape record psychic readings otherwise minor but important details can be lost to consciousness. It also means that details can be later checked by the inquirer and time given for the effects of the reading to anchor into brain awareness.

At the end of the session make sure that you have released all figure of eight connections to the inquirer before they leave the healing space and centre yourself. Cleanse the space after each session.

Psychic readings can have powerful healing effects for the inquirer, depending on the ability, character and consciousness of the reader. They primarily affect the inquirer's mental body and brain consciousness, where attitudes and ideas tend to become fixed. They catalyse change in the mental body which reflects onwards in changes in the emotional and etheric bodies. They help people to see where and how they may have become stuck in their thinking and help bring clarity to confused minds.

Psychic Reading

All psychic readers can have off-days, when we focus upon ourselves rather than the inquirer. Our aim as readers is ever to improve concentration and focus of attention as well as listening and trusting absolutely our intuition. The inquirer is learning to discriminate for themselves between reality and unreality, and learning to listen to their own intuition about the truth or otherwise of the reading they are given. No-one else can truly know another's destiny and purpose in life, no matter how certain they may appear to be when they are telling us how things are for us. Our destiny is our own. A psychic reading can facilitate the discovery of that destiny.

CHAPTER NINE

Self Healing

The free flow of Soul energy through our vehicles creates health. We become ill when the flow of this energy into or out of the chakras is inhibited. When we are ill by the very nature of disease we often don't have the strength, the mental concentration or the will to clear the disturbed chakras ourselves. We just want to feel better again, to feel ourselves once more. So we go to the doctor, holistic practitioners or healers, to help us get better.

Healing always comes essentially from the self, whoever helps us to get better. If we are able to recognise this fact when we are dis-eased, then there are steps we can take to bring about our own healing. How much we are able to do for ourselves depends on the nature and degree of the illness and its meaning and purpose in our life.

As we all know when we are feeling good about ourselves, free flowing and creative, when we have things we really want to do, we do not usually *catch* the numerous minor infections that are ever present in the air we breathe. When we want to, when we have more interesting things to do, we can often prevent a tickle in the throat from becoming a sore throat, or a runny nose from becoming a full-scale cold in the head. We use our will and determination not to become ill, to move our attention away from the point of friction and to draw healing energy into our bodies. In essence we are using our will to invoke Soul energy, increasing the flow of life energy into our bodies and thereby removing the cause of the disease.

It is this creative use of our will to bring in the healing energy of our own Soul which is the basis of all self-healing. How we use our will depends on the nature of the disease and whether it is a minor or major illness. Many minor illnesses we half consciously create in order to give ourselves a rest from stressful situations and also as a cleansing process for the subtle bodies. They provide a means of discharging pain, anger or grief, which we are unable to express in any other way. In a sense the disease itself is a form of self-healing as it creates the space for healing to take place in the subtle bodies. The disease naturally resolves itself with time and rest.

With many minor diseases all we need to do is to let the disease take its course, while allowing ourselves to feel emotions and thoughts which have been restricted. The disease is their means of expression. There are also cleansing exercises for the etheric body which are helpful in clearing the chakras. If we choose to we can accelerate the process of self-healing in the same way that we prevent ourselves from getting sore throats and head colds. We can use our will to invoke our Soul's energy, drawing it into the etheric body and thereby removing restrictions and clearing the chakras.

With a major disease whose cause lies hidden deep within our psyche the resolution of any imbalance may not be so simple. It is easy to make trite suggestions as to how to deal with a major illness, when we aren't suffering from it. For much of the time we may be too ill, in too much pain and distress to feel that we can do anything for ourselves. There may be nothing that we can do. Many diseases after all are the result of living in a poisoned environment where pathogenic and carcinogenic substances can enter the body and destroy it from within. But there is no way of knowing if yours is a disease which can be healed or not. The attempt to heal is an important part of the transformatory process of disease. Even in the midst of much discomfort there are still moments when we feel a little better and it is these moments which we can use for self-healing.

For our own purposes, hidden deep within our own reality we contract diseases. Why did *I* get this cancer, arthritis, heart disease, etc.? Why me? And not you? The nature of disease is such that it completely transforms the way we live, think and feel and this is part of its purpose.

As human beings we are ever expanding into ourselves through Self expression. As we live our lives we limit this self expression by our ideas, mental attitudes, emotional condition and etheric vibration. Whenever these limits become fixed and cease to expand with the flow of life energy within us, then disease comes to crack through those limits we have placed upon ourselves. Disease is *fire by friction* - a fire which burns through limitations of form and purifies the matter within the subtle bodies.

Although it may be painful, disease is an agent of personal and spiritual transformation. We are transformed through the recognition of its deep purpose in our lives. This does not necessarily mean that we are cured, the disease may itself be too potent. Sometimes if we are prepared to release ideas, ways of thought and feeling that have ceased to serve us, disease is the prelude to initiation and the expansion of consciousness. At other times disease lingers on and may result in physical death, when our Soul takes its ultimate step in breaking through the limitations of our form life.

Healing Ourselves

When we make the conscious decision to heal ourselves there are two approaches we can take. The first is to shift our focus of attention away from the point of friction that is the seat of our disease and return our attention to the Soul. If we are ill this may prove hard to do since we are distracted from our centre. The second approach is to find and experience the root causes of our disease. We can look for the ways in which we restrict our life energy so that we can release ourselves from that restriction. If we let ourselves fully experience a restriction and express it, then that restriction is automatically transformed and released. Restriction may be part of our personal growth pattern; it may be due to being part of the body of humanity as a whole as in the case of infectious diseases, pollution or war; or it may be due to our being a small unit in the planetary body as in the case of natural disasters.

What we require of ourselves is an insight into the nature of our disease, which comes out of a degree of honesty with ourselves that few of us possess. It is part of the purpose of the disease to evoke that honesty and truth from within, bringing the recognition of *what is* in our life. By becoming naked to ourselves we may be able to realise the point of friction within our personality vehicles and the meaning and purpose of our disease.

Several of the diagnostic techniques which we use as healers, can be used on ourselves. We begin by remembering in as much detail as possible the beginning of the disease. We try to locate the exact time and place where we first noticed symptoms and attempt to re-experience any thoughts and feelings we were having at that time. There is often one point, one sentence, one argument, one repression that catalysed the whole experience - the straw that broke the camel's back. This straw holds a key to our release and healing.

Next we can look at what the disease gives to us in our lives. What are the advantages in being ill? What needs are satisfied by being immobilised or bedridden? A disease may bring us time and space to think, to ruminate on life, to be looked after as if we are children. It may give us a break from a boring job or from too much stress and anxiety. We may experience dependency and power over others, or feel our common human suffering. We feel devotion and love or the lack of it from family, friends and strangers, our fears of death and life, and many more basic human experiences we have not noticed before.

In life we invoke the experiences that we need for our Soul's purposes. By recognising our needs we can then decide whether they can be fulfilled in another way - other than by being ill. In this way we can begin to reassert ourselves within our illness. Rather than feeling ourselves to be the victim of a disease that comes to us from the outside, we begin to recognise the causes which are within us about which we can perhaps do something.

Self-healing comes from the Soul. It comes with the will to get better - the will to survive, one of humanity's primary drives. This will is a quality of the Soul. It is not a wanting or desire, but a surrender to the true purpose of Being, knowing that it is our birthright to be healthy. Any activity, physical, emotional or mental which invokes the Soul's presence within our personality vehicles, aids the healing process.

Depending on the severity and duration of the disease, we can heal ourselves if we are able to invoke the healing power of the Soul and see ourselves as whole and free from disease. I am not suggesting here that this is a simple and easy thing to do because we would probably not be ill in the first place if it was. For long lengths of time we may withdraw our consciousness from our physical bodies, because the pain and discomfort is too great to bear. We may feel our minds and emotions are completely befuddled and we can't think straight or we just don't have the energy, but there are moments when we are conscious. We use these moments to call in our Soul energy, connecting ourselves to the earth and the heavens and opening our Heart Chakra. Each time we do so we increase the energy in our bodies, which can bring healing and the removal of suffering.

Self Healing

There are many exercises that we can do in a sick bed that will change the way we are feeling and which bring healing energies into our bodies. These include simple breathing exercises which follow, such as pranayama or controlled breathing, which increases the circulation of oxygen in the physical body and prana in the etheric body. We can use the exercises given in Chapter Three for stimulating the chakras and other visualisation exercises, in which we create our own health. All these exercises are based on the premise that energy follows thought.

Below are several exercises designed to promote self-healing. They can all be performed lying down if necessary, although we are more likely to stay awake and conscious if we are sitting upright.

EXERCISES:
The Pranayama Circle or Cleansing Breath

The breath brings us oxygen and prana and removes stale air and energies from the body. Pranayama or cleansing breathing has a long history in the Yogic traditions and I recommend it as a healing practice.

1. Sit or lie comfortably with the back as straight as possible. Let the left hand relax and place the right hand, palm facing inwards, so that the middle finger is resting between the eyebrows on the forehead. Place the thumb on the right nostril, closing the nostril, and take a deep breath in through the left nostril to the count of four.

2. Place the ring finger of the right hand over the left nostril, so that both nostrils are closed and hold the breath for a count of four.

3. Release the thumb from the right nostril and breathe out through the right nostril to a count of four.

4. Hold the breath out for a count of four.

5. Take a breath in through the right nostril for a count of four and place the right thumb on the right nostril, so that both nostrils are closed

6. Hold the breath in for a count of four.

7. Release the ring finger from the left nostril and breathe out through the left nostril to a count of four.

8. Hold the breath out for a count of four.

9. Repeat the exercise for 20 breaths or as long as desired. Once the rhythm of the pranayama circle has been established, increase the count for each part of the cycle from 4 to 6 and then 8.

This exercise balances the energy in the ida and pingala, the two energy channels that pass up the spine between the chakras. It brings prana to the nadis and thence to the nervous and endocrine systems of the body. It brings oxygen to the tissues and removes stale carbon dioxide, cleansing the body of toxins and generally speeding the healing process. It helps us to become centred in our bodies and experience peace.

Cleansing Visualisation for minor and major disease

This exercise brings prana into the etheric body and begins to balance the energies in the chakras.

1. Lie comfortably on your back and allow your body to relax and sink into the bed. Close your eyes. Feel your limbs becoming heavy. Watch your breath as it moves in and out through the nostrils. Don't attempt to alter the rate of breathing but watch it until it has quite naturally slowed and deepened.

2. As you take a deep breath in visualise a wave of silver light flowing into your body through your feet and up your legs. Watch it move up through the body and out of the top of your head. Hold the breath and feel your body bathed in silver light.

3. As you breathe out see a wave of golden light flowing into your body through the top of your head. Watch it move down through the body and out through the feet. Hold the breath and feel your body bathed in golden light.

4. Repeat the process for at least ten breaths or longer, visualising alternating waves of silver and golden light flowing up and down the body. Keep your attention focused on this visualisation for as long as you are able.

Clearing Congested Chakras

This exercise is most effective when performed with an awareness of the different qualities of energy carried by the chakras.

1. Sit or lie down comfortably. Let your body slow down and relax. Watch the breath as it slows and deepens of its own accord.

2. Focus your attention in your Heart Chakra and visualise threads of light energy moving down into the centre of the earth, from the Heart via the Base Chakra and up to the heavens via the Crown. Feel yourself centre in your Heart Chakra and Soul energy radiating out through the aura.

3. Focus your attention in the chakra governing the diseased area, e.g. in the Throat Chakra for a sore throat or the Ajna for a headache across the eyes or the Solar Plexus for a stomach ache, etc.. Visualise the energy in the chakra as a tangled ball of string with lots of knots in it.

4. Take a deep breath in and see white light flowing into your body from the heavens via the crown. See it flow down through the body to the chakra governing the diseased area. Hold the breath and see this light as it moves through the ball of string, untangling the threads and loosening the knots. On the outbreath see the light, which may have become grey and discoloured flow down out of the body, carrying with it the congested energy from the diseased chakra down to the earth.

5. Repeat this visualisation until you clearly see that the threads have become disentangled and smoothed out.

This exercise can also be carried out as follows using colour, rather than the ball of tangled string, to symbolise the congested energy in the chakra:

1. Begin as above by centring in the Heart Chakra and feeling its energy. Focus your attention on the diseased chakra and see its colours. Take the first impression that comes to be the actual condition of the chakra.

2. Take a deep breath in and visualise white light or a complementary cleansing colour, flow in through the Crown Chakra and down to the diseased chakra. The complementary colour can be one of those given below or it may come directly from your own intuition.

Chakra	Colour	Complementary Colour
Base	red/black	green/light
Sacral	violet	orange
Solar Plexus	yellow/orange	blue
Heart	blue	gold
Throat	green	red
Ajna	pink/yellow	turquoise/blue
Crown	white/rainbow	indigo

3. Hold the breath and see the colour flowing through the chakras neutralising and removing distorted colours. On the out breath see any distorted colours flowing out of the body into the earth. Repeat the process until only the clear colours of the true energy of the chakra remains.

Visualisation of the Healing Forces of the Physical Body

The main healing force in the human body is the auto immune system which discriminates between foreign and body proteins, rejecting material which is foreign to the body, including invasive bacteria, poisons and damaged tissues. This system is controlled by the thymus gland and is governed by the Heart Chakra. When the Heart Chakra and/or thymus gland is stimulated, the production of white blood corpuscles and other particles increases. These travel to the physical site of the disease where they ingest foreign, damaged or dead material and carry it to the liver for breakdown and subsequent elimination from the body.

Another major healing force in the body is the natural regenerative quality of all living cells, whether they are skin, muscles, nerves or bones. The ability of living tissue to repair damage to itself, to replace itself periodically and to make whole, ensures our survival as living organisms.

Our ability to visualise, sense and feel these processes in action in our physical bodies greatly speeds recovery from disease. Such visualisations are particularly important in the treatment of long term degenerative diseases, such as cancers, diseases of the joints and muscles, and also for bone fractures.

The following visualisation exercise is for cancer in any part of the body.

1. Lie comfortably and relax the body. Watch your breath as it flows in and out through the nostrils until your breathing slows and deepens.

2. Centre yourself in Being and focus your attention in your Heart Chakra and feel it filling with an electric blue light. As it fills become aware that the

thymus gland, which lies on top of the physical heart, is being stimulated by inflowing energy. As the thymus is stimulated, chemical messengers are released, which can be visualised in any form you like - as chemicals, as little people carrying messages, as letters, etc.. Visualise these messengers moving from the thymus gland to the lymph glands, which are situated in the arm pits, groin and sides of the neck; and moving to the bone marrow in the centre of the long bones of the arms and legs. These messengers instruct these tissues to increase the production and flow of white blood cells into the blood stream. White blood corpuscles are similar to red blood corpuscles, but are slightly larger and have no pigment to carry oxygen or carbon dioxide. White blood cells ingest dead and damaged tissues and foreign material and remove it from the body. They can be visualised as cells or more visually as sharks, or anything which will engulf harmful cells.

3. Now move your attention to the site of the disease. In as much detail as you are able, visualise the disease site and give it an image which is meaningful to you. This may be a blob of colour, a beetle, a piece of metal, an octopus, however your disease looks like to you. Visualise the healthy tissues which surround it. Then see the white corpuscles flow in great numbers to the blood vessels in the healthy tissues which surround the disease site. See individual white blood cells or sharks swallowing diseased cells and watch the disease site shrink and grow small as the cells are ingested and removed by the white blood corpuscles. Visualise the dead cells being taken via the blood stream to the liver where they are broken down into harmless elements. Some of the debris is broken down into urea and excreted by the kidneys and other elements leave the body as faeces from the bowel.

4. Return your attention to the healthy tissues surrounding the disease site and visualise an increased flow of red blood cells bringing oxygen, sugars, antioxidants (which help remove ionised particles which create cancers) and proteins, to build in healthy new tissues and to remove carbon dioxide and waste products of this building activity. Take care only to send energy to healthy tissue and not to the disease site itself, which may stimulate its growth.

5. Detailed visualisation enhances the healing process. This exercise should be carried out at least twice a day by those with major diseases. It is also effective with lesser ailments.

Visualisation of the Building Devas of the Etheric/Physical Body

See the exercise in Chapter Six on Devas.

Self-Healing when Hope is Fading

For some people disease is more than a minor inconvenience and discomfort. It can drastically alter a person's way of life and if it is unresolved can lead to death and release from the limitations of form life. Before this happens there are often times when all outside help seems to be exhausted, when we feel we have tried everything that is offered, when we have done everything we can to make ourselves better and nothing seems to work. We stay the same, chronically ill or our illness gets worse.

When this is the case, we have only one recourse, which is to move directly to the creator of our disease, to the Soul who is seeking expression. Here the disease and its healing are not minor disturbances in our lives but are the catalyst for Self transformation and the expansion of consciousness. The disease fundamentally alters our way of life and its healing comes as the result of a definite change in how we see ourselves in the scheme of things - of how we view ourselves as human energy beings.

Our Soul is seeking our conscious recognition of its existence, of its divine, limitless, multidimensional nature, of its glory, power and wisdom. That is our essence and is the energy which seeks recognition and expression. It is what we are, no matter how small and insignificant and awful we feel ourselves to be. When our disease is overwhelming, it is this reality which we need to search for. It is this reality which is calling to us.

We have one direct means of getting in touch with the Soul and its reality and that is in meditation. Meditation is a here and now space which we enter when we still our minds, emotions and body. We still our body by sitting comfortably with an upright spine. We can sit in the traditional lotus position or cross-legged or we can sit in a chair. If sitting is too painful or uncomfortable we can lie down, but there is always the possibility that we will fall asleep. It is more important for a sick person to be comfortable than upright, so that the experiences of a painful body can slip away.

We still our emotions through the simple practice of breathing slowly and deeply down into the Solar Plexus, into the tummy. As we continue to breathe we gradually find our emotions becoming calmer and less intense.

We still our minds in the first place by giving it something constant to concentrate on. This can be a word, a sound, breathing, etc.. Several suggestions are given in Appendix Three. Once we have learned to concentrate the mind we can move to a space where there is no thought only the energy of our Soul.

Many of us find the process of learning to meditate rather difficult, especially if we are unwell. We find that we fall asleep as we relax, we get bored, nothing seems to happen, we don't feel as if we are getting anywhere. For others it is relatively easy and a space we have already experienced in other situations - while painting or writing or making something from within, or when we are in nature. Whatever your reaction is remember that your aim is to experience your own Soul. There is no rule that says that you must continue with a technique for stilling the mind which doesn't work for you. Change methods rather than give up trying altogether. Follow your intuition.

The sick person is at a disadvantage in that when we are ill it is often difficult to concentrate on anything. It may also be hard to relax physically, which is necessary for meditation, if we are in pain. The advantages are that we have usually developed a facility for leaving our bodies when we are ill and in some ways we are connected to the energy of our Soul during an illness although it is repressed. However when the need is there, we will find a way.

We are going in search of our Soul so that we can know and experience the truth of our nature. It is the realisation of this truth which can make us whole, which will heal us or allow us to complete our earthly experience in reality.

Finally there are two methods of self healing from Tibetan Buddhism which I personally found to be beneficial when I was severely ill with a life threatening disease. One is the practice of Tantric Self Healing developed by Lama Gangchen Tulku Rinpoche, the other is the practice of Tonglen described by Tsogyal Rinpoche in *The Tibetan Book of Living and Dying (Harper San Francisco)*.

Tantric Self Healing

Lama Gangchen Tulku Rinpoche is the current incarnation of a long line of Tibetan Healing Lamas. He has developed a system of Self Healing which involves the use of visualisation, invocation, mudras - movements of the hands and body, and sound. He has adapted ancient Tibetan healing knowledge for modern western minds and created a system of self healing that is beneficial for healing oneself, others and the planet. The system he teaches is rather complex to consider here and requires initiation into some of the practices in order to gain the full benefit.

Lama Gangchen travels the world teaching about peace and the practices of self healing and more information can be obtained from Lama Gangchen World Peace Foundation at Via Marco Polo 13, 20124 Milan, Italy, or from Tashi, 1 Trinity Church Hall, The Gill, Ulverston, Cumbria LA12 7BJ.

Tonglen

The main elements of the Tonglen practice of giving and receiving can be found in *The Tibetan Book of Living and Dying*. In this practice we take on the suffering and pain of others and give them our happiness, well being and peace of mind. I found this practice to be very helpful when I was feeling particularly unwell and unable to do anything much more than lie in bed for many days and hours without energy. I found that by trying to help others, I could feel that there was some point to my own suffering. Tsogyal Rinpoche recommends the practice of Self Tonglen first.

Self Tonglen

1. Divide yourself into two parts A and B. A is the aspect of you which is whole, compassionate, loving and forgiving - your Soul. B is like your shadow, the part of you that has been hurt, misunderstood, is frustrated, bitter and angry.

2. As you breathe in imagine that A opens her heart completely and warmth and compassion flow outwards embracing all of B's suffering, negativity, pain and hurt.

3. Moved by this B opens her heart and all pain and suffering melt away in this compassionate embrace. As you continue to breathe imagine the Soul sending the Shadow all her healing love, warmth, comfort, confidence and happiness.

4. Continue this practice of breathing and sending love for as long as you are able to hold your focus.

Tonglen for Others

In the Tonglen practice we take on through compassion all the mental, emotional and physical sufferings of other beings - their fear, frustration, pain, anger, guilt, bitterness, doubt and rage and we give to them through love all our happiness and well-being, peace of mind and healing. We can use this practice for healing our friends or our enemies so dissolving separation and negative karma.

1. Begin by centring yourself and quieting the mind and allowing the love of your Soul to flow into the Heart Chakra and out so that it fills the aura.

2. Imagine in front of you as vividly as possible someone you care for who is suffering. Imagine what it is like to be them and try to feel every aspect of their suffering. As you feel compassion for them in your own heart visualise their suffering coming together in a great mass of hot, black, grimy smoke.

3. Then breathe that hot black smoke into your own body and visualise it dissolving into the very core of your own dis-ease, neutralising the darkness that is your own suffering. Here it destroys completely all traces of separation between you and purifies all negative karma.

4. As you breathe out send out the cooling light of peace, joy and happiness and ultimate well-being to your friend in pain, and clearly visualise its rays purifying all their negative karma which has created the disease.

5, Continue the practice of breathing in their suffering and breathing out to them love and compassion for as long as you are able to hold focus.

Again as with all healing practices although we are breathing in another's suffering, because our hearts are open and love is flowing out from us we cannot take on their disease.

CHAPTER TEN

Death and Conscious Dying

Death is a mysterious transition which we will all meet and which many of us fear. Western cultures have generated a great fear of death, pushing it into the background, not speaking about it, hoping it will go away and not happen to us. Death however is essentially a matter of consciousness. At one moment we are conscious in the material world and the next we have withdrawn into another world and are actively conscious there. As long as we identify ourselves with our physical form, we are afraid of death as it means our extinction. When we know ourselves to be primarily energy beings and learn that we are capable of focusing our consciousness in any form or any world at will, then we no longer need to fear death.

For many people death is seen as a cataclysmic ending to life, involving the termination of all human relationships, the end of all physical activity, the severing of all ties of love and affection and the passage into the unknown and the dreaded. We feel as if we are going to leave a warm, light, friendly and familiar room and go off into the cold, dark night alone and terror-stricken, hoping for the best and sure of nothing.

We forget that every night when we go to sleep, we die to the physical world but are alive and functioning somewhere else. We forget that we already know how to leave our physical bodies easily, because we don't bring into brain consciousness the memory of passing out of the physical body and of the active life we lead while the physical body is asleep. We get some idea of this activity from the dreams that we can remember, and the feelings, thoughts and intuitions we have when we awaken. Anything which helps us to recall our dreams, such as keeping a dream diary, brings this life into waking consciousness.

The processes of falling asleep and of dying are virtually the same with one important difference. In sleep the sutratma, the magnetic thread of energy along which life energy streams into the body, is held intact and is the path along which we return to our physical bodies. In death this life thread is broken so that we can't return to our physical body and the body without the coherent life force, disintegrates.

Life force flows into the body via the sutratma. This current is differentiated into two threads, one carrying the consciousness aspect and the other carrying the life aspect. The consciousness thread anchors into the brain in the region of the pineal gland and is that principle which makes us rational, self-conscious, self-directing human beings. The life aspect of the sutratma, which animates every atom in our bodies and which constitutes the principle of coherence, integration and self-determination, is anchored in the heart. The third earth thread is anchored in the Base Chakra, its energy animating the material form.

Death is literally the withdrawal of the two streams of energy from the heart and the head and the return of etheric/physical energy via the earth thread to the earth. Medical science recognises that death is a function of both the head and the heart, shown in the clinical tests of both heart and brain function which must be made when a person is thought to be dead. Death occurs when the life has withdrawn from the heart and the head producing complete loss of consciousness and physical energy returns to the earth, resulting in the disintegration of the earth thread and the physical body.

In sleep only the thread of consciousness anchored in the brain is withdrawn and focused elsewhere. Our attention is no longer directed to this world but is turned to another world of being and we centre in another part of ourself.

In death both streams in the sutratma are withdrawn and unified in the life thread. The heart stops beating and the brain stops recording. Silence settles down. The house is empty. Activity ceases except for the process of physical decomposition which takes over immediately. Once the life force which holds us together has gone, the physical body returns to the reservoirs of the natural world.

In the new born baby the consciousness thread is not completely anchored into the brain. The baby sleeps a lot and its consciousness is focused for much of the time in the energy space from which it has come. The baby carries this energy in its aura and it is this beautiful feeling of the pure electric energy of the world of being which we can experience in the presence of new born babies. There can also be a similar experience in the presence of the old and the dying, who spend gradually increasing amounts of time focused out of the body in other realms.

When we become really old our focus of awareness gradually withdraws from the brain. We are preparing ourselves for a new point of focus beyond death. We may appear to be functioning intelligently, but this is due rather to old habits and established patterns of behaviour and not to present coordinated purpose. We spend longer and longer amounts of time focused on where we are going rather than on current physical reality.

In senile dementia and Alzheimer's Disease, the consciousness thread withdraws gradually from the brain, while the life impulse remains anchored in the heart. There is life but no intelligent awareness. In certain cases of mental retardation from birth, the life thread is anchored in the heart, but the consciousness thread has not anchored properly in the brain, so that while love and feeling can develop, intelligent, reasoning awareness is not possible without special care and healing.

Death occurs under the direction of the Soul. For most of us death is a process which happens automatically. When our Soul withdraws its attention from the physical world, death is the result, either by the abstraction of the dual thread of the sutratma or by the abstraction of the consciousness thread, leaving the life thread intact and still functioning in the heart although there is no intelligent awareness. Here the patient is in a coma and a decision must be taken as to whether this withdrawal is permanent and life support can be discontinued.

There are numerous cases now documented of people who have died momentarily, for example during an operation or after an accident. One of the remarkable things about the descriptions that people give of these experiences is their similarity. In nearly all cases the person who dies is at one moment alive in the physical world and the next finds themself viewing the scene of which they were a part only a moment ago, as if they were on the ceiling or several feet above the scene. They can see their own body clearly either on the operating table or at the scene of an accident and the activity going on around them. Sometimes they try to talk to people who are there but find that people cannot hear them. Usually the person who has left their body does not realise immediately that they have in fact withdrawn from their physical body into the astral realm. They may also be able to later describe accurately what was going on around them while they were dead, activities which are later verified. Such experiences are usually completely involuntary.

Another common experience of momentary death is of a clear, welcoming, blissful light, a feeling of peace and being at home, that draws the departing Soul onwards. Here a choice is made to return to earthly life often with the help of a being of light. This experience and those that follow it in the afterdeath state are described in the death teachings of many religious traditions, such as the *Bardo Thodol* or *Tibetan Book of the Dead*, or the *Egyptian Book of the Dead*.

For most of us, death is literally a sleep and a forgetting. For others it is a continuance of the living processes going on within consciousness. The interests and tendencies of our lives are carried on into the future. Death is an entrance into a fuller experience in which we are free from the limitations of life in a physical body. The rending process which we dread does not exist for most people, except for those for whom death comes suddenly and violently. For such people just before death there is an instant and overwhelming sense of imminent peril and destruction. In an experience like receiving an electric shock the person literally jumps out of their body.

Most people know when they are about to die. This knowledge can even include knowing the day of death itself together with a preservation of self-determination up to the moment of withdrawal. By understanding the way in which death occurs and how we withdraw from our bodies, we can learn to make this withdrawal consciously and in full waking awareness, moving out of the physical body to function in the astral realm. We can have continuity of consciousness so that there is no hiatus between our awareness in the physical world and the afterdeath state. Much religious teaching particularly in Tibetan Buddhism is a preparation for the conscious experience of death.

After death we continue but without an instrument for contacting the physical world. We are aware of the feelings and thoughts of those we love although we cannot contact the dense physical body. If we are en rapport with the people we leave behind we can communicate with them through feeling in the astral realms or telepathically, but communication using any of the five senses is out of our reach. However, astral and mental communication can be closer and more sensitive than it ever was in physical life, because some of the handicaps of being in a physical body have gone. The gateways to direct communication remain open

175

initially until the time of cremation or burial, when the physical body is completely discarded. The Tibetans read the Bardo Thodol to the dead person for 49 days to guide the soul through the Bardo states between death and a good rebirth. Some telepathic communication seems possible long after physical death has occurred.

Two things can prevent communication between the dead and the living. One is the overwhelming grief of those left behind, which means that they cannot sense or hear clearly our communication from beyond physical reality. The other is our own ignorance and bewilderment as we face the seemingly new conditions of the after death state. As every birth brings us into a new world, so every death we are born to a new life. If we view our life as a series of incarnations these conditions which seem to be new are really old and familiar, if we can realise it.

Once our fear of death is diminished and we have established an understanding of the after death world, which is not based upon hallucinations or the conclusions of mediums who are often controlled by their own thoughtforms, the experience of death will be conscious. The people who are left when we die will be given help in maintaining the relationship with no false expenditure of energy. At the present time there is a big difference in the way in which science and human feeling are used to usher us into incarnation and the unconscious and uncontrolled way we are sent out of incarnation. This is changing with the growing Hospice movement for the dying, but there is a long way to go for most people.

When we are finishing our life on the earth, when we have worn out our bodies and pain has reached the limit, we need to be allowed to prepare ourselves, even if we are unconscious, for the great transition. The act of dying can be a triumphant finale to life when the hours we spend on the death bed may be a glorious prelude to a conscious exit. Letting go of our physical body can be a joyous event, shared by the dying person and our loved ones. Instead of fear and tears we could mutually agree the hour of our passage and we could share this with happiness. So far many of us pay lip service to the idea of our immortality, not realising what it means in reality and how it applies to our own deaths.

Underlying the human physical body is the interpenetrating etheric body. This energy body is composed of force centres and nadis or energy channels. In the etheric body there are three places of exit for the life force. One opening is at the Solar Plexus, one is near the apex of the heart and the other is in the brain at the top of the head. All these exits are protected in life by closely woven webs of etheric matter composed of interlacing strands of life energy.

During death the pressure of the abstracting life force as it beats against the web produces a puncturing or opening in the web. As the Soul calls in its energy the life force pours out of the etheric body through the hole in the web. If we are polarised in our emotions or are infants, we use the exit in the Solar Plexus. If we are polarised in our mental or causal vehicles, we use the exit in the head in the region of the fontanelle. If we are dedicated to the divine in our hearts we use the exit in the heart.

In psychics and mediums the Solar Plexus web is usually permanently ruptured early in life, and they are therefore able to pass easily in and out of the body in trance, functioning in the astral world. However there is no continuity of consciousness and there is usually no relationship between what they relate while in trance and every day life. The information they give is often purely astral with its attendant illusions. With conscious clairvoyance, there is no trance or mediumship. The web in the brain is punctured, allowing the inflow of light, information and inspiration. This puncturing also allows us to pass into the state of samadhi, when our Soul is in deep meditation, dissolved in formlessness. The sensitive medium has access to the truths of feeling while the conscious seer explores the world of spirit.

In a parallel sense when we are exploring our emotions through visualisation we lie down horizontally so that we can exit via the Solar Plexus to the world of emotion. When we are exploring the world of thought in meditation we usually sit with our backs straight so we can exit via the head, or the world of the Soul via the heart.

Conscious Dying

We can die consciously. We can approach the doorway that is death and in awareness pass through it to the other side. Instead of seeing death as the final breakdown of life it can be the grand finale, the climax of all that has gone before. Every religion and culture has stages of preparation for death and it is only our own barren culture which has denied the necessity for such preparation through its fear of death. *The Tibetan Book of the Dead* and *The Egyptian Book of the Dead* are two such traditional approaches to death and we can learn much from these works.

There are several things which we can do to prepare ourselves for conscious death, in which we leave our bodies through the exit in the heart or the head. We can:

1. Learn to focus our attention at will in the heart and head, through visualisation, concentration and meditation. Develop the capacity to live in the moment viewed in the light of the eternal, dedicating the personality to the life of the Soul.

2. Give the love in our hearts in service to others. This balances the energy in the Solar Plexus, making it less likely to be used as a door of exit.

3. Learn as we fall asleep to withdraw consciousness into the head or the heart. This can be a definite exercise which we can practice as we fall asleep, endeavouring to keep our consciousness intact until there is a conscious passing into the astral realm. We need to be relaxed and attentive as we steadily draw our awareness upwards to the centre in the centre of the head or inwards to the heart.

4. Record and watch all the phenomena which happen as we withdraw our consciousness out of the body either in meditation or as we are falling asleep. For example, sometimes as we fall asleep we jerk awake suddenly after a few moments. This is due to consciousness slipping out of an exit which is unclear or partially closed. The consciousness cannot exit properly so returns suddenly, waking us up again. We may hear sounds as we fall sleep, due to an aural sensitivity which

allows us to hear sounds that are always present but which we do not usually register. We can often find ourselves returning to the place of our dream from the previous night as we fall asleep. Other people see lights, colours, streams of violet, all of which are etheric phenomena.

5. Keep a dream diary to record the events and experiences of our dreams to bring that world into awareness, so that we can become conscious within it.

Practice of these exercises over a period of time can help us to make our dying conscious and easier for ourselves and others.

The Healer and the Dying Patient

When a patient is dying, as healers we place ourselves at the patient's head, centre ourselves and the patient and then direct all the radiations from our own Soul to the seat of the disease in the patient's physical body. This causes a great acceleration of vibratory activity within the patient's vehicles. The patient will then either consciously through recognising that they are dying, or unconsciously through the direction of their own Soul, begin the process of withdrawing their energy out of the etheric/physical vehicle. We can sense this process of withdrawal as a drawing off of energy. Once this withdrawal has begun, we sever our links with the patient and resume control of our energy field.

The patient on their own automatically completes withdrawal of the consciousness thread from the head centres and the life thread from the heart, releasing the earth thread at the base. Where the antahkarana has been built through experience and meditation the process of withdrawal and dying can be experienced consciously by the patient, as the life energy is withdrawn from the personality vehicles into the causal body and then via the spiritual triad back to the spark of life.

There are several things which we can do to make this process of transition out of the physical body easier if we are caring for someone who is dying.

The dying person should be positioned so that the top of the head is symbolically facing east, towards the rising sun. The feet and hands are crossed so that the final energy circulation in the body is whole and complete. We can burn sandalwood incense to invoke the energy of the first or destroyer ray of energy and the presence of destroying devas. The Soul is in process of destroying its habitation.

There should be quiet in the room where the patient is dying. Often when someone is dying they may be unconscious but this is more apparent than real. Brain awareness may in fact still be present with full consciousness of what is happening, but the person is completely unable to communicate that awareness. The will to express that awareness and to generate the energy to indicate aliveness, has gone. With silence and understanding the departing Soul can communicate and can hold onto its physical expression until the very last moment and can make all its necessary plans for departure.

Colour and sound can be used to aid the dying person. Orange light in the room will help the person to focus their awareness in the Head. Red light stimulates

178

the Solar Plexus and green has a definite effect upon the Heart. Use your intuition. Certain sounds are also helpful, again choose intuitively. Sounding the dying person's note, for example, assists in unifying the two streams of life and consciousness and eventually ruptures the sutratma. Mantras can be used by the dying person and those who are assisting. This is part of the ritual of extreme unction reserved by the Catholic Church and most religions have a final ceremony. Any sacred word can be chanted in a low tone or in a chosen key to which the dying person is known to respond.

Pressure on certain nerve centres in the head and on the major arteries also aids the dying, but this science is unknown in the west. It is part of the Tibetan art of dying preserved in the *Tibetan Book of the Dead*, which also describes the states of consciousness encountered after death. This knowledge is available to us intuitively if we are able to follow our inner sensing.

Death is the final major initiation of life. It is not a failure for the patient or the healer. It can be the supreme healing. The more that we know of death and our dying, the more we know of life and how to live fully in our physical bodies.

EXERCISE:
Practice of Phowa

There are certain practices which help prepare us for the moment of death such the Tibetan practice of Phowa described in *The Tibetan Book of Living and Dying* by Tsogyal Rinpoche (Harper Collins), which can be carried out by anyone whether they are Buddhists or not.

Phowa means the transference of consciousness. This practice needs to become second nature so that at the moment of our death which may come suddenly or otherwise, our consciousness is automatically transferred into the one light. In its simplest form the practice involves first of all:

1. Centre yourself in Being. Then in the sky in front of you visualise a holy being who is important to you. It may be the Goddess or Buddha or Jesus or Mary, or it can be a sphere of golden light which is for you the embodiment of truth, wisdom and compassion. Fill your heart with their presence.

2. Then say a prayer to this being asking that all your negative karma, destructive emotions and blockages may be purified and removed, that you may be forgiven for all the harm you have done in your life and that you may feel this forgiveness, that you may die a good and peaceful death which may benefit all other beings.

3. Imagine that the holy being you have invoked is so moved by your prayer that she/he responds with a loving smile and sends out love and compassion in a stream of light from her or his heart to you. As the rays touch you they cleanse and purify all your negative karma and destructive emotions and you see and feel yourself totally immersed in light.

4. You are now completely purified and cleansed by the light streaming from the presence. Visualise your body which is itself created by karma, dissolving

completely into light.

5. The body of light you now are soars up into the sky and merges with the holy being.

6. Remain in this state of oneness with the presence for as long as possible.

This Phowa practice can be adapted to help the dying patient. It can be repeated often during a loved one's last illness and especially when the dying person is breathing their last breath, or as soon as possible after breathing has stopped and before the body is disturbed in any way.

1. Visualise for the patient the presence of the holy being who is important to them, or to us if we don't know whom they love, above them in the sky.

2. Imagine rays of light pouring down onto their body purifying their whole being, dissolving all their negative karma.

3. See them dissolve into light and merging into the spiritual presence.

CHAPTER ELEVEN

Soul Healing and the Divine

"And Isis came with her craft, whose mouth is full of the breath of life, whose spells chase pain away, whose word maketh the dead to live. She said: "What is it... ? Tell me thy name for the man shall live who is called by his name."
Ra at first gave evasive answers. Now the poison burned like fire, it was hotter than the flame of fire.
The god said: "I consent that Isis shall search into me, and that my name shall pass from my heart to hers."
And Isis the witch spake: "Flow away poison and depart from Ra. It is I, even I, who overcome the poison and cast it to the earth. Let Ra live and let the poison die."
Thus spake the great Isis, the queen of the gods, she who knows Ra and his true name. And Ra did not die."
(The Golden Bough, Sir James Fraser)

Love is the healing power of the Goddess that lies in the touch of the hand of a friend in our moment of need. It is that warm comforting glow that fills our bodies, a sunburst in the solar plexus, the tears in our eyes that shares and eases our pain. Healing is the ear that listens, the soft voice that murmurs, the voice that gives without doubt or a trace of hesitation, that does not fear for itself. Pain is the resistance of limitation. Certainty is a start of hope that heals and expands the binding behind which lurks disease. Healing is love in action, the power of transformation that eases disease. And need is the cry for help that releases love.

"Touch us, feel us, love us, heal us, O Isis, Astarte, Inanna."

We concentrate the skill of unravelling, revealing the patterns of harmony, the experience of being. We look and listen to the voices of the bodies as they speak. If the eyes are blind we are not seeing. If the heart is attacked, our life is breaking free. If our legs are in pain, we need to slow down. The bodies do not lie, they express what we may not like to accept. Disease is responsive to the past, progressive to the future, the body's way of creating change. Healing is in the now.

"Touch us, see us, love us, heal us, O Jesus, Buddha, Krishna, Baba."

In the now we connect with life, consciously interlacing the energy webs and balancing. As tools we use our aura, our hands, our earth wisdom, herbs, massage, colour, light, pressure and touch. Through these we facilitate change. We are energy beings and we respond to the touch of other energies. We can all touch each other with love. We can all heal.

> *"Touch us, be us, love us, heal us,*
>   *O Bridie, Tara, Ariadne, Morgen la Fey"*

We are never alone in our disease. The cat sitting on our lap purring/ pouring/withdrawing energy, balances our chakras for us. Watch where she sits. The dog that rubs our legs touches our heart with his love. The child's hand in ours opens our heart. And the angels, ethereal beings of radiant hue are here to help, flashes of electric blue, magenta, violet, green and yellow. Just call in the heart. Their quality is to respond automatically to the note sounded, disentangling, redistributing, rebuilding the unseen bodies, bringing health to the physical body. And there are goddesses too and gods, waiting. Let them know your secret names. Just call.

> *"Touch us, love us, heal us, O Serapis, Nodens, Mercury*
> *O Ereshkigal, Ninti, Shatagat, O Isis, Great Queen*
> *Hear our secret names. Let us live in you."*

Appendices

APPENDIX ONE

The Energy System of the Universe Visible and Invisible

Any attempt to describe the nature of the universe in an appendix is obviously inadequate, but I shall nevertheless try, with the aim of placing all that has gone before in this book within a wider energetic context. It is not necessary to believe or follow the detail of this plan in order to practice esoteric soul healing.

This plan of the universe is based in the western esoteric tradition and that given by Alice A. Bailey in her 'Treatise on the Seven Rays' (Lucis Trust). However, rather than being a masterplan of the universe which overrules all others, it is the msplan - the reawakened, feminine, non-hierarchical (no white brotherhood here), independent perspective on reality. This msplan is merely an indication of the range of energies and forces and their relationships in manifestation in our universe. It is not meant to be gospel, but a guide, providing a framework within which we can view our own energy systems as human beings.

Energy is not amorphous and unstructured but obeys certain laws of its own - the laws of nature visible and invisible. In our everyday lives we experience different qualities of energy all the time. We learn about energy by being alive on this planet. On the whole this learning is unconscious and automatic. We can consciously investigate energy and the laws which it follows in meditation and through creativity. We can develop a sensitivity to energy which is by its very nature subtle.

Energy has neutral value. Of itself it is not good or bad it just *is*. No one quality of energy is *better* than any other. Value is determined by the motivating force - the purpose of the being from whom it emanates, and by the way in which it is expressed and experienced. A tidal wave crashing on the shore is the effect of natural forces moving within the earth's crust. It can have devastating consequences without a *bad* motivation. So too with psychic energies. So-called negative human energy is on the whole, energy which has been suppressed and turned in on itself, becoming distorted. If this energy had been allowed its natural flow it would have been experienced as positive. For example, unexpressed love can become hatred. Behind negative energies jewels are waiting to be revealed.

The Energy System of the Universe

Energy vibrates at different frequencies. Sound is energy vibrating at a frequency which we are able to hear with our ears. Light waves move with a faster frequency which we can see with our eyes - we see the aeroplane before we hear its engines. Emotional or astral energies vibrate at a faster frequency which we can feel in the solar plexus chakra as warmth or *butterflies* or *cramps* in the stomach. Mental energies we register in our minds. More subtle energies we sense with the inner ear and see with the third eye.

Just as no hierarchical value is placed on the faster light waves as compared to slower sound waves - they are just different and give variety to human experience, so no hierarchical value is placed on faster moving subtle energies as compared to slower moving dense matter. Spirit is not better than matter. The Mother is not better than the Father. The Father is not better than the Mother. They are two sides of a coin, inseparable, complementary and intrinsic parts of our life experience on earth and both are vital for manifestation to occur.

According to the teachings of the ancient wisdom and the inspiration of Madame Helene Blavatsky and Alice A. Bailey, the energy in our universe is differentiated into seven streams (*Seven Spirits before the Throne of God* in the Bible) which flow from the *First Cause* and are known as the *Seven Rays*. These seven rays are named as follows :

1st ray of power
2nd ray of love
3rd ray of light
4th ray of harmony
5th ray of pattern
6th ray of devotion
7th ray of rhythm

The name of each ray describes its characteristic energy. The numbers are just numbers, first does not mean best. These seven rays manifest themselves through *Seven Cosmic Realms.* Each realm is characterised by matter vibrating at a different set of frequencies. On the whole this matter is non-physical.

These seven realms are known as :

the cosmic logoic realm
the cosmic monadic realm
the cosmic atmic realm
the cosmic buddhic realm
the cosmic mental realm
the cosmic astral realm
the cosmic physical realm

These seven rays and seven realms encompass all of life in our universe from the tiniest atoms to the greatest galaxies. All are created by the interaction between these two sets of energies. *As human beings we live and move and have our being within the cosmic physical realm.*

The Cosmic Physical Realm

On our planet Earth, the range of energies which are available to us as human energy beings are all to be found within the cosmic physical realm. We are created as a result of the interaction between the seven rays and the energy/ matter of the cosmic physical realm. Other beings, including those which ensoul planets and suns, solar systems and galaxies, live out their lives in other cosmic realms, as well as the cosmic physical. We can very occasionally contact these energies and beings by coming into resonance with them. The energy of such beings affects us via the planets, the sun, the stars and constellations.

The Seven Spheres of Energy

The cosmic physical realm is composed of *Seven Spheres* of energy, which are interpenetrating and inclusive and known as the :

logoic sphere	- planetary logos, word, goddess, god
monadic sphere	- where dwell the sparks of life
atmic sphere	- atma, spiritual will
buddhic sphere	- buddhi, intuition, pure reason
mental sphere	- manas, imagination, mind
astral sphere	- emotion, feeling
physical sphere	- including etheric energy & dense physical matter

Our planetary logos is known as *Mother Earth,* as *Gaia the Earth Goddess*. She is the being who ensouls planet Earth, who is now recognised by science to be the sum of all the interlocking energy systems of the world. She is also known as *Ertha*, or as *Geb the Earth God*. Different names in different cultures.

Creation

Energy ever precedes form. Energy spirals out from Gaia through the seven spheres into physical manifestation. As human beings alive on earth we are all part of the expression of that ensouling being, we are all part of Gaia. Similarly our earth along with all the other planets in the Solar System is part of the expression of the *Solar Logos,* the being who ensouls the solar system, sometimes imaged as a *Sun God,* such as *Helios, Lugh, Surya* or the Egyptian *Ra,* sometimes as a *Sun Goddess,* such as *Sulis, Brigit, Greinne* or *Amaterasu.* The Solar Logos is itself an expression of the central Logos of our Galaxy, the *Galactic Logos, the Central Spiritual Sun* imaged by the Egyptians as *Isis* who rules Sirius, or *Hathor* who created the Milky Way or as *Nuit* the starry night sky, and so on back to the *First Cause.* The ancient peoples of the world had many more names for Planetary, Solar and Galactic Logoi than we do nowadays, recognising essences of divinity of which we are no longer aware. They had complex mythologies which described the energetic relationships between these mighty beings.

The Energy System of the Universe

Manifestation is the result of the movement of energy outwards from a centre, the logos, goddess or god through the seven spheres of energy. Creation, the beginning of this process of manifestation is the mystery of the First Cause.

Emanating from Gaia, our essence as human beings is found within the monadic sphere, the home of the individual *Sparks* of life which we are. These Sparks are also known as Monads. There are seven basic types of sparks, differentiated according to the seven rays, i.e. there are 1st ray sparks, 2nd ray sparks, etc.. We move out into manifestation from the monadic sphere, through the spheres of atma, buddhi and manas to the astral sphere, and from there into etheric and physical manifestation. Our experience as human beings encompasses these six spheres.

Seven Types of Activity

Each of the seven spheres of the cosmic physical realm is differentiated into *Seven Types of Activity* which are related to the seven rays and also to the five elements used in many native traditions from Britain to native America to China. The space/aether element encompasses 1st, 2nd and 3rd ray activity.

These types of activity are known as follows :

atomic activity	1st ray	aether/
sub-atomic activity	2nd ray	space
super-etheric activity	3rd ray	
1st ether activity	4th ray	air
gaseous activity	5th ray	fire
liquid activity	6th ray	water
dense activity	7th ray	earth

Thus the physical sphere of manifestation is differentiated into seven types of activity, ranging from dense physical matter which is characterised by the 7th ray of rhythm found in the ancient rocks and crystals of the earth's crust, to the electric atomic activity of the 1st ray of power found at the earth's core, in nuclear power plants and bombs. The astral/emotional sphere ranges from dense *gut* feelings and reactions to the atomic activity of communion. The mental sphere includes everyday mechanistic repetitive thought as well as spiritual telepathy.

This differentiation of each of the seven spheres into seven types of activity creates a mandala of forty-nine different *qualities* of energy, which are in manifestation in the cosmic physical realm. These forty-nine qualities can be depicted as a spiral unfolding from a creative centre, the power of Gaia, outwards through the spheres of activity into physical manifestation and the limitations of dense matter. The different qualities of energy are not actually separated from each other into discrete blocks but rather flow from one into the next, in the same way that sound and radio waves are two expressions of the same energy. These forty nine informing qualities of energy can be further subdivided according to their expression in time and space, e.g. 7 subdivisions of dense activity, etc., but we shall stay with this basic set of forty-nine.

AMH

   In reality this spiral is multidimensional and is visible in many forms in nature - in the shells of sea creatures and snails, in waves, in the way plants grow, in the DNA molecules in our genes which carry the instructions for all life on earth, and in the spiral formations of the galaxies.

Sound, Colour and Light - Aspects of Energy

Every energy has three aspects -
its *Sound* or *Note*,
its *Colour* or *Quality*,
its *Light* or *Luminosity*.

   Sound or *Note* represents the creative potential of an energy - *"In the beginning was the Word"*, and all of life proceeds from the Word or Logos. In Eastern traditions the *OM* or *AUM* is the sound which is said to encompass the whole of creation. This threefold note brings the universe into manifestation, maintains it through the aeons and when the last note of the OMmmmm........... dies away returns it to the source. The notes of the seven rays are mirrored in the western musical scale - doh, ray, me, fa, so, la, te, doh - the top doh beginning a new cycle.

   Light or *Luminosity* represents the degree to which an informing being is expressing itself in manifestation. The greater the being the more light it emits. Imagine the greatness of the being who ensouls our sun which supports and includes all life within the solar system. The physical light of the sun is a reflection of the inner light of the solar logos. As we unfold our true nature as human beings we become more luminous and radiant.

   Colour and *quality* are synonymous in terms of energy. Each of the seven rays carries a different quality of energy and therefore has a different colour, but

191

the rays express themselves through different spheres of activity and types of matter which have their own intrinsic qualities and therefore colours. Its not just a simple matter of saying the seventh ray is violet. All energy is modified by the matter through which it passes . Yellow is a fifth ray colour and also of cowardice, green is healing but in astral matter denotes envy. Red is a power colour and also of anger. Blue is the colour of the heart chakra and of space. It is more important to follow what *you* see/feel developing your own colour systems.

The Energies of the Cosmic Physical Realm

Viewed cosmically our planet and all life upon it can be seen as an ever changing, multidimensional mandala of sound, colour and light, impossible to describe in physical terms. The spiral of the forty nine informing energies of the cosmic physical realm which follows is a pale representation of the truth of creation, but here we go. The forty nine energies can be named in words which describe the quality of energy created by the interaction between the seven rays and the seven spheres, manifesting through seven types of activity or matter. For example, 7th ray energy in the physical sphere expresses itself in dense matter - earth. In the astral sphere, this dense type of energy is raw gut feeling. In the mental sphere it is repetitive thought, and so on.

The more subtle the matter of the sphere the less likely we are to have experienced it consciously and therefore these qualities are difficult to describe in single words. I have made the attempt and these are given below, together with the rays, spheres, types of matter or energy of the forty nine energies of the cosmic physical realm.

Ray	Type of Matter	Quality
Physical Sphere		
7	dense	earth
6	liquid	water
5	gaseous	fire
4	1st ether	air
3	super-etheric	ether
2	subatomic	electron
1	atomic	proton
Astral Sphere		
7	dense	raw emotion
6	liquid	attraction
5	gaseous	passion
4	1st ether	art
3	super-etheric	expression
2	subatomic	empathy
1	atomic	communion

Mental Sphere

7	dense	thought
6	liquid	belief
5	gaseous	intelligence
4	1st ether	telepathy
3	super-etheric	discrimination
2	subatomic	soul love
1	atomic	oneness

Buddhic Sphere

7	dense	intuition
6	liquid	magnetism
5	gaseous	pure reason
4	1st ether	healing
3	super-etheric	inner vision
2	sub-atomic	beauty
1	atomic	bliss

Atmic Sphere

7	dense	synthesis
6	liquid	service
5	gaseous	realisation
4	1st ether	perfection
3	super-etheric	all-knowledge
2	sub-atomic	wisdom
1	atomic	will

Monadic Sphere

7	dense	ritual
6	liquid	ideal
5	gaseous	awareness
4	1st ether	relationship
3	super-etheric	truth
2	sub-atomic	attraction
1	atomic	purpose

Logoic Sphere

7	dense	rhythm
6	liquid	devotion
5	gaseous	pattern
4	1st ether	harmony
3	super-etheric	light
2	subatomic	love
1	atomic	power

Human Experience

Human beings are composed of energy from six of the spheres of the cosmic physical realm, that is, all spheres excluding the logoic, though we are all beings alive within the body of Gaia. As human beings we all have the same basic combinations of energy from the six spheres, for our expression outwards into manifestation. This *matrix* of energies which we are, provides an almost endless variation of different qualities of energy unfolding through time according to the rhythm of the informing being. We all carry the same energies as human beings yet we are all unique and individual, from the self-realised sages who consciously create their own vehicles of expression to the majority of us whose current expression is created automatically through need.

Every night in sleep we withdraw our consciousness from our physical bodies and become focused elsewhere, for example, experiencing the astral sphere in dreams. Occasionally we have glimpses of other dimensions of reality through spiritual, religious or drug-induced mystical experiences. Sometimes we invoke Fate to confront us with the mystery of life through coincidence, accident, birth and death. Out of incarnation our awareness is focused in spheres other than the physical and our experience is purely one of energy.

Most of our experience of energy is unconscious. It comes to us automatically via our five senses and we don't think about it. We feel energy to be concrete even though essentially it isn't. The table feels solid but is composed mainly of space and energy. We can experience energy directly in meditation through conscious awareness. Meditation is a process of creating space within our personality vehicles of mind, emotion and body; of quieting ourselves so that we can experience energies which are subtle and normally lost in the noise of the dense vehicles. One of our purposes as human beings is to experience the full range of energies which are available to us while in human form, i.e. the energies of the cosmic physical realm.

For most of us consciousness is focused mainly in our feelings, thoughts and physical bodies. These are the energies of which we are aware and which we can experience directly. There are however a vast range of energies of which we are not conscious. We can experience these energies by opening a space within ourselves which vibrates harmonically or in resonance with the energies we are attempting to contact. We create an energy link along which subtle energies can flow into the dense vehicles and thus we can experience them.

The spiral of the forty nine energies of the cosmic physical realm can be used as a form in meditation for experiencing energies. By placing ourselves at the centre of the spiral in our physical bodies we can see ourselves expanding outwards into evermore subtle qualities of energy as we move inwards in meditation.

In meditation we use the conceptual name for each energy as a key word to describe their quality and help us tune into the energy itself. We move from the natural elements of the physical world - earth, water, fire and air, through the etheric energies of the physical sphere to the astral sphere and so on. Each concept is contemplated sequentially and the energy it describes experienced until it unfolds within us, moving from one to the next. The concepts given, like the energies themselves, are not truly separate and discrete, but merge from one value into the next like waves in the ocean. The point at which our concentration goes in this meditation gives us some idea of the limitations we have in our experience of energy - the limits of our consciousness.

Of course, our unfoldment as human beings is not actually linear or sequential except in a generalised sense. Life is not a process of learning first about all seven types of physical energy before we move on to the next seven types of astral energy. We all unfold according to the rhythm and purpose of the energy of our own being and its interaction with the outside world. At any time we may be conscious of say five physical energies, three astral energies, three mental energies and one buddhic, and all these to lesser or greater degrees. Each of us has a different pattern of awareness and unfoldment.

The spiral meditation is very useful in helping to bring a wider range of energies into brain awareness. It can help us expand our conscious experience of life on earth, by learning to discriminate between different qualities and types of energy. We can gain an idea of how large we really are as energy beings and what a small part of our potential we have contacted, let alone realised and expressed.

Healing and Energy Discrimination

Esoteric Soul Healing is an energy experience. The more that we know about different energies and how they move within our own bodies and within the world, the more effectively we can heal. When we know which energies are which, we are able to perceive several essential facts about our patients.

We can know what kind of energy they are putting out - mental, astral or physical and therefore can perceive their focus of consciousness - whether they are mentally, astrally or physically polarised. We can know something of an individual's pattern of unfoldment and we can be aware of the energies which are in conflict at any particular time, which are creating disease. It is often helpful to the patient to be able to describe to them the forces which are in conflict causing the illness, as well as working directly with the energy itself. Often we are ill because this conflict is unconscious and we have a need to know mentally what is going on.

Our knowledge of healing and how it works is limited by the degree to which we can perceive and discriminate between different energies. It all depends on how deeply we have explored our own and other psyches.

Many healers have a natural talent for healing, say through the hands. When we begin to develop this talent and learn more about what is going on, there is often a time when our talent seems to get lost in the jargon of any system we adopt for understanding. Perseverance furthers. Clarity and expanded awareness will come.

EXERCISES:
The Cosmic Physical Realm - Meditation

The aim of this meditation is to experience the range of energies in manifestation in the cosmic physical realm. We are using single words to describe particular energy qualities. These words are not the energy itself, they are stepping off points for the imagination, to bring us into resonance with the individual energies. When you feel you have fully experienced one energy move on to the next in the sequence, being aware of a distinct change in the quality of the energy.

As you progress through the spiral the concepts become more abstract. You may need a dictionary to understand some words. As energy becomes more subtle it is more difficult to describe, because we don't know what certain energies are. However each energy is a combination of at least two different elements and this can help us to know them. For example, in the astral sphere, art is the result of the fourth ray of harmony passing through astral matter. And so on for each energy.

1. Find a quiet place and sit comfortably with an upright spine. Close your eyes and let the cares of the world slip away. Feel your body, your emotions and your mind beginning to relax. Notice your breath as it flows in and out of your nostrils. Count the breath for 20 complete breaths. Keep the mind focused on the breath. If your attention wanders return it to the breath.

2. Turn your attention to the spiral of energies listed below. Begin with the concept of EARTH. Let your thoughts move all round the idea of earth. What does earth look like, feel like, to you? What is its texture, smell, its qualities, its forms? Sense into what earth means. Think into earth until no more thoughts come, then return your attention to the breath and let the mind go blank. After several breaths, let the seed thought of EARTH drop into the vacant space in your consciousness and feel the energy of the earth. Hold the feeling. When you have sensed the energy of earth, let it go.

3. Take a deep breath in and move on to the energy of WATER. Breathe out. Repeat the whole process for the concept of water. What does it look like, feel like? What is its colour, texture, taste and smell. What is the difference between water and earth? Again, when you have run out of thoughts on water, return your attention to the breath and let the mind go blank. After several breaths, allow the seed thought of WATER to drop into your consciousness and feel the energy of water. Hold the feeling for several moments and then let it go.

4. Take a deep breath in and move on to the energy of FIRE. Repeat the whole process for FIRE. Slowly work your way through the forty nine different concepts in the meditation spiral :

earth, water, fire, air, ether, electron, proton;
raw emotion, attraction, passion, art, expression, empathy, communion;
thought, belief, intelligence, communication, discrimination, soul
    love, oneness;
intuition, magnetism, pure reason, healing, inner vision, beauty, bliss;

synthesis, service, realisation, perfection, all-knowledge, wisdom, will;
ritual, ideal, awareness, relationship, truth, attraction, purpose;
rhythm, devotion, pattern, harmony, light, love, power.

Remember to breathe. Notice the changes in energy as you move from one concept to the next and the changes in quality between one sphere of energy and the next. See how far you are able to move through the spiral before your concentration finally breaks and you are unable to understand or feel the concepts any longer. As you move through the spiral you will experience increasingly subtle qualities of energy. As you experience the energy you will feel changes in your awareness and certain pressures within the physical body, in particular in the head.

Daily practice of this meditation will expand your consciousness. It will bring into brain awareness those energies which you can experience at will. It will extend the range of your energy experience and increase your ability to discriminate between energies.

Each of the forty nine energies has a different *colour* and a different *note*. See if you can open your inner vision to the colour of each concept. The notes of each energy are sounds which are soundless and heard in the silence as you experience different qualities of energy. You can try anchoring this note by opening your throat and mouth and letting out the sound which comes as you attune to each of the different energies. Sounding the note helps anchor the experience of the energy.

APPENDIX TWO

Condensed Instructions for Magnetic and Radiatory Healing Sessions

The first six points apply to both Magnetic and Radiatory healing sessions and then each form of healing follows its own path.

1. Welcome patient, make them feel safe and secure. Face to face discussion and record of disease symptoms and history. Note the location of the diseased chakras in the patient's body. Note the degree of soul unfoldment and whether the patient is physically, astrally or mentally polarised. Note the possible location of the point of friction. Describe what will happen during the healing session. Ask for the names of supportive beings the patient would like to be present.

2. Make the patient comfortable seated or lying down and stand or sit next to them as appropriate.

3. Set up personal energy connections to the centre of the earth and the farthest star and radiate energy out from the Heart chakra.

4. Speaking aloud invite guides, goddesses, gods and patient's personal beings to be present. Recognise the entrance and presence of your particular healing angel.

5. Create figure of eight connections between healer and patient at the Base, Heart and Crown chakras. Connect the patient to the earth and farthest star and see their Heart Chakra open and radiate energy.

6. Connect healer's soul to patient's soul to healer in physical form.

Magnetic Healing

7. Using one or more of the four diagnostic methods of sensing with the hands, clairvoyance, registration in the healer's body or direct perception, make your energetic diagnosis of the condition of the patient's aura and chakras. Note the condition in particular of diseased chakras.

8. Create a triangle of energy linking Soul, Heart and brain. Move energy through the triangle and rotate to create a sphere of energy. Generate and amplify Pranic energy. Using the Ajna as a distributing centre send energy down the arms and into the hands.

9. Place hands on the physical body or on the aura. Lay one hand on the chakra governing the diseased area and the other on the part of the body which is diseased, and circulate energy. Or place one hand on the diseased chakra and the other on the etheric location of the point of friction. Circulate energy through the hands and the patient's body until there is a change in the energy condition. Or when the patient is seated place one hand at the front of the body and one at the rear over the diseased chakra and pass energy through the chakra. Or if the

chakra contains excess energy remove energy from the chakra by withdrawing one hand at a time from the chakra towards the healer's body. Continue until there is a definite change in the condition of the chakra.

10. Check and balance related and other chakras. Smooth the aura.

11. Give thanks out loud to the healing beings and ground the patient.

12. Discuss all experiences with the patient. Communicate with compassion any insights you may have into their disease. Withdraw all energy connections. Clear the healing space energetically.

Radiatory Healing

7. Using direct perception on the awakened Third Eye make an energetic diagnosis of the condition of the patient's aura and chakras. Note the condition in particular of diseased chakras.

8. Focus attention in the Heart chakra and radiate energy to the Soul and from there via the sutratma to the pituitary gland. Circulate energy rotating the triangle to become a sphere of radiating energy.

9. Using figure of eight energy connections hold the healer's chakra in rapport with the parallel chakra governing the diseased area in the patient's body. View the point of friction illuminated within the patient's aura.

10. Focus on healing the point of friction sending in yellow devas to heal the mental body, green devas to heal the astral body and violet devas to heal the etheric/physical body.

11. Holding the healer's chakra in rapport with the patient's diseased chakra, sound the note of the Soul within the parallel chakra

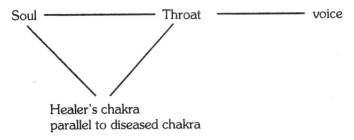

12. For depleted chakras send in a ray of your own Soul energy into the chakra. Remove excess energy from an overstimulated chakra by increasing the potency of the healer's parallel chakra and abstracting and absorbing energy. Or hold parallel chakras en rapport until there is a distinct change in their energy condition. Check through related and other chakras and balance as necessary.

13. Allow the energy space between healer and patient to deepen and listen and watch for significant information. Follow your intuition.

14. When healing is complete and/or your attention shifts away from the patient, thank the beings who have helped with the healing process.

15. When the patient returns to consciousness ask them how they are feeling and discuss experiences. Communicate with compassion any insights you may have into their disease. Withdraw all energy connections. Cleanse the healing space.

APPENDIX THREE:

Concentration and Meditation Exercises to Awaken and Develop Conscious Soul Contact

Most disease is caused by loss of contact with the Self, with the Soul that is the source of all that we are in the world. The following exercises aid the development of concentration and meditation and awaken conscious contact with the Soul, helping us to become more truly ourselves and to aid our healing practice.

For all the exercises find a quiet place to be, free from interruption. Sit comfortably, if possible with an upright spine to enhance the energy flow in the physical and subtle bodies, except for those exercises which specifically suggest another posture. Let your emotions subside and the cares of the day slip away. Use each technique for at least 20 minutes at a time and longer if possible. Practice them twice a day, once in the morning and once in the evening until they are easy.

Relaxation

a) Lie on your back with your arms and legs apart and relaxed. Beginning with the toes, focus your attention on your toes and curl them tightly. Then tell them to relax. Feel them relax. Move slowly up through the different parts of the body, telling each in turn to tighten and then to relax, feeling each part relax. Move up through the body from the feet and ankles, through the shins, knees and thighs, genitals, hips and sacrum, trunk, breasts and chest to the shoulders, down the arms to the hands and individual fingers, to the neck, through the parts of the face and out through the top of the head. Take your time to recognise all the different parts of your body and how they feel tense. By the end of the exercise you should feel relaxed and may even fall asleep.

b) Lie on your back and imagine that your body is a long thin tube, something like a drainpipe, only larger. Imagine that black/grey dirt and gravel, cinders, oil, tar, etc., are flowing down through this tube from your head down and out through your feet. Gradually see the flow of dirt being blown out of this tube by cool clean air, streaming through the tube and the body, until all the dirt has gone. Feel this air in your body.

Be a Tree

Stand with your bare feet slightly apart and your body hanging loosely and easily. Let your arms swing and your knees bend and feel tension draining out of your body into the earth. Feel the contact between the earth and your feet as they touch the ground and feel the energy of the earth entering your body through the soles of your feet. Feel the earth energy moving up through your legs and anchoring in your Base Chakra. Feel rooted in the ground.

Feel the earth energy moving up through your body and as it does so slowly raise your arms up above your head like the branches of a tree, reaching to the sky. Feel your chest open out and your fingers stretch out to touch the sky, releasing the earth energy into the air above you.

Hold this image for a short while and then feel the energy of the heavens moving into the top of your head and the tips of your fingers, down your arms and into your body. Feel the energy of the heavens flowing through you down into the earth.

Focus your attention at your navel and feel yourself to be a tree with your roots down into the earth to receive nourishment and your branches into the air to receive space and light. Feel your energy stream out from your navel down into the earth and up to the skies and out to the world.

Practice this exercise slowly and with focused attention.

Walking

Remove your shoes and socks or stockings and stand with your feet placed firmly on the ground. Become aware of how your feet touch the earth - where they touch and where there are gaps. Feel what the earth feels like to your feet. Very, very slowly begin to walk. Lift one foot up becoming aware of how your foot leaves the ground, the way in which the pressures in your standing foot change as you balance on it for a moment. Feel how the moving foot comes into contact with the earth once again becoming a support for the body. Feel how the standing foot changes position and contact as it begins to leave the earth in turn.

This is an exercise in being completely present in the moment during activity. See how long you can maintain your concentration on the movement of your feet when walking, extending your awareness to the movements of all the parts of your body. Walk for half an hour, attempting to remain completely focused on the actions of your feet and body in walking.

Watching the Breath

Watch your breath as it flows in and out of the body, feeling the air as it moves in and out of the nostrils and down into the lungs. Focus your attention completely on your breathing. If your mind wanders bring it back to the breath as soon as you notice it has shifted. This is a simple and effective exercise for stilling the mind, but can be very difficult to maintain in the initial stages. Practice for twenty minutes at a time.

A variation on this exercise is to count the breaths for 30 or 40 rounds. One round is one complete cycle of breathing in and breathing out. Hold the in or out breath as intuition dictates.

Pranayama

This is a cleansing, balancing and focusing exercise for the personality vehicles. Breath in and out at the rate of one round a second for about 30 rounds of breathing. Increase the rate of your breathing until it doubles to about 2 whole breaths per second, but without hyperventilating. The symptoms of hyperventilation are giddiness, nausea and spots in front of the eyes. If any of these begin to appear decrease your rate of breathing.

As your rate of breathing increases, the breath will move higher into the chest. Practice daily and in the first month aim for 55 rounds of breathing at 2 whole breaths a second. In the second month aim for 88 rounds at 2 rounds a second and in the third month aim for 108 or 120 rounds.

Mantra

One of the most common methods given by spiritual teachers to help still the mind and enter a meditative space, is the use of a mantra - meaning literally to engrave on the mind. Any word or words whether they are personally significant or not can be used as a mantra. They will be more effective if they do have some spiritual relevance for you, for example, the name of a guru or teacher - *Buddha, Ma, Babaji,* or a name for divinity, *Isis, Allah, Gaia,* etc., or they may be sounds - *AUM, OM, SO HAM, AMEN, AWEN,* etc.

A mantra is used in conjunction with the breath and is repeated constantly giving the mind something on which to concentrate. The mantra can be repeated aloud or more usually silently, on the in breath or out breath or both.

Choose your own mantra and practice its repetition for 20 minutes at a time. If your attention wanders bring it back to the mantra. In some religious practices the aim is the constant repetition of the mantra throughout the whole of everyday life, even in sleep, bringing a stillness to the mind and freedom from constant mental chatter.

Mandala

A mandala also gives the mind something on which to concentrate, using vision rather than sound. Any picture which has a definite centre and a regular balanced shape i.e. it is round, square, hexagonal, octagonal, etc., can be used as a mandala. There are many paintings of mandalas of the Tibetan and Hindu traditions now available as posters, but any modern painting which fulfils the conditions above, can be used.

Place the mandala with its centre on a level with your eyes 3-4 feet away for a two foot diameter mandala, so that you can take in the whole picture easily without moving your head. Sit comfortably and focus your attention in the centre of the mandala.

Whenever your attention shifts away from the centre bring it back as soon as you notice it happening. At first strange things will happen to your eyes - you may feel you are going cross eyed, light, colour and darkness may blur in and out depending on the original colours of the mandala. Keep looking at the centre of the mandala. Quite soon your attention will lock into a space of concentration where other things begin to happen.

Moving Needles with your Mind

This is a concentration exercise which demonstrates the power of the focused mind to move material objects. Fill a glass or bowl with water. Place a sewing needle on the surface of the water so that it floats, held there by surface tension. This part of the exercise can be difficult enough in itself. Once the needle is floating wait until it comes to rest on the surface of the water. Focus your attention on the needle and try to move the needle with your mind 180 degrees to the left and then 180 degrees to the right. As you concentrate notice all the sensations that you feel in your body and head. These may include tension (relax) and strong feelings of pressure in the top of the skull and behind the eyes.

Some people find it very easy to move the needle and many find it very hard. This exercise sharpens concentration and demonstrates psychokinesis. You may surprise yourself with your own abilities.

Clock Watching

Concentrate your attention on the face of a clock or watch with a second hand. Follow the second hand as it moves around the dial without breaking your concentration. Begin by concentrating for 30 seconds at a time, then one minute, then two minutes. This exercise sounds simple but is in fact quite difficult. It can be attempted on trains and buses, in bed, in spare moments of time.

The Candle Flame

Place a lighted candle about 3-4 feet in front of you. Sit comfortably and focus your attention on the candle flame. Notice its different layers of light and space and concentrate upon the centre of the flame for as long as you can without losing your focus. Notice how the candle flame symbolises you and your own life in the world.

Horizon Gazing

Sit comfortably outside and gaze at a distant horizon, preferably several miles away. Maintain your gaze upon the horizon for at least twenty minutes without losing focus.

Listening

Sit comfortably in a quiet and peaceful space outdoors. Close your eyes and feel yourself sitting on the earth. Feel the air all around your body. Listen to the sounds of human activity, the distant buzz of traffic. Listen to the sounds of nature, of insects, animals and birds. Reach out with your hearing beyond these familiar sounds into the space beyond. Listen to that space for as long as you can.

Five Finger Exercise

Sit with your hands held in front of you, palms facing inwards and slightly apart.

For each of the five phrases given below, which can be recited aloud or silently, bring together the tips of the appropriate parallel finger of each hand, so that they touch each other. Begin with the thumbs. Ponder on each phrase.

Thumbs	Peace is my real nature not conflict
Index fingers	Truth is my real nature not falsehood
Middle fingers	Love is my real nature not hatred
Ring fingers	Strength is my real nature not weakness
Little fingers	Freedom is my real nature not bondage

Then bringing the palms together, press the palms and fingers gently for each phrase beginning with the thumbs.

Thumbs	Peace only peace
Index fingers	Truth only truth
Middle fingers	Love only love
Ring fingers	Strength gentle strength
Little fingers	Freedom total freedom

Visualisation

Visualisation is one expression of the imagination, the creative aspect of mind. As children we all possess the capacity to visualise, but it is often repressed or deadened as we grow older. These exercises are designed to develop and enhance our natural abilities. All are carried out with closed eyes.

Oranges

Imagine eating an orange. What does it feel like? Which senses do you use to experience eating an orange? Dwell on its taste, shape and texture. Let the associations you have with these qualities arise in your mind. What do they remind you of? Are the cells in your feet aware of the orange? Let your mind and imagination go free and follow where they take you. Repeat this exercise with other fruit and vegetables.

Today

Starting from now, go back in your imagination through everything that has happened to you today. Remember in as much detail as you can the sights, sounds, smells, tastes and touches of today. Notice those things which you remember easily and those that come up less easily.

A Journey

Remember the last journey that you made, e.g. from work to home, from the shops to home, etc.. Visualise the beginning of that journey and remember in as much detail as you can what you felt and saw and experienced on that journey, even down to the texture of the road which you apparently didn't notice.

Personal Problem Solving

This a good exercise for gaining insight into personal difficulties using the imagination. Focus your attention at the back of your head. Visualise a triangle with its apex pointing away from the back of the head into the distance. See yourself standing in the triangle on the base line and then beginning to move through the triangle towards the apex. As you reach the apex you come face to face with three closed doors. One door is the door to the past, one is the door to the present and the other is the door to the future. Look at the shapes, designs and colours of these three doors.

Bring the problem you have into your conscious mind. Formulate it as clearly as you can and then approach the door to the past. Open the door to the past and see what is on the other side concerning your difficulty. Take the first image that comes to you when you open the door as being relevant to your problem, although you may not know what it means immediately. If the image is vague keep looking until it clears. Trust what you see and hear. If a person or an animal appears ask them what they want to tell you. Listen for the answer. Use what you get directly or as a symbol of the cause of your difficulty. Let the images which come flow freely, without judging if they are right or wrong. When they have ceased, go out through the door again and close it behind you and turn to the door to the future.

Open the door to the future and see what lies immediately on the other side concerning your present problem. Trust that what you see and feel here is real and the future reality you would like to create. Try not to think, but to let the images float into your consciousness as they will, of how you would like things to be. When this flow ceases go back through the door to the future and close it behind you. Turn to face the door to the present.

Open the door to the present and go through into the present. The immediate step in resolving your current problem awaits you there on the other side of the door. When you have found it, return through the door, close it and move back through the triangle into the back of your head.

In addition to this visualisation it is also helpful to write down, draw or paint the images of the three doors and what you saw when you opened them, anchoring the images and messages into consciousness.

Opening the Chakras

This exercise opens and energises six of the seven major chakras in the etheric body in the sequence 2 with 3, 4 with 1, and 5 with 6, where 1 is the Base Chakra and 6 is the Ajna Chakra. In the Vedas, a symbol is given for each of the chakras, representing the way in which energy moves in the chakra. This exercise

Exercises in Consciousness

uses these symbols in conjunction with the breath. Carry out each pair of openings once per day for six days and then move on to the next pairing taking eighteen days to complete the cycle.

Begin by sitting comfortably and allowing the breath to slow and deepen naturally. Count the breaths for 30 rounds of breathing in and out.

Chakra 2 - Sacral Centre - *The Crescent Moon*
Imagine a crescent moon lying on its back across the pelvis dipping down between the hip bones. On the inbreath visualise a line moving along the top edge of the crescent moon from right to left across the stomach. On the outbreath move back along the bottom edge of the crescent moon from left to right so that it includes the pelvis and the internal sexual organs. Do not hold the breath at all, but make it continuous, in and out. Repeat for nine rounds concentrating your attention on drawing the line clearly.

Chakra 3 - Solar Plexus - *Inverted Triangle*
Imagine an inverted triangle. Take a breath in and visualise drawing a line from your navel to your left breast. Hold the breath and continue the line, moving from your left breast across to your right breast. On the outbreath, draw a line from the right breast back to the navel completing the triangle. Repeat for nine rounds of breathing with focused attention.

Chakra 4 - Heart Chakra - *Upright Triangle*
Breathe in and imagine drawing a line from your right breast to the back of your throat. Breathe out and draw a line from the back of the throat to the left breast. Hold the breath out and draw a line from the left breast to the right breast. Repeat for nine rounds.

Chakra 1 - Base Chakra - *The Square*
Breathe in and imagine drawing a line from your right hip up to your right shoulder. Hold the breath and draw the line from your right shoulder across to the left shoulder. As you breathe out draw the line down from the left shoulder down to the left hip. Hold the breath out as you draw the line from the left hip across to the right hip, completing the square. Repeat for nine rounds.

Chakra 5 - Throat Chakra - *The Oval*
Breathe in and imagine drawing a large oval shape moving anticlockwise from the Base chakra to the Throat chakra. On the outbreath continue the oval shape from the Throat back to the Base Chakra. Do not hold the breath. Breath in and out slowly, deeply creating a continuous oval flow. Repeat for nine rounds.

Chakra 6 - Ajna Chakra - *The Circle*
Take a breath in and imagine drawing a circle, moving anticlockwise from the Base of the Spine to the Crown of the head and back to the Base. Draw the circle as slowly as you can. On the outbreath draw the circle in the opposite clockwise direction. Do not hold the breath at either end and breathe as slowly and deeply as you can. Repeat for nine rounds.

Love Meditation

Sit comfortably and let your breathing slow and your body relax. Focus your attention in your heart and feel your heart opening and filling with the love that is there inside you. See it fill with love until there is no room left to fill and your heart begins to overflow. Gently let the love in your heart begin to radiate outwards through your body. See your whole body and being fill with love.

Then visualise a person that you love seated in front of you and see your love flow outwards towards them and fill them with love. Next visualise a person that you dislike seated in front of you and send the love in your heart towards that person, filling them with your love. Finally imagine people that you do not know in the world, and feel your love flowing out towards them, filling them with love.

Fear

When you feel afraid, take a deep breath in and as you breathe out through the mouth allow your teeth to chatter, at the back of the mouth and the front. Continue to breath until the chattering ceases of its own accord.

Take a deep breath in and repeat the following phrase or another to yourself, as you release the breath through the mouth;

Let reality govern my every thought and truth be the love of my life.

Green Tara is the Tibetan Goddess of Compassion who protects against fears of many kinds. Try repeating her mantra and see her rushing towards you at great speed to protect you from all harm.

Om Tare Tuttare Ture Svaha

Concentration and Contemplation

Concentration of the mind is the first step in the process which leads to contemplation, viewing ideas and thoughtforms in the light of the eternal and allowing intuition to penetrate to the truth of the matter.

Begin by sitting comfortably and relaxing, allowing the breath to slow and deepen. Watch the breath for thirty breaths. Choose the subject on which you want to contemplate (see below) and think around it. View it from all different angles that you are aware of, until no more thoughts come. Then allow the mind to become still by watching the breath flowing in and out of the nostrils. Let the seed idea of the subject you have chosen float in your consciousness. Focus your attention in the centre of your head and listen and look to see what drops into your awareness. Take whatever comes as relevant.

Subjects for contemplation include :
Nature
The earth, fields, plants, trees, streams, lakes, the ocean, mountains, valleys, volcanoes, fire, air, sky, crystal, birds, animals, continents, the whole planet.

Exercises in Consciousness

Centres of Consciousness
A rock, a plant, a fish, an animal, a bird, a human being, a deva, the earth, the planets, the solar system, the galaxy, the universe.

The Chakras
The different qualities of energy which they carry :
Base Chakra   - the latent fire of matter
Sacral Centre - creative sexual energy
Solar Plexus   - emotional energy
Heart Chakra - love, compassion
Throat Chakra   - mental energy
Ajna Chakra - insight, integration
Crown Chakra   - spiritual energy

Japam
Names of divinity - the First Cause, Goddess, God, Inanna, Persephone, Demeter, Hecate, Brahma, Vishnu, Shiva, Isis, Io, Allah, Gaia, Krishna, Christ, the Breath, the Word, etc..

Breath
Watch the flow of breath in and out of the body. Do not alter it, merely observe and consider the nature of breathing.

Abstract Concepts
Space, time, movement, energy, etc..

Dynamic Self-Opening
Concentrate on different aspects of yourself and open that aspect up to the energy of your being, e.g. the physical body, emotional make up, intellect, mind, aesthetic urges, morality, ethics, etc..

Self-Surrender
Offer yourself to the transcendent within your own nature. Offer every action to the direction of your Soul, seeing yourself as an active centre for its expression.

Cosmic Love
Fill your heart with the spirit of oneness and feel that love joining you with all people, races and nations in the world.

Free Self Enquiry
Ask yourself questions about your self, e.g. Who am I? Where do I come from? Where am I going? What do I mean when I say I? Do I exist? Consider *I* as knower, doer, enjoyer. Consider the deeper consciousness which is aware of *I*, the unconscious and the superconscious. Consider consciousness as different from the body, emotions and mind, where the being is a self contained spiritual entity, which is part of an interrelated whole.

Detached Self Observation

Relax the body, emotions and mind. Do not focus your mind on anything in particular. Allow it to move around as it wants and watch its movements without being involved in them. Observe. Become aware of yourself watching your mind, eventually leading to a transcendental awareness of yourself as the observer as well as the observed and the field which is being observed.

Suggestions from Zen practice

Look inwardly at your state of mind before any thought arises. When a thought does arise, cut it off as with a sword and bring the mind back to no thought. Try to look at the mind all the time.

Try to remember what it feels like to look at the mind during daily activities. Put your mind into a state as though it had just received a tremendous shock, i.e. when it is extremely alert. In the midst of the most tumultuous activities, stop and look at your mind.

Meditate for brief periods of time with your eyes open.

Experiencing Consciousness

Attempt to experience the consciousness of the ink on this page, of the page itself, the book, the room you are in, the building, the garden, the field, the sky, all that is.

Experience different types of consciousness by becoming aware of them. Let your imagination go free and move from one type of consciousness to the next. Take a deep breath in before each move and allow yourself to sink deeper and deeper into the experience.

Types of Consciousness

Waking consciousness - feel the space around you with your five physical senses, touch, taste, sight, smell and hearing. Become aware of what you are presently feeling, thinking and sensing around you.

Dream consciousness - remember your dreams, write them down when you wake up. Attempt to fall asleep consciously. Be aware of returning to the same place when you fall asleep that you left when you awoke, just as you wake up in the same place in which you fell asleep.

Objective consciousness - this type of consciousness can be imagined as being parallel to everyday consciousness but slightly to one side of it. Close your eyes and focus your attention at the back of the head and in your imagination move out through the back of your head. From this perspective allow yourself to experience what reality is for your hand, your stomach, your heart. In this space we can be more objective and are able to see through the physical bodies of other people if we choose to. Try it and see.

209

Exercises in Consciousness

Group consciousness - this is our awareness of ourselves as members of different groupings e.g. family, community, work, social status, ethnic grouping, nation, continent, hemisphere, planetary group and solar system. We have a consciousness which is aware of our relationships within the group, of the relationships between these groups and of the different probabilities of events occurring because of these relationships. For example, in a family group we can all be totally opposed to the use of nuclear weapons, but as part of a larger national group there is a greater probability of using them.

Soul consciousness - awareness of the different groupings of which our Soul is a part, for example, humanity, particular energy or ray qualities, planetary and solar groupings. This awareness is an extension of group consciousness, but has greater mobility to probe into the cause and effects of events.
These last three types of consciousness can be viewed as lying adjacent to each other, the main difference being one of focus.

Consciousness of the past - this is a deep level of consciousness. Allow the breath to slow and deepen and let yourself sink into the past within you. Here you can rediscover and explore your own reincarnational past if you choose to.

Mass past consciousness - sinking deeper into yourself, but broadening your perspective, it is possible to come into touch with the past viewed from the perspective of humanity as a whole.

Ideational consciousness - this is where the archetypes which determine our behaviour are created - the concepts which underlie matter. Personal conversion takes place here and all initiatory experience.

Communication consciousness - deeper still is the consciousness in which we are able to communicate with other forms of conscious existence. This is not astral or mental telepathic communication, but one that comes through a shared resonant consciousness.

Centre of the Head

Focus your attention in the centre of the head. Concentrate upon this space until the mind is completely stilled and a smooth black velvet centre appears which takes over and holds your awareness. This involves feelings of intense pressure in the head as you attempt to concentrate, which eases once concentration is achieved. Peace is held here in space by being.

Energy Oriented Action

All action becomes a meditation, being present in the moment, free, spontaneous, whole, healthy and relaxed. Meditation as a way of living.
Achieve this state of being by :
1. Focusing on the energy beneath all action, its quality and nature.

2. Experiencing your own way of being and that of other people. Create circumstances which are favourable for the growth in expression of your own Soul and other peoples.
3. Observe how you are in everyday action.
4. Offer every action to the glory of the divine in all things, nature and people.

All the exercises which have been given previously in this book can also be used in your search for yourself. All of these exercises can be used by the healthy - healers as well as sufferers

Don't stop until you know your Soul.

Ariadne Publications

Other Publications by Kathy Jones:

In the Nature of Avalon : Goddess Pilgrimages in Glastonbury's Sacred Landscape

A beautifully illustrated book of Goddess pilgrimages in Glastonbury's sacred landscape providing an excellent guide for those who wish to journey through the Veil separating this world from the magical Otherworld of the Isle of Avalon. With detailed route directions, maps, Goddess historical and mythic information, and suggestions for prayers , rituals and visualisations all designed to bring you into closer contact with the Goddess.

224pp pbk illust. 2000 £9.99

Breast Cancer: Hanging on by a Red Thread

A strong story based on diary extracts of Kathy's journey through the experience of having breast cancer, looking at the physical, emotional and spiritual aspects of this dangerous disease. With ideas on how to help yourself.

124pp pbk illust. 1998 £8.95

On Finding Treasure: Mystery Plays of the Goddess

An exciting autobiographical account of the transformative work of Ariadne Productions which regularly presents original sacred dramas in Glastonbury. Includes five performed playscripts.

264pp pbk illust. 1996 £9.99

Spinning the Wheel of Ana by Kathy Jones

A spiritual journey to reconnect with the Primal Ancestors of the British Isles, examining the earliest myths and legends and bringing their meaning into the present to create the Ancestral Medicine Wheel of Ana the Great One, ancient Goddess of the British Isles.

262pp pbk illust. 1994 £11.95

The Ancient British Goddess - Her myths, legends and sacred sites by Kathy Jones

A wonderful introduction to many of the lost Goddesses of the British Isles, showing us how to rediscover the divine feminine part of our heritage, bringing her into the present.

109pp pbk illust. 1991 £6.95

Audio Tapes:

The Goddess in Glastonbury
A reading by Kathy Jones from her original book *The Goddess in Glastonbury* (now out of print), with atmospheric music from Mike Jones
     35mins   £6.50

Hanging on by a Red Thread
Songs and speeches of Wisdom from the 1997 production of *Hanging on by a Red Thread* Written by Kathy Jones with music from the Ariadne Players - Jana Runnalls, Oshia Drury, Lydia Lite and Katrina Brown.
                                               £6.50

Visualisation tape:
The Cauldron of the Morgens, aJourney to meet the Underworld Goddesses of the Isle of Avalon.
Devised and spoken by Kathy Jones with music from Mike Jones
                                               £6.50

Post and Packing 2001
UK : add £2.00 per item except SWA £3.50.
EEC: add £3.00 per item except SWA £5.00
Rest of World : Surface mail add £4.00/item,
                        Airmail £5.00/item except SWA £8.00.
Cheques in £ sterling to:
      Ariadne Publications, 61 Tor View Avenue
      Glastonbury, BA6 8AG, Somerset, UK.

Courses in Esoteric Soul Healing with Kathy Jones

Kathy Jones teaches a year long intensive training in Esoteric Soul Healing for the Isle of Avalon Foundation in Glastonbury. She also teaches a One Year Training to become a Priestess or Priest of Avalon dedicated to the Lady of Avalon. For further details of when trainings please contact::

The Isle of Avalon Foundation, 2-4 High Street,
Glastonbury, BA6 9DU, Somerset, UK
Tel 44 (0)1458 833933
email ioafoundation@ukonline.co.uk